WHEN ANIMALS DIE

ANIMALS IN CONTEXT
General Editor: Colin Jerolmack

When Animals Speak: Toward an Interspecies Democracy
Eva Meijer

Just Like Family: How Companion Animals Joined the Household
Andrea Laurent-Simpson

The Creative Lives of Animals
Carol Gigliotti

When Animals Die: Examining Justifications and Envisioning Justice
Edited by Katja M. Guenther and Julian Paul Keenan

When Animals Die

Examining Justifications and Envisioning Justice

Edited by

Katja M. Guenther *and* Julian Paul Keenan

NEW YORK UNIVERSITY PRESS
New York

NEW YORK UNIVERSITY PRESS
New York www.nyupress.org

Library of Congress Cataloging-in-Publication Data
Names: Guenther, Katja M., 1975– editor. | Keenan, Julian Paul, editor.
Title: When animals die : examining justifications and envisioning justice /
edited by Katja M. Guenther and Julian Paul Keenan.
Description: New York : New York University Press, [2024] | Series: Animals in context |
Includes bibliographical references and index.
Identifiers: LCCN 2023028408 (print) | LCCN 2023028409 (ebook) |
ISBN 9781479818884 (hardback) | ISBN 9781479818891 (paperback) |
ISBN 9781479818907 (ebook) | ISBN 9781479818914 (ebook other)
Subjects: LCSH: Dead animals. | Animals—Mortality. | Animal rights. |
Pets—Death. | Human-animal relationships.
Classification: LCC QL87.5 .W44 2024 (print) | LCC QL87.5 (ebook) |
DDC 591.6—dc23/eng/20231117
LC record available at https://lccn.loc.gov/2023028408
LC ebook record available at https://lccn.loc.gov/2023028409

This book is printed on acid-free paper, and its binding materials are chosen for strength and durability. We strive to use environmentally responsible suppliers and materials to the greatest extent possible in publishing our books.

Manufactured in the United States of America

10 9 8 7 6 5 4 3 2 1

Also available as an ebook

CONTENTS

Introduction

How Can We Make Sense of Animal Death?

KATJA M. GUENTHER AND JULIAN PAUL KEENAN

Humans are responsible for the deaths of billions of animals each year, through active practices like slaughtering, hunting, culling, and exterminating and through more passive practices like contributing to, and failing to stop, climate change that is having catastrophic effects on animals from a range of species. As the Animal Studies Group (2006) notes, there is nothing historically new about humans killing animals; rather, "what has changed is the scope of the technology involved and the intensity of its global impact on species" (4). Industrial technologies facilitate the swift slaughter of millions of animals each day for food, while industrial toxins and mechanized encroachment on animals' habitats for human gain are key contributors to the current sixth extinction, in which a large number of distinct species are dying out because of human activity (Kolbert 2014).

The acceleration of animal death has given rise to greater interest in it, especially in the context of industrial agriculture (e.g., Pachirat 2013; Striffler 2007) and extinction (e.g., Parreñas 2018; Kolbert 2014). Further, shifting social views about animals, in large part the outcome of the animal rights movement's challenges to Western ways of thinking about animals as soulless and without insight, as well as research focused on how different animals think, act, and feel, have resulted in greater human awareness of animals as sentient beings who experience anxiety, fear, pain, and grief and who, perhaps most importantly, want to live. This in turn has contributed to more attention to how other-than-human animals experience dying and death (Pribac 2021; King 2014) and how human and other-than-human animals make sense of, and often grieve, animal death (Dave 2014; Gillespie 2016; Stanescu

2012). Scientific and popular attention to human grief for companion animals in particular has ballooned (for one set of scholarly engagements with human mourning of animals, see DeMello 2016), with other works elaborating how animals grieve for one another and why we should pay attention to such grief (e.g., Beckoff 2009; Bradshaw 2004; Pribac 2021).

This volume contributes to the growing field of what we identify as animal death studies, which centers questions around animal death and human involvement in it (as other exemplars, see Desmond 2016; Johnston and Probyn-Rapsey 2013). An interdisciplinary undertaking, animal death studies explores and analyzes animal death and dying and the structural and psychological mechanisms that help humans and other-than-humans make sense of animal death. Contributors to this field include scholars and practitioners who adopt a range of positions vis-à-vis such deaths and who are interested in understanding better the historical and contemporary dynamics of animal death.

What causes death, how others respond to death, and even whether death is seen as a loss vary significantly. The contributions to this volume consider who dies, how they die, how others make sense of those deaths, and what transpires after death, including both what happens to animal bodies and whether deaths are grieved and memorialized. We think about animal death within its social context and as reflective of the prevailing power relations between humans and other-than-human animals in a given society. Elucidating the many interconnections between structures of inequality involving humans and claims about animality and humanness (i.e., who is animal or animal-like) is critical for understanding inequalities; these interconnections often emerge most powerfully through discussions over who is considered deserving of life (such as humans belonging to dominant groups and some high-value animals) and who is not (such as marginalized types of humans and most animals). We also recognize the urgency and importance of advancing knowledge about animal death during this moment of climate crisis: it is imperative that we stop turning away from humans' involvement in the killing of animals and instead face it head-on, now.

Theorists of racial inequality have traced how settler-colonialist logics of racialization involve articulating race "in part as a *metric of animality*, as a classification system that orders human bodies according to how animal they are—and how human they are not—with all of the entitlements that follow" (Kim 2015, 18). Settler-colonialism has also undertaken massive violence against both Indigenous peoples and other-than-human beings, disrupting communities, undermining Indigenous sovereignty, and, in some cases, pushing Indigenous people and other-than-human animals to extinction. The experiences of humans and other-than-humans in the face of this complex violence vary across many parameters and invite careful theorization that avoids simplistic substitutive logics, a core area of continued scholarship within animal studies and of the work that we highlight in this volume.

Veganism and vegetarianism have become relatively mainstream dietary practices in many parts of the world where traditionally they have not been widespread. While some who adopt these diets do so for health or religious religions, ethical veganism and vegetarianism generally interlink with critical approaches to how food systems, and capitalism more broadly, exploit animals and some groups of humans. Theory and research on vegetarianism and veganism often recognizes the enmeshment of human and other-than-human animals and the interfacing characteristics of social structures of inequality that shape all of our lives (e.g., Adams 2010; Deckha 2020; Dickstein et al. 2022; Ko and Ko 2017; Wrenn 2017; Wright 2015, 2018).

Even as what Claire Kim describes as the "synergistic" (2015, 18) relations of race and animality harm both people of color and animals, these relations also open possibilities for resistance (see also Ko 2019). One of the contributors to this volume, Bénédicte Boisseron, writes in her earlier work, "Looking at connections between racism and speciesism reveals the inextricable entanglement of the black and the animal. But even though the two may mutually—or alternately—elide each other, they can empower each other as well by turning this intersectional bond into defiance" (2018, xix). Engaging with the synergies of inequalities between humans and between human and other-than-human animals produces opportunities to resist social and physical and death and the violence that leads to it. To this end, in this volume, we explore the circumstances and conditions of animal death *and* possibilities for resistance and change. David Pellow, in his contribution, advocates working toward a multispecies ecological democracy in which humans recognize and value the multispecies lifeworlds of which we are a part and seek just approaches to organizing those worlds. Chapters by Matthew Calarco, María Elena García, Katja M. Guenther, and Lisa Jean Moore all include attention to how such recognition and valuing of animal lives could occur, in part by pointing out the invisibility of many animals' lives. Foundational to this book is the belief that we need to continue to build attention to animal death and its varied consequences in scholarly and political work.

Who Are Animals? What Is Death?

Conceptualizing animal death means starting with an exploration of who animals are and what death is. From a Western scientific perspective, long ago in evolutionary history, a multicellular organism was created from unicellular ones, probably a choanoflagellate, and the result was a jellyfish-like organism with many separate but similar parts. Soon those similar parts started performing different functions—one focused on movement, another on reproduction. This organism was a heterotroph and motile. It was bound in sexual reproduction. In the early stages, animals were similar to other multicellular entities like plants and fungi. But soon, the need for gathering food changed everything, and bigger differences started to emerge, such as unique sensory systems, consumption behaviors, and movements. Consider that even early in evolution there were animals as different from each other as corals, sponges, and jellies. When is debated, as is how and the details, but the big picture seems established. And note, all animal life started underwater. Some animals stayed, some left for land, and some have come back and forth more than once.

What all animals share is that they tend to be heterotrophs. That is, they do not typically photosynthesize or use any other autotrophic tricks to produce their own food or consumables. Instead, animals are connected by their search for food. For hundreds of millions of years, animals have been stalking, entrapping, killing, eating, hiding, camouflaging, creating, and using tools, all in the name of seeking sustenance. Almost all animals also breathe oxygen, have a capacity for movement, and reproduce offspring that begin in an embryonic stage.

Animal death took on the many forms we see today around 550 million years ago. During what is termed the "Cambrian explosion," animals started to diversify into new and wonderful forms, turning into, over the next millions of years, fish, insects, amphibians, reptiles, and mammals. That these animals had new ways of living also meant new ways of dying. Death comes by natural internal causes, external forces, accidents, invaders, predation, and suicide. The demands of hunting and defending led to the evolution of wings and gills, claws and scales. Luck, of course, like today, played perhaps the biggest role in survival: the only dinosaurs to survive the Chicxulub asteroid and the K-Pg extinction some sixty-six million years ago were those birds that seem to use their beaks to exploit seeds, because this food source remained.

While most people probably believe that we can define or explain what death is, there is no scientifically or socially agreed-upon definition of death. Nor is there an agreed-upon definition of life. Instead, necessary conditions for life are established (e.g., all life is cell based, all life must evolve, all life metabolizes). The debate about when human life begins and ends, visible in abortion politics in the United States, evidences the disagreement about when life begins and what constitutes the end of life. Likewise, conversations that take place around end-of-life care throw conflicts about what a life is and what a death is into stark relief.

Most scholars in the sciences note that the passage of deoxyribonucleic acid (DNA), ribonucleic acid (RNA), or other genetic coding material across generations constitutes the continuation of an organism. That does not mean in a real sense that a being will live as long as it reproduces, that even if it stops breathing and regulating, its offspring carry on its existence. We can trace human origins to a "Mitochondrial Eve" of at least 150,000 years ago in Africa, an individual that passed her genes on to all humans in existence. The revelation that many of us are carrying around Neanderthal DNA (around 2 percent of their DNA for many) indicates that Neanderthals may have never gone extinct; in fact, almost two hundred million people with Neanderthal DNA exist today. If beings can extend across generations, are those beings somehow still among us and still alive?

A universal definition of death may thus not be possible. We conceptualize death as the ending of the self, the end of one's existence. When a deer has been fatally hit by a car or an earthworm is consumed by a bird, their nervous system is no longer active, and thus the separation of self and other breaks down. Cognitive processing stops, as does metabolism. Some part of the self ends. But the finality, a singular point, may not be how humans think (i.e., the afterlife) or animals act (i.e., kin altruism).

Ultimately, death is biological *and* social insofar as human interpretations of biological processes determine who considers an event to be a death. Volumes can be written on the definition of death and its practical application. Here, we ask simply that the reader contemplate the notion that life and death are not binaries but rather exist within a spectrum of possibilities. The spectrum captures both the differences between individuals and groups in their thinking on death and the idea that all deaths may not have the same end result.

The contributors to this volume, for instance, explore and analyze different ways of thinking about death. The chapters by Katja M. Guenther and by Lisa Jean Moore both engage with the cessation of reproduction as a type of dying. Bénédicte Boisseron explores who is alive and how imagined and real technologies both give and take life. David Pellow considers social as well as physical death in his analysis of how carceral institutions harm humans, other-than-humans, and ecosystems. Paola A. Prada-Tiedemann's chapter on the science of decomposition illustrates how even after death, bodies actively undergo change and transformation, much of it involving forms of life. What constitutes death is thus slippery and mysterious, and opening ourselves up to the myriad possibilities reveals otherwise-hidden aspects of dying and death.

Considering Animacide and Specicide

Part of the challenge of engaging with animal death is the sheer scope of it and the lack of language we have to make sense of that scope. We have only partial knowledge about what impact humans have had on other-than-human animal death. There are agreed-upon trends (e.g., climate change and certain extinctions) and some strong data, but we often lack specifics precisely because the universe of other-than-human animals is so vast that humans have yet to classify much of it. For example, most evolutionary biologists acknowledge that we are in a sixth extinction, but the numbers of species at risk are unknown. Given that most species on this planet remain unclassified, we can only grossly *under*estimate the scope of animal death.

What we can establish is that animals are dying at vastly higher numbers than humans are and that a far-greater percentage of animals die from direct human assault than do humans. About sixty million humans die each year, many of them from causes we would consider natural, such as old age. Only about four hundred thousand humans die globally each year from homicide, and fewer than one hundred thousand die from military conflict. In contrast, animals are dying by the hundreds of millions, specifically from human violence. This is animacide, a concerted campaign on the part of humans to kill animals for human gain, whether financial, political, or other gain. Specicide refers to the killing of members of a species with the goal or outcome (intended or not) of species annihilation. Cows, pigs, and chickens, then, are ongoing victims of animacide as humans keep them in a constant cycle of death and reproduction for profit. Monarch butterflies, an endangered species endemic to western North America, are experiencing primarily specicide because their near extinction is the outcome of herbicide use that has not targeted them but that has harmed them to the point of endangerment nonetheless. The two terms are not always mutually exclusive: because the use of toxic pesticides has worked to uphold the profits of industrial agriculture, monarch butterflies are also victims of animacide.

Animacide and specicide serve the constant demand under global capitalism for land, animal flesh that can be repurposed as various products like meat and leather, and animal presence as companions, characters, or objects of admiration. Every known phylum includes species already extinct or at risk for extinction, and all due to human activity. This is, in fact, one of the markers of the Anthropocene, or the current geological epoch in which human domination over the natural world—including animals, the atmosphere, waters, land, forests, and more—is the most significant influence on that world. Measuring the scope of animacide is a challenge because the institutions of global capital conceal it; specicide is sometimes easier to measure because its outcome is, at worst, extinction, which is often documented. Global economic data do not recognize a category of industry dependent on animals' bodies, and estimating one seems near impossible. So, here we briefly consider some information from just a few industries that rely in some way on animal death to demonstrate how expansive the practices of animacide and specicide are.

The US beef industry alone slaughters thirty-five million cows annually; pig and poultry bird deaths are far higher. Land clearing, a practice that results in the deaths of many types of species, for cattle ranching, an industry organized around giving life to animals and then slaughtering them, has been responsible for upward of three-quarters of the deforestation in the Amazon region in the past decade, displacing Indigenous people and other-than-human animals. Demand for leather products continues to increase year after year, and China now leads as the world's largest producer of leather, producing over six billion square feet of leather each year. Given that an average cowhide is about fifty square feet, this export is composed of the bodies of some 120 million cows annually. Somewhere between one and two trillion free-swimming saltwater fish are pulled from oceans each year (FishCount 2022); this does not include farmed fish. The exotic pet industry, in which untold numbers of animals perish in transit and storage each year, is thriving (Collard 2020). An exotic pet is useful as property *because* it is alive and because of its "*not* thingness: its liveliness and sentience, its capacity to respond to and interact with humans, its ability to be *encountered* as a living being, as a companion" (Collard 2020, 5). Yet, the exotic pet trade is a site for death both of animals directly traded and of those in ecosystems damaged by disappearing animals. In Hawaii, for instance, the aquarium hobby industry took almost nine million fish from reefs between 1976 and 2018, probably contributing to the destruction of reefs there, as these fish play an important role in algae production that sustains other forms of sea life essential to the reefs (Knoblauch 2022). The damage to reefs parallels damage on land, both of which are also a violence perpetrated by white settlers and their institutions against native Hawaiian people.

How can we make sense of so many living beings subjected to violence and killed? *Can* we make sense of it? What can we know about the way other-than-human animals experience death? Where can we see the interconnectedness of human and animal lives and deaths? And, perhaps most urgently, what can we do to stop the horrific rates of animacide and specicide? Rather than turning away from these questions, animal death studies—and the contributions to this volume—move toward them.

Several existing concepts help in approaching animacide and specicide analytically. Scholars in the humanities and social sciences engage critically with death as a location of human power over other humans and also over animals and as part of a structure of human domination over the natural (including animal) world, or anthroparchy (Cudworth 2011). Two central concepts in social scientific and humanistic engagements with theorizing life and death are biopolitics and necropolitics. Biopolitics most simply refers to the struggles, contestations, and practices around the optimization of life (Foucault 2009). Necropolitics, developed by Achille Mbembe (2003) in part as a corrective to biopolitics, refers to "technologies of power that (re)produce social relations of living and dying, such that some populations are ushered into the worlds of life and vitality, while others are funneled into the what Mbembe calls deathworlds—worlds of slow living death, and dead living. . . . Death here includes literal physical death, but also social, political and civil death—the social relations of death, decay, and dying that emerge from prolonged exposure to violence, neglect, deprivation and suffering" (Lamble 2014, 161).

Branching out from necropolitics illuminates how social and political power determines which beings live and under what conditions and which are killed or left to die. Carrie Ducote's chapter in this volume, for instance, illustrates how farmed chickens in the United States are considered entirely disposable in the event of disease outbreaks like avian influenza. Considering necropolitics also helps us interrogate the invisibility of animacide and specicide. Industrialization moved the site of animacide out of agrarian households and into mass slaughterhouses and processing plants. Outside of global biosecurity networks seeking to slow the spread of contagious diseases, there is little public information to monitor the overall status of the planet's nonhuman life—that is left to research institutions and teams whose findings, while important and urgently needed, are rarely aggregated in ways that help the public understand, let alone observe, the scale of animal death on this planet.

Ethical and Interdisciplinary Issues in Examining Animacide and Specicide

Our central goal in curating this volume has been to recognize and incorporate scholars who might not otherwise find opportunity to appear together on the topic of animal death because of disciplinary boundaries. In assembling this collection, we sought to include work that engages with central questions around animal death from a range of vantage points. To that end, the volume includes contributions from scholars across a number of disciplines—anthropology, biology, Black study, environmental studies, feminist studies, food studies, forensic science, Native studies, philosophy, psychology and neuroscience, and sociology, among others—who engage with death and animality in different ways. We were deliberate in including scholars from the field of animal studies, as well as those who may not identify primarily as animal studies scholars. This is important because the work of animal studies cuts across so many intellectual and political projects and because we can only continue to build the fields of animal studies and animal death studies by expanding our conversations and opening the fields to many perspectives.

The field of animal studies has also struggled in attracting and retaining scholars of color, and we sought to develop this volume so that it would amplify and showcase the works of scholars of color whose engagements cut into animal studies with the specific intention of revealing the complex interconnections between structural violence against groups of humans and groups of other-than-human animals. We believe one of the many ways we can expand who participates in animal studies and animal death studies, and what we learn in these areas, is to broaden the circle, to welcome people who may not identify themselves primarily as animal studies scholars but who are doing work in which animals and animality are central, and to recognize and appreciate that work and to incorporate it into the field. We aspire for this volume to contribute to the growing tradition in critical animal studies of thinking about and working toward what contributor David Pellow calls "multispecies abolition democracy" or "total liberation." We hope the book contributes to efforts to make animal studies more inclusive by building stronger bridges between and across theory and research on anti-Blackness, carcerality, settler-colonialism, gender oppression, capitalism, and anthroparchy.

As editors, we approach the broad topic of animal death from different vantage points. Guenther is an interdisciplinary scholar trained as a sociologist and working in gender and sexuality studies. She engages in feminist multispecies ethnographic work that interrogates inequalities of species, gender, race, class, and dis/ability. Keenan is a neuroscientist who additionally studies animal behavior. His work centers around states of knowing and self-awareness. What we share is a recognition of the current climate catastrophe and its roots in human activities, which threaten members of all species. We also share deep concern about human disregard for animal lives and the brutal violence carried out against animals and humans, often in the name "progress" and "health" for some humans. As we worked on developing this volume together, we approached our conversations as opportunities to learn and to encounter ways of thinking that we all too often otherwise do not in the siloed structure of higher education in the United States.

As is true for the field of animal studies, those who are engaged in animal death studies take different ethical and theoretical positions, including some who support animal liberation or abolition, or an end to human domination over nonhuman animals, and some who advocate various welfarist approaches that center on eventuating meaningful reductions in animal suffering. This necessarily marks animal death studies, like animal studies more broadly, as a contentious field and one in which ethical and political principles across participants often conflict. Whether animal death studies develops as a field committed to reducing or eliminating death remains to be seen. Our stance is that it generally *should*: we cannot continue in our current relationships with animals without increasingly devastating consequences for humans and animals together.

We work in this volume to set a tone such that disagreements can be discussed further, respected, and resolved. But agreeing to disagree is usually giving up, often coming out of frustration of multiple parties not understanding each other. Instead, we hope to pay attention to one another in ways that shift our entrenched positions. As editors, both of us learned and changed through reading and listening as we shepherded this volume through the editorial process. Our own ethical approaches toward human-animal relations are not necessarily reflected in all of the chapters included. We believe that if we want to make progress on reducing animal suffering and death, we need to be in conversation with people and communities working from different perspectives on human-animal relations. However crooked and bumpy our pathway may be, there is a path forward through disagreement.

In the field of animal studies, consensus can break down around foundational terminology. We use the term "animal" in the title of this book to refer to those living beings not understood as human. In the field of animal studies, these beings may also be referred to as "nonhuman animals," "other-than-human animals," "more-than-human animals," "anymals," or "creaturely kin," among other terms. The contributors to this volume use different language with specific political and cultural valences, and we embrace the diversity of that language for expressing how each author conceptualizes living beings not understood as human. The choice of language is meaningful because it reflects any one author's specific epistemology of human-animal relations and also often is an important act of refusal to participate in the maintenance of human domination of animals through language.

We also want to acknowledge that one concern about talking about animal death has been the fear of creating spectacles around such deaths and/or rallying even greater resistance to engaging with animal death. The contemporary animal rights movement relies extensively on images and videos depicting animal suffering and death as important tools for mobilizing support for animal liberation. But these same images may further polarize people with already-divergent ideologies about human-animal relations, leading those who endorse human domination over animals to react with anger or disgust rather than with empathy or understanding. Yet another issue with the emphasis on suffering and death common among animal welfare and animal rights groups, both in their public-facing work and in the labor their employees and volunteers undertake, is potentially contributing to what is widely regarded as compassion fatigue, or the emotional, psychological, and physical toll of attempting to help others. Exposure to images and narratives about animal death may also contribute to a type of secondary trauma and reactivate grief among those who have witnessed animal death.

We recognize those challenges here but stress the need to engage with animal death as important on many fronts. We did not ask authors to limit their descriptions or language in any way, but none of the chapters, in our reading of them, contain graphic examples, although many have moving moments. Certainly, the book poses many uncomfortable questions and is likely to elicit emotional responses from some readers. We collectively need to engage with any discomfort we have with thinking and talking about animacide and specicide as such engagement itself can be instructive. We do not have to be comfortable; indeed, we expect that most empathic people will not be. But we can be uncomfortable *and* hopeful, thoughtful, and proactive.

Organization of the Volume

We organize the volume into three parts, "Before," "During," and "After," with each part representing a stage of dying: what happens before death (including what might be done to prevent it or stop it), how events and perceptions emerge during death, and, finally, the processes that unfold after animal death. We developed these parts to draw attention to how animal death itself is a process that happens within particular contexts, largely of human creation. Most of the chapters contain some content pertaining to each of the stages of death yet make central an aspect of sense-making that occurs at a particular moment vis-à-vis animal death, that is, before, during, or after.

The first part of the book, "Before," includes works that focus on the physical, social, and/or cultural production of animals for death or dying. "Before" begins with María Elena García's engagement with the politics of *cuy* (guinea pig) production in Peru, where cuy are cultivated as a food product layered with sociopolitical and cultural meanings. García analyzes the discourses of cuy producers, discourses that center efficiency, (re)production, and gender. She also, importantly, works to center the experiences of cuy in the production process, proposing a strategy of "looking away" to make it possible to see animals who are bred to die as individuals. Next is Guenther's analysis of the discourses around and practices of sterilization of community cats in Los Angeles, including abortive sterilization. Community cat caregivers trap and sterilize cats living on the street as a strategy to limit the amount of future suffering or death. Drawing on reproductive justice frameworks, Guenther's chapter elucidates how the violence of sterilization stops new life so that existing life can flourish. The final chapter in this section is Matthew Calarco's engagement with why road-killed animals are considered sacrificeable. In the US, animals who die in traffic collisions constitute the largest group of killed animals annually, following animals trapped in industrial agriculture, yet their lives and deaths are rarely a site for conversation and debate among animal rights advocates or, really, anyone. In this chapter, Calarco presents three critical approaches to thinking about, responding to, and acting on roadkill and proposes a pathway to moving away from thinking of some animals as road-killable and sacrificeable.

The second part of the book, "During," includes works that, in different ways, center the process of death and dying and current questions and crises. "During" begins with Bénédicte Boisseron's theorization of the racialized human-animal divide in the context of technology. In her analysis of how Black slaves were the first cyborgs, or human-machine hybrids, Boisseron engages with the potential of photography and video to humanize Black people subjected to white-supremacist violence but also shows how technology can be used to displace the lives of animals and humans alike. Carrie Ducote's chapter examines how farmers and the US Department of Agriculture (USDA) respond to outbreaks of highly pathogenic avian influenza (HPAI), more commonly referred to as "bird flu." The chapter analyzes efforts to limit the spread of disease and the financial consequences to farmers for the loss of their flocks, the members of which are "depopulated," or killed en masse using methods even more problematic than what happens in slaughterhouses. The USDA governs the response to avian influenza using policies and practices that center economic concerns and sideline humane considerations. Yair Dor-Ziderman and Julian Paul Keenan explore the question of whether animals understand death from the perspective of cognitive neuroscience. The authors use evidence from recent neuroimaging to demonstrate that humans themselves have quite a difficult time conceptualizing death, particularly their own passing. Charlotte Coté's presentation of Indigenous cultural understandings of killing animals for food and her analysis of the Nuu-chah-nulth and Makah whaling tradition completes this part. Coté situates the Nuu-chah-nulth conceptualization of ʔiisaak, or being respectful, as part of food sovereignty and a reflection of a symbiotic relationships between humans, land, water, and other-than-human beings.

The final section, "After," focuses on what happens—and what *could* happen—in the wake of animals' deaths, physiologically, socially, and politically. Paola A. Prada-Tiedemann introduces us to the world of forensic taphonomy, showing what we can learn about the death of an animal when confronted with their remains. Lisa Jean Moore then reflects on and analyzes the individual and collective fates of spider goats, or goats who have been transgenically modified to produce spider silk protein in their milk. But scientists' and businesses' investment in these goats was fleeting, and after several generations, the spider goats were repurposed for another research project and pushed into a type of latent extinction in that they could be easily reengineered at any time. Finally, David Pellow unpacks the synergies between social and physical death for humans and other-than-humans (including nonanimal species) in the prison-industrial complex. Pellow maps out four terrains of harm that carceral institutions inflict on human and other-than-human beings. Pellow's work illuminates why a multispecies abolition democracy is necessary to understand and, crucially, to address dying occurring in the many locations of industrialized carceral violence.

While the authors included in this volume bring varied perspectives, address different subject matter, and operate within diverse disciplinary frameworks, we collectively make visible ways and consequences of animal death. Further, the chapters we have written are all laced with deep concern for our other-than-human fellows and with hope for eventuating multispecies lifeworlds in which other-than-humans do not face animacide and specicide.

REFERENCES

Adams, Carol J. 2010. *The Sexual Politics of Meat: A Feminist-Vegetarian Critical Theory*. New York: Bloomsbury Academic.

Animal Studies Group, ed. 2006. *Killing Animals*. Urbana: University of Illinois Press.

Beckoff, Marc. 2009. "Animal Emotions, Wild Justice and Why They Matter: Grieving Magpies, a Pissy Baboon, and Empathic Elephants." *Emotion, Space and Society* 2:82–85.

Boisseron, Bénédicte. 2018. *Afro-Dog: Blackness and the Animal Question*. New York: Columbia University Press.

Bradshaw, Isabela Gay. 2004. "Not by Bread Alone: Symbolic Loss, Trauma, and Recovery in Elephant Communities." *Society & Animals* 12 (2): 143–58.

Collard, Rosemary-Claire. 2020. *Animal Traffic: Lively Capital in the Exotic Pet Trade*. Durham, NC: Duke University Press.

Cudworth, Erika. 2011. *Social Lives with Other Animals: Tales of Sex, Death, and Love*. New York: Palgrave Macmillan.

Dave, Naisargi. 2014. "Witness: Humans, Animals, and the Politics of Becoming." *Cultural Anthropology* 29 (3): 433–56.

Deckha, Maneesha. 2020. "Veganism, Dairy, and Decolonization." *Journal of Human Rights and the Environment* 11 (2): 244–67.

DeMello, Margo, ed. 2016. *Mourning Animals: Rituals and Practices Surrounding Animal Death*. East Lansing: Michigan State University Press.

Desmond, Jane C. 2016. *Displaying Death and Animating Life: Human-Animal Relations in Art, Science, and Everyday Life*. Chicago: University of Chicago Press.

Dickstein, Jonathan, Jan Dutkiewicz, Jishnu Guha-Majumdar, and Drew Robert Winter. 2022. "Veganism as Left Praxis." *Capitalism, Nature, Socialism* 33 (3): 56–75.
FishCount. 2022. Home page. http://fishcount.org.uk.
Foucault, Michel. 2009. *Security, Territory, Population: Lectures at the Collège de France, 1977–78*. Edited by Michel Senellart, Francois Ewald, Alessandro Fontana, and Arnold I. Davidson. Translated by Graham Burchell. New York: Picador/Palgrave Macmillan.
Gillespie, Kathryn. 2016. "Witnessing Animal Others: Bearing Witness, Grief, and the Political Function of Emotion." *Hypatia* 31 (3): 572–88.
Johnston, Jay, and Fiona Probyn-Rapsey, eds. 2013. *Animal Death*. Sydney: Sydney University Press.
Kim, Claire Jean. 2015. *Dangerous Crossings: Race, Species, and Nature in a Multicultural Age*. Cambridge: Cambridge University Press.
King, Barbara J. 2014. *How Animals Grieve*. Chicago: University of Chicago Press.
Knoblauch, Jessica A. 2022. "The Big Catch: How Earthjustice Stopped Hawaii's Deadly Aquarium Pet Trade." *Earthjustice Quarterly Magazine*, Spring, 16–23.
Ko, Aph. 2019. *Racism as Zoological Witchcraft: A Guide to Getting Out*. Brooklyn, NY: Lantern Books.
Ko, Aph, and Syl Ko. 2017. *Aphro-Ism: Essays on Pop Culture, Feminism, and Black Veganism from Two Sisters*. New York: Lantern Books.
Kolbert, Elizabeth. 2014. *The Sixth Extinction: An Unnatural History*. New York: Henry Holt.
Lamble, Sarah. 2014. "Queer Investments in Punitiveness: Sexual Citizenship, Social Movements and the Expanding Carceral State." In *Queer Necropolitics*, edited by Jin Haritaworn, Adi Kuntsman, and Silvia Posocco, 151–71. New York: Routledge.
Mbembe, Achille. 2003. "Necropolitics." *Public Culture* 15 (1): 11–40.
Pachirat, Timothy. 2013. *Every Twelve Seconds: Industrialized Slaughter and the Politics of Sight*. New Haven, CT: Yale University Press.
Parreñas, Juno Salazar. 2018. *Decolonizing Extinction: The Work of Care in Orangutan Rehabilitation*. Durham, NC: Duke University Press.
Pribac, Teya Brooks. 2021. *Enter the Animal: Cross-Species Perspectives on Grief and Spirituality*. Sydney: Sydney University Press.
Stanescu, James. 2012. "Species Trouble: Judith Butler, Mourning, and the Precarious Lives of Animals." *Hypatia* 27 (3): 567–82.
Striffler, Steve. 2007. *Chicken: The Dangerous Transformation of America's Favorite Food*. New Haven, CT: Yale University Press.
Wrenn, Corey. 2017. "Toward a Vegan Feminist Theory of the State." In *Animal Oppression and Capitalism*, edited by David A. Nibert, 201–30 . Santa Barbara, CA: Praeger.
Wright, Laura. 2015. *The Vegan Studies Project: Food, Animals, and Gender in the Age of Terror*. Athens: University of Georgia Press.
———. 2018. "Introducing Vegan Studies." *ISLE Interdisciplinary Studies in Literature and Environment* 24 (4): 727–36.

PART I

Before

1

Guinea Pig Life, Death, and Dying in Peru

MARÍA ELENA GARCÍA

In 2012, when I was seven months pregnant, I visited a guinea pig (or *cuy*) breeding farm about an hour north of Lima, Peru's capital city. The trip was part of research I was conducting on Peru's so-called gastronomic revolution, a phenomenon that has by now received sustained attention from academics, journalists, food writers, bloggers, and many others captivated by the transformation of that country from a place of violence and upheaval to a high-end culinary destination (García 2021). What few of those writers note, however, is that alongside the culinary explosion of Peruvian cuisine, there was also a boom in guinea pig production sweeping the country.

Producing guinea pigs for national consumption and export—breeding them, killing them, marketing and selling them—was becoming one of the most popular ways to make money in Peru, especially for people living in the periurban districts of Lima. There were (and still are) countless conferences and courses, seminars and workshops, all dedicated to discussions about best production practices and breeding techniques, the significance of "postproduction" (killing and marketing), the latest research on the modification of guinea pig bodies for profit. While research on cuyes and commercialization efforts had been ongoing for decades before Peru's food revolution took off in the middle of the first decade of this century, it was during this moment of culinary nationalism and economic possibility that cuy production emerged as a profitable business opportunity. The cuy, it seemed, had suddenly become a national symbol of hope and pride, a small but powerful development engine. I was fascinated by this less prominent dimension of Peru's gastronomic boom. I was also concerned about the clear trend toward the intensification of cuy production: the move away from traditional—rural, Indigenous, familial—relations with the cuy and toward industrialized production in cities.

It was in this cultural, political, and economic context that I visited the breeding farm. As I have written about elsewhere (García 2019), that visit had a powerful impact on me. My encounter with hundreds of pregnant cuyes while I, too, was experiencing pregnancy (albeit in entirely distinct ways) called into question the "multispecies" research I was conducting (Kirksey and Helmreich 2010), even as it also opened up possibilities for connection. But it was a particular encounter with one small pregnant female that really shook me. She was not doing well, and after a quick examination, the owner of the farm (my guide that afternoon) took her from her enclosure and tossed her onto the dirt floor outside, leaving her to die alone. Without another thought, he moved me away from her to show me some of the other enclosures that held cuy mothers and their newborn pups. And I let him. I let him move me away, because I was worried about what might happen to my research, how signaling discomfort or anger or sadness about his actions might imperil access to these kinds of sites. The violence of that moment, the matter-of-factness of it, and my complicity have stayed with me.

It took me years to be able to write about that experience. When I finally did, my focus was on the politics, possibilities, and limitations of multispecies ethnography; it was a meditation on methods and ethics in research with and about more-than-human life. In this chapter, however, I critically explore the discourses of guinea pig breeders and researchers as a way to consider the impacts—bodily and emotional—on guinea pigs experiencing production. Doing fieldwork in Peru, listening to researchers discuss how to squeeze out as many offspring as possible from female cuy bodies, reading production manuals describing the best castration methods, or watching videos demonstrating the main steps in killing cuy, such as sticking a needle through a guinea pig's neck to stun them before cutting their throat, bleeding them, and tossing them into a pot of scalding water—all of these modes of accessing production discourses and practices can offer a glimpse into what these beings are made to endure.

The first section of this chapter offers some important context for understanding guinea pig production in Peru today, while the second offers a critical reading of cuy producer-researcher discourses. The third, and concluding, section is an exploratory attempt at conveying the phenomenology of guinea pigs subjected to industrialized production. In this effort, I draw from studies of guinea pig behavior and physiology, but I also consider animal experience through writing that is speculative and that emphasizes imagination. It is also writing that tries to foreground individual animals and not only species. In this effort, the work of the anthropologist Lisa Stevenson was helpful. In a move that gestures toward a deeper understanding of others, Stevenson calls for "looking away" from those whom we are trying to understand, in order to more fully "see." For her, "looking away"—from a photograph, a person, someone we are trying to represent—can be a form of "seeing with our eyes closed" that gestures to "the singularity of another being" (Stevenson 2020, 8). As she writes (following Roland Barthes and John Berger), this form of looking—or not looking—might "allow us to go beyond seeing someone as a specimen from a social category" (11).

Stevenson is writing about photographs she encounters in the archives of McMaster University's Health Sciences Library, photographs from the mid-1900s of Inuit patients in Canadian sanatoriums. She explores the idea of "looking away" as one form of refusing the "look" of the colonial gaze, refusing "categorical ways of looking" that reduce lively beings to specimens, ethnic categories, anthropological types. She is searching for an "un-stately, unseemly, un-fixative" way of looking, for a way to move "beyond the clinical label or social category [that] involves a play between seeing with our eyes and seeing with our soul" (Stevenson 2020, 11). As I drafted this chapter, I found inspiration in Stevenson's invitation to look away to more fully "see" individual beings. And yet, the privileged focus on sight raises important concerns about this approach. Indeed, as one of the editors of this volume pointed out, we must find ways to push beyond ableist language and framings that are so often part of critical animal studies discourse.

Perhaps, then, we might read Stevenson in multisensorial conversation with Tina Campt's powerful work on "listening" to images.[1] For Campt, "'listening to images' . . . designates a method of recalibrating vernacular photographs as quiet, quotidian practices that give us access to the affective registers through which these images enunciate alternate accounts of their subjects" (2017, 5). "To listen to them," she writes, "is to be attuned to their unsayable truths, to perceive their quiet frequencies of possibility" (45). This last point, "to be attuned to their unsayable truths, to perceive their quiet frequencies of possibility," is what I think

Stevenson is trying to do through her play with the language and practice of looking and seeing. And it is similar to what I am trying to think through in this chapter. I am trying to move us away from discussions of "multispecies research" or even of "guinea pigs" in the plural and toward an attunement to individual beings who are brought into life only to be made to live slow deaths, only to be made to die. I want us to move toward a multilayered affective attunement to nonhuman animals, one that perhaps allows for a more complex relation to and with animals, one that recognizes the emotional richness of their lives, as well as their multifaceted experiences of death and dying.

Finally, these stories of cuy life and death provide an opportunity to think through the gendered rhetoric and logics of cuy production. Jokes about body types, reproduction, and sexuality permeate the pedagogy of cuy production workshops. They serve to euphemize the violence that is necessarily part of the process of cuy production but that is also connected to the broader workings of society. As I explore more fully elsewhere (García 2021), gendered dynamics cannot be disentangled from racial formations, colonial structures, and hierarchies of power. These discourses and practices not only make guinea pigs killable but also reinforce many human hierarchies and heteronormative/colonial orders that make clear the relative value of "productive" (and reproductive) bodies. In this chapter, then, I suggest that we can apprehend the complexities and violence of colonial heteronormativity through multisensorial engagement: seeing and more-than-seeing the lives and deaths of cuyes.

INTERLUDE

Many of the cuy researchers and producers I met in Peru often referenced two people: Roberto Moncayo, a cuy producer in Ecuador known as having the largest cuy commercial farms in the world, and the director of a cuy production and research center in Bolivia whom I will call Claudia. I was interested in visiting the cuy institute in Bolivia because it had a close working relationship with Peruvian producers and with the National Institute for Agrarian Innovation in Peru (INIA). According to several producers, they were particularly interested in the "super guinea pig" (the genetically modified cuy that was often bred to be twenty times as large as a "normal" guinea pig), in breeding them with Bolivian cuyes in order to export them to Europe as lab and fur animals. With all this in mind, I traveled to Bolivia in June 2018 to meet Claudia and learn more about the work at this institute. Much like producers had described, Claudia gushed about the "advances" coming out of Peru, particularly the INIA, and emphasized especially the superior qualities of the Peruvian cuy. The institute did indeed use the Peruvian cuy "as a base" for their "interracial breeding experiments," but she also noted the importance of protecting the native Bolivian cuy.

After we had talked for close to an hour, she leaned in and said, "We have been talking a lot about the genetic research we do here and our work with local communities, but what I am most excited to show you is our *camal* [killing area]. My friend Roberto [Moncayo] has been an amazing supporter, and he has taught me about the importance of postproduction. Efficiency is key, and technology is crucial. And he just gave us the most amazing gift: a peeling machine [*una maquina despeladora*]. This has cut our defurring time from two minutes to ten seconds. Come! Let me show you." We walked through the institute offices, through the *galpones* full of cuyes, to the *camal*, where Moncayo's machine stood in the center. She walked over to it, caressing the machine's side, and told me about the killing process. "We usually stun the animals with electricity before scalding them, but there is also a woman in town who can calm an animal by rubbing her fingers on its head. Then it is easy to cut their throat and bleed them before we scald them in water with lime [*cal*] to allow for the skin to soften. At this point, we can use the peeling machine, and then we move to gutting, cleaning, and packaging."

The emphasis on postproduction is an increasingly common one as businesses compete with each other and as boasting the "best-quality cuy" becomes ever more important for sales. Claudia's delight over Moncayo's gift was certainly related to a genuine appreciation for their collaboration and his support. But it was also appreciation for the ways this machine would aid in their production and postproduction of cuyes, as the sale of cuyes, both as breeders and as food, was one way the institute supported the research taking place there. This focus on postproduction also brought back a lecture at a cuy production conference I had attended a couple of years back. The talk, by an agronomist working on milk and meat production at the Agrarian University, was on the impact of postproduction on the quality of cuy meat. "You might have excellent production," he told the audience, "but if your postproduction techniques are not well conceived, you have failed." The agronomist was particularly fascinated with the use of electricity in the postproduction process. Noting "electronarcosis" (or electric stunning) as the preferred way to stun cuyes before killing them, he began describing the studies conducted at his lab. "We have worked extensively on this, conducting studies to see how much electric current is necessary to kill, to stun lightly, to stun appropriately. Sometimes, if not done properly, the electric current can cause males to ejaculate. And we have had cuyes wake up during scalding because they were not stunned enough. That is not good because the stress of the pain ruins the meat."

Backstories

We had just moved to the United States after spending several years in Mexico City. It was 1985, and at that time, Virginia did not have the robust Latinx community that is there now. Today, in northern Virginia (or in Paterson, New Jersey; Miami, Florida; or Shoreline, Washington), you could make your way to a "Latin" grocery store and find many of the ingredients necessary to replicate food from home, dishes that connect us—those of us who left, and miss, home—to our families and ancestral lands. One of these "ingredients" would be cuy. The animal would be sold defurred, packaged and frozen, next to frozen yuca and corn, near counters full of queso fresco and bins packed with limes and tomatoes and cilantro. But in 1985, frozen cuy was not yet available. And when my grandmother came to visit us from Peru that year, she wanted to cook for us. She wanted to cook what she knew, take us back home. And so after church one Sunday morning, when my mother had to pick up groceries, she told me to entertain my grandmother while she shopped. It was one of those sprawling outdoor shopping centers, with a grocery store and a nail salon and, in this case, a pet shop. My grandmother was not amused, but we walked in and looked around. I got distracted by some puppies, and I suddenly lost her. By the time I found her, she was about to purchase five guinea pigs. She did not speak English, but she had managed to make herself clear; and the young woman helping her was pointing at the guinea pigs, asking her which ones she wanted.

I will never forget my grandmother's smile that day, at that moment. She was picking out our dinner. Even if frozen guinea pig had been available to us, she would most likely have preferred to buy them fresh, these animals—fresh so she could twist and break their necks and defur them and scald them and open them up and stuff them with herbs and butter and roast them in our modern kitchen. I gestured frantically to the young woman (my English was not so great either back then), told her not to sell my grandmother anything, that we were just looking. We didn't end up buying any guinea pigs that day. And I'm sure instead of roast cuy, we ate lentils or spinach soup or *ají de gallina* (Peruvian chicken curry), something that was still Peruvian, even if it did not include the cuy, this quintessentially authentic Peruvian animal at the center of so many hopes and dreams and debates in Peru today.

The guinea pig has been an important figure in the Andean world for centuries (Archetti 1997; Morales 1995). This small mammal was domesticated by Native peoples at least three to five thousand years ago in the Andean region of South America, and cuy remains can be found in archaeological sites and in colonial art across the region. A famous example is the painting of the Last Supper hanging in Cusco's cathedral, where cuy is the main dish. Despite this historical significance, because the guinea pig has been associated with Indigenous peoples and communities in Peru, it has been derided by many (especially by Peruvian elites) as a dirty rodent, one that belongs in the homes of rural Andean peoples and not in the capital city of Lima; they belong in the space of "savagery," not sophistication.

Racialized geographies in Peru mark the Andes (and Amazon) as backward and dangerous, while coastal Lima is imagined as a modern, cosmopolitan city. The gastronomic boom of the past several years has reinforced the centrality of Lima as a sophisticated culinary destination. Indeed, three of the restaurants on the prestigious "50 Best" list are located in the Peruvian capital. But part of this moment of culinary nationalism also brought with it renewed discourses of social inclusion and the recognition of Indigenous tradition and cultural production. Elite chefs conspired with state tourism agencies, academic institutions, publishing houses, and private industry to promote a gastropolitical project that sold Peru to the world as a place of magical and harmonious racial and cultural fusion, a nation brought together through food, made possible by the encounter of multiple worlds, through conquest, slavery, and migration (García 2021). These are sanitized histories, in which the violence of colonialism, the ongoing racial, gendered, and extractive violence in the country, is erased or obscured. In its place, we find stories about love between elite (white, male) chefs and Indigenous producers, stories about a nation reconciled, appreciative of the Indigenous, African, Arab, Japanese, Chinese, and other contributions to Peruvian cuisine, stories about the value and worth of Native ingredients, such as the cuy, especially in their power to authenticate the country's high-end gastronomy as *Peruvian*.

The story I am sharing here, about the production (exploitation) of the Peruvian guinea pig, cannot be understood outside of this context. It also cannot be understood without knowing that the gastronomic boom has, in many ways, been a powerful response to the years of terror in Peru. There are countless accounts, studies, and reflections about the war between Sendero Luminoso (Shining Path), a ruthless Maoist-Marxist-Leninist organization, and the Peruvian state (Degregori 2012; Stern 1998). Officially, the so-called internal conflict in Peru lasted two decades (1980–2000), and the violence most directly impacted Indigenous peoples in the Andes and Amazon.[2] The Peruvian Truth and Reconciliation Commission estimates that almost seventy thousand people lost their lives (CVR 2004). Of those, at least 75 percent were from the poorest regions of the country and Indigenous. Given the elusive nature of Sendero and the fact that it initiated its armed struggle in the highland department of Ayacucho, counterinsurgency forces treated all Indigenous peoples and peasants as potential terrorists, subjecting them to kidnapping, torture, displacement, disappearance, and death. Sendero Luminoso was also a brutally violent organization that, like military and paramilitary forces, committed unspeakable acts against anyone who did not support its cause. Significantly, animals did not fare much better. They were stolen, maimed, killed, burned alive, used as decoys to deploy bombs, and much more. As with most examples of settler-colonial violence, part of the brutality of this war had to do with the ways it impacted relations between people and their kin, human and nonhuman.[3]

To return to Peru's gastronomic revolution, this is a movement that from the start was framed as a national project of reconciliation, one that recognized the centuries of colonial subjugation of Indigenous Peruvians and that vowed to do better. An important part of this was the foregrounding of Indigenous producers as central to the success of Peru's gastronomic revolution. Without the Native products Peru's high-end restaurants offered—so the story went—they simply could not work. Chefs relied on purple potatoes and quinoa and *ajíes* and cuy. As the world of high-end cuisine increasingly revolved around Indigenous ingredients and became hyperfocused on biodiversity and authenticity, Peruvian chefs needed something to distinguish their work from that of colleagues in other Latin American countries; they needed to mark their cuisine as authentically Peruvian. It is here that the guinea pig becomes suddenly central and useful to urban chefs and that space opens up for their consumption outside of Indigenous or migrant households. Cuy researchers and producers noticed and used this moment to expand their work, launching breeding and business projects with renewed emphasis.

Indeed, while research in guinea pig production has been supported by the Peruvian state since the late 1960s, the *business* of cuy production has only taken off recently. These efforts are in keeping with the forward-looking aspirations of the gastronomic boom, the hope of moving beyond precarity and toward the promise of seemingly more inclusive modes of modernity, cosmopolitanism, and development. Along these lines, the focus in cuy production has been primarily on developing cuy research and breeding. In practice, this has meant moving from *familial* production (in which cuyes live with families, usually housed in a corner of the kitchen, and are eaten mostly on special occasions) to small-, medium-, and large-scale *commercial* production (in which animals are kept outside the home and there is a focus on more selective breeding and production to sell the animals for profit). It has also meant moving from domestic spaces in which women were the protagonists toward commercial ventures dominated by men. And of course, this process disrupts the familial/kinship structures of cuyes themselves.

As the guinea pig boom began in earnest (first few years of the 2000s), the focus for many cuy breeders and producers was on export. As the head of one cuy business in Lima told me, there was particular excitement about the promise of what he termed "markets of nostalgia," referring to the large communities of Andean migrants who had left their countries (Peru, Ecuador, and Bolivia) and were now living in cities in the United States, Spain, and Japan. However, while some producers do work with large companies to export their products, the primary focus of cuy production in Peru today is domestic consumption. There are various reasons for this, such as the challenge of global consumption of the guinea pig, an animal who is seen not as a food animal but as a companion animal in many countries. But an important reason for this shift also has to do with the association between cuy production and both rural and urban development. During interviews with state and private producers, it became clear that only large companies with the financial means to pay for certification and to navigate the bureaucratic process required for export could participate in this market. Rural families or small cuy businesses are unable to compete. One cuy researcher put it starkly: "Exporting [cuy] hurts the country; it hurts Peruvians." Unlike other products such as quinoa, it is hard to think about an organic fair-trade business for cuy (for example) given that most of those who are purchasing cuy abroad (Andean migrants) do not have the means to pay for the cost of business. Instead, most cuy producers have identified the national market as the most promising. This has proven to be a smart move, as demand for cuy meat has soared, and the small animal's meat is the most expensive in the nation. This is the context in which one cuy business owner told me about his vision for a cuy-based fast food chain: "If there is a Ronald McDonald, there can be a Johnny McCuy."[4]

In some ways, the revalorization of native Peruvian products has reframed the association of the guinea pig with Indigeneity. Rather than disparaging the animal because of its connection to Indigenous or poor migrant households, the cuy is now upheld as a quintessentially Peruvian animal. Newspapers, Facebook posts, magazines, and blogs tout the health benefits of guinea pig meat (e.g., it is low in cholesterol; it has medicinal, even anticarcinogenic, properties), with some doctors even prescribing a daily dose of cuy soup to counteract chronic headaches and improve digestive health. This has led to an astounding surge in small cuy production businesses. There are multiple seminars, workshops, and courses offered by universities, private companies, and state institutes to train people interested in becoming cuy producers. There are also regular producer conferences in Lima and other provinces. And in 2013, the Peruvian Ministry of Agriculture declared the National Day of the Guinea Pig, an effort to promote and increase cuy consumption in the country.

INTERLUDE

It is a Friday in November (2016), and I'm at the auditorium of the Universidad Nacional Agraria in La Molina, a quiet middle- and middle-upper-class district in Lima. It is the first day of the national symposium "Advances and Perspectives on Cuy Production," and the place is packed. Most of the people in the auditorium are young men—university students, cuy producers, researchers—and of the fifteen or so featured speakers that day, there was only one woman, a researcher from INIA. Discussions that day ranged from a focus on genetic improvement and meat quality to the most effective slaughter techniques and marketing strategies to the historical and contemporary significance of the cuy in Peru and beyond. The INIA researcher's lecture moved familiarly through the beginning of the Cuy Project in the 1960s to the INIA's pioneering research on cuy genetics and its work with rural families in developing cuy production. Then she began offering more details about the INIA's current research.

Researchers at the institute were working on manipulating muscle fibers in order to minimize fiber and increase the amount of cuy meat, and they were seeing some exciting results; they were working on further reducing the time between birth and kill weight and were close to reducing this to fifty days. The goal was forty-five days. And then she moved to a discussion about female cuyes and birthing. "You all want more and bigger babies, but imagine a woman weighing sixty pounds giving birth to a baby of thirty pounds." She continued, "We need to keep in mind the female's body, her breathing capacity, the size of her thorax. And you want them to produce more milk, but we need to think also about mastitis. You men never think about this. The poor females have larger teats full of milk, but that means they are rubbing against the floor of their *pozas*, next to shit, getting infected. Do you treat this condition? No. You don't even notice. This is a problem." I was fascinated by her projection of blame—for "having" to manipulate cuy bodies for maximum production, for not caring properly for birthing mothers—onto the male producers present. And then she suddenly said, "And also, we need to start thinking about killing certain babies. We need to determine key qualities, such as size and strength, that we can use to know which ones to kill in order to maximize the survival rate of others. It breaks my heart [*me parte el alma*], but it has to be done."

Making Cuy

> The tremendous evidence found about the origins of the cuy in the Andes allows us to affirm, quite properly that the cuy is our animal. In other words, he is from the Andean regions of Peru, Ecuador, Bolivia and Colombia, and—as he is ours—he obliges us and commits us to not only improve his exploitation and quality, but also to create our own technology that deserves, in the future, our very best efforts
> —from a guinea pig production manual (Rodriguez et al. 2009, 27)

In October 2016, I attended a daylong cuy production seminar at the National Institute for Agricultural Innovation, one of the most important sites for guinea pig research in Peru. These courses, offered since 2004, are aimed at the increasing numbers of working-class men and women in Lima who see in the cuy a means of support and the possibility of increased income. I arrived at the institute early and was waiting by the guarded entrance gate with other men and women when a technician came to take us to the Cuy Project offices. On this day, the seminar began promptly at eight thirty in the morning. Most of the others present were young men, with only a handful of women in the group.

As is usually the case, the focus of the seminar was on the cuy as raw material for profit-seeking business. Speakers addressed cuy production, nutrition, reproduction, commercialization, and biosecurity. The workshop began with a lecture by a lead researcher I will call Veronica, who spoke about the history of the Cuy Project and the origins of the cuy, before noting the important work the INIA had done in moving guinea pig breeding in Peru from familial to commercial breeding, contributing greatly to the national economy along the way. "The guinea pig is only good for meat," she stated and then asked the seminar participants if they knew Donald Duck's uncle Scrooge McDuck, "whose eyes turn into dollar signs when he sees potential for profit. *That* is cuy production." With an image of Scrooge McDuck on the PowerPoint slide behind her, Veronica continued her discussion by reminding her audience, made up of mostly men, that women have been central to cuy production.

"Women saved the cuy," she stated, "because they took them to the kitchen." Veronica was referencing the traditional way that cuy husbandry, to use another curiously gendered term, relies largely on women, who in Andean communities tend to care for cuyes, keep them in the home, and use them for food on special occasions. In the move from (primarily) rural contexts of familial production to (increasingly) urban spaces of commercial production—a developmentalist move that the INIA is invested in—she emphasized that in production, it was important to "disassociate the cuy from women, because men are the ones more interested in production." "Women treat cuyes better," she noted, "but cuy production is about business and efficiency, not care, unless it is profitable."[5] Gender ideologies are very much at work here, as discussions of efficiency and profit emphasize the importance of men in this moment, while essentialized understandings of women confine them to familiar contexts of domesticity, reproduction, and care.[6]

While in retrospect it is not surprising, on that day, I was struck by how much of the discussion about production, profit, and business was entangled with ideologies of sex and gender. The discussions throughout that day and in other spaces of conversation about cuy production revealed the intimate linkages between development and gender and sexuality and, more specifically, the masculinist dimension of development initiatives such as this one. For example, during a conference on cuy production in November 2016, a technician working with Antamina, one of the largest copper- and zinc-mining companies in the southern Peruvian highlands, told the large, mostly male, audience that the company's cuy project (part of the mine's corporate social responsibility initiatives) emphasized the importance of "bringing men in" and getting buy-in from communities, from families, and in particular, from husbands. "People still think cuyes are for women, but we need to change men's thinking and move away from the prejudice of this, away from the idea that caring for the cuyes is women's work. We need to masculinize cuy production and move from the participation of women to that of their male children and eventually to the participation of the head of the household." The "head of the household," of course, referred to the man in this context. In a similar vein, the INIA team, despite being led by a female researcher, provided innumerable examples of not only centering masculinist perspectives but also minimizing the suffering of female bodies.

During another lecture at the cuy production workshop, Veronica highlighted her team's efforts to synchronize cuy estrus so that all cuyes in one farm could give birth at the same time, thus streamlining cuy "harvest" and postpartum care.[7] She also proudly shared the work that went into lessening the time from birth to kill weight (from 120 to 56 days). And it was during this discussion about efficiency and reproduction that Veronica offered a striking comparison between female guinea pigs and herself and her two daughters. She began by saying, "Look at me. I am short and chunky. One of my two daughters is also like me, short and prone to gaining weight." She then said that while we might think this means that they eat a lot, in fact she and her daughter do not really eat much. Her second daughter, however, "is tall, skinny, and can eat all she wants and not gain weight. This is genetics," she said. And she continued, "If we were cuyes, my overweight daughter and I, we would have been chosen as breeders because we don't consume much. This means we are low cost, but we still gain weight; so we can give birth to higher numbers of young and then have more meat once we are spent and ready for slaughter." She went on, "My skinny daughter would have been sent to slaughter quickly, because she eats a lot—too much production cost—but does not gain weight. This is not efficient." In a strikingly effective performance, Veronica was figuratively serving up her body, and the bodies of her daughters, for consumption. In addition to the technical and scientific information she conveyed, Veronica's words also served to reinforce the heteronormative order in which women are controllable, consumable, and disposable.

In another fascinating, if disturbing, discussion about the importance of uniformity in cuy production, Veronica told the men and women at the workshop that efficient production meant that cuy populations had to be homogeneous. "In the military, the entire population is the same. They all must weigh the same and be equally tall. They don't let in short or fat men. Same with the cuy. They must all be the same size, weigh the same, have the same leg dimensions." And she continued, "We want convex carcasses. What kind of girl would you like? A girl with nothing in the front or back or a convex one, with a curvy body? That is what we want with the cuy." Both the men and women in the room laughed heartily at this. Such humor certainly makes Veronica an effective teacher, but it also makes her part of the hegemonic masculinist ordering of the nation.

The way in which human bodies can stand in for cuy bodies might seem remarkable, but in fact, practices and discourses of animal reproduction are always linked to gender ideologies and imaginaries about human bodies (Adams [1990] 2015, 2003; Davis 1995; Gillespie 2018; Ritvo 1987, 1997). And as others have noted in scholarship on the violence of animal industries, humor—and very often sexualized humor—plays a significant role in uncovering these connections and masking unease around the violence of breeding (Cassidy 2002; Gillespie 2013; Blanchette 2020).

It is also worth noting that, as Kathryn Gillespie writes, "while female animals are more obviously subjects of gendered commodification and violence, male animals, too, experience a gendered appropriation of their lives and bodies" (2013, 1325).[8] This is certainly the case in the context of cuy production. Discussions about efficiency during this workshop and other lectures I attended had just as much to do with breeding female cuyes for maximal reproductive efficiency as they did with selecting the "best" male specimens. One producer's lecture at a conference was representative of this. With a slide of a cuy penis on the projector behind him, the producer discussed the importance of "a good working penis," noting that there are some males who do not work as they "should": "They don't work. They are worthless. Or maybe they just don't like females [laughter and applause from the crowd]. You have to check the penis every month, measure the testicles, make sure they are working. If they are not, you must take them out of the reproductive space. Why should I let him rest? He has to work. If he doesn't, he is just wasting my money." This kind of "breeders only" comment reflects not just the familiar misogyny already noted but also homophobia and particular ideas about masculinity.

Additionally, much as Gillespie found for cows and bulls in the dairy industry, the male animal body is not only commodified but "simultaneously discursively employed to take responsibility for the sexual violence against the female body through the construction of the hypermasculine, virile *male*" (2013, 1325; emphasis in original). There was one discussion in particular during the INIA workshop that offers a telling example of just this kind of simultaneous discursive and material commodification. The discussion was about the "postpartum estrus period," a period two to three hours after females give birth when they are once again able to be impregnated. Many producers take advantage of this period, a method called "continuous" or "permanent mating," described as providing no sexual rest for the female cuy. This means that she will be continuously impregnated during the course of one year. This usually leads to four or five births before the animal is "spent" and slaughtered. During Veronica's lecture at the INIA workshop, she put it this way: "Two to three hours after giving birth, the female has another reproductive cycle, and the male can penetrate her once again. She sometimes does not want this, but she has no other choice; and we need to take maximum advantage. Efficiency—remember the eyes of Scrooge McDuck." As she spoke, the slide on the screen showed a cartoon image of a female cuy holding hands with a male cuy. With her other hand, she is swatting away her newborn baby, who is presumably in the way of her amorous liaison. The male cuy, who is holding a beer with his other hand, looks at her lasciviously, while a red heart over the female cuy's head signals that she is in love (or at least willingly responsive to the male's desires).[9] Immediately after this comment, Veronica continued by reminding those of us in the workshop that the male cuy was the most important part of the reproductive space:

> Remember, there are seven females and only one male in the *poza*. This is the male's harem [again laughter]. He is the first to enter the *poza*, and he is the owner. This is his territory. Once he is in, you slowly begin bringing in the females, two by two, until you have seven. You have to be creative, because the males will easily get bored with the females. They are just like men. They have to smell new things every so often; they have to smell new meat. So you need to move him once in a while to different *pozas* so he can smell new blood. This gives him energy. And then the females are happy too because they want a young stud, not an old man. This male works better if he is excited and energized, and that makes females happy.

"They are just like men." While one might have imagined such a statement to be the start of a critique of the familiar misogyny in so many places in the world, here it works to naturalize male dominance across human and nonhuman divides. Another technician at the INIA noted that guinea pigs will sometimes resist and refuse mating: "She does not always allow the male to mount her, unlike rabbits who are . . . crazy, like prostitutes or like those women from the jungle who do not only consent to be mounted but in fact they are the ones seducing the male. The male is the one with no choice really. They put him to work all day long." Listening to this facile racism and misogyny was difficult for me, but in this masculinist space, it played all too well. There is no doubt that it was so effective because it reinforced the everyday misogyny found not only in daily conversation but also in the ideologies and colonial structures that validate violence—sexual and otherwise—against certain bodies.

Policies across Latin America, from the criminalization of miscarriage in El Salvador to the state-led forced sterilization of Indigenous women and men in Peru in the 1990s, show that this kind of violence operates at the intersections of race, class, and gender; it demonstrates the ways in which it is a central dimension of the coloniality of power in Peru (Quijano 2000). For example, let us consider the terminology that the INIA has used to discuss cuy breeding. In the 1970s, for example, the institute moved from what it called its "improved race" (*raza mejorada*) of cuyes to developing three different cuy "races": Peru, Inti, and Andina. (In Spanish, "race" and "breed" are both signified by *raza*). In descriptions of each "race," gender and sexuality quickly come into play. Many cuy breeders and researchers within and outside the INIA recommend cuyes from *la raza Andina* for production, as they are more "promiscuous" and have been bred to be more "reproductively efficient." This means that they can reproduce more frequently, and deliver larger numbers of offspring, than either cuyes from the Peru or Inti "races" can. But even though Andinas would make better economic sense (given their reproductive efficiency), researchers at INIA often note that "no one wants them." "Everyone wants *la raza Peru*. No one wants *la Andina*. Not even *la Inti*. This is why we had to develop the 'interracial' lines, to improve certain qualities and expand the market." These interracial cuyes are cheaper than others, but as they are bred with cuyes from *la raza Peru*, some people, especially those with less funds to invest in their business, are more open to buying them.

It is striking how the specter of eugenics, the science of "racial improvement," and *mestizaje*, the nationalist ideology of racial mixture, haunts this space of guinea pig production. A preference for some races ("the Peruvian") over others ("the Andean") is observed and quickly assimilated as a way to reframe and literally repackage racial mixture. While the language of racial mixture was in many ways a Latin American response to North Atlantic rhetoric of white supremacy, in the end, the ideology of *mestizaje* is a celebration of homogeneity, heteronormativity, and anti-Indigenous racism. In a word, it is an extension of the settler-colonial project of the elimination of the Native.

INTERLUDE

> Regarding carcass yields and quality, no statistical differences were found [between castrated and noncastrated animals]. But when considering behavior, the castrated animals showed less aggressiveness than the whole animals, and the latter obtained a lower carcass rating due to the injuries presented.
>
> —cuy researcher, from presentation at a conference on cuy production (in Lima, 2018)

The video shows three men and a young woman in a conference room in front of an audience. Two of the men are wearing white gloves, and one is holding a microphone, pointing to a whiteboard, and talking to the audience. The young woman remains in the background, looking ahead but not participating. One of the men walks over to a small box on a chair and looks down toward it. I can't tell what he is thinking or feeling from the look on his face. He opens the top of the box, then closes it. As the man with the microphone approaches, the man by the box reaches in. The video cuts, and we see only the two men and the woman holding something and hovering over it. Another man is erasing something on the whiteboard while the man with the microphone continues to speak, but his attention is on what he and the others are holding. He examines what we will soon learn is a guinea pig.

The woman watches on without participating, and the man who had been near the box helps by holding the animal. The camera zooms in, and we then see the cuy. He is held belly up, his head forcefully and tightly pulled backward. In the background, the third man (who had been erasing the whiteboard earlier) moves to a table behind them and opens what looks like a large, black medical bag, taking out instruments. The man with the microphone then begins to describe the process of chemical castration, pulling at the animal to expose his testicles. As the camera zooms in, we can detect a slight and subtle smile on the woman's face. As one of the men reaches for something, we see the cuy struggle, moving his paws and trying to pry his head from the man's grasp. The camera cuts again, and then we see the needle.

The man with the microphone continues talking, describing what he is doing, as he impassively injects a chemical into one of the cuy's testicles. As he does this, the other man, who is holding the animal tightly, looks away with a grimace, but noticing the camera on him, he offers an uneasy smile and then looks back toward the cuy. The animal continues to squirm and screeches. The man finishes one injection and moves on to the next. At this point, the woman very quickly dabs the area with a small gauze pad, and we see that she is now holding the microphone. Once the second injection is done, the camera zooms in on the cuy's inflamed testicles. We can see the animal breathing hard but no longer struggling. The man who had looked away then takes the cuy and puts him back in the box as the other man continues speaking to the audience.

Experiencing (Re)Production: Concluding Reflections

Journal entry, May 17, 2015. On this day three years ago, my love, you were born. You were born, and I remember the bend of your knee, the first part of you I saw as you came out of me. I remember feeling so strongly about the trauma of your birth. Society puts so much emphasis on the pain of labor for women. But who talks about the pain of labor for the one being born? The violent ripping from a womb, a warm, safe space; the bruising and the sudden light and the cold; the handling and weighing and cleaning. And being forced to breast feed then and there; then moved to another room, not allowed to hold you. Sleep with you. Which, after thirty hours of labor, is all I wanted to do. Today we celebrate your birthday, and I only want to say that I adore you. I don't have the words to describe this feeling, something I had never felt before and that fills me up in an indescribable way. Listening to you, looking at you, feeling you, smelling you—you are my life.

I had finally returned to Peru. It was February 2022, and because of the ongoing global pandemic, this was my first trip back home in over two years. Away from the demands of academic and home life, I was able to turn my attention to research for a new project on the impact of political violence on more-than-human life. For two weeks, I would immerse myself in the testimonies collected by the Peruvian Truth and Reconciliation Commission, looking for incidents that involved animals, thinking about how earth beings figured in the archives, imagining how it might have felt to be forced to kill your chickens and dogs, to watch soldiers or Senderistas mutilate your donkeys, cows, or alpacas. I also spent time thinking through ways we might approximate what it might have felt like *for the animals themselves* to experience the brutality of this war, to witness the killing of their kin, to be chased and caught and hung, to be abandoned and left to roam the Andean valleys in search of sustenance.

I also needed to carve out time to write this chapter. My focus was (and is) on the discourse of breeders, researchers, and business owners around the production and management of guinea pig life for death. But perhaps because I was so focused on imagining animal experiences of violence in the context of my next project, I wanted to find a way to weave in guinea pig experiences of production. I wanted to imagine what cuy females might feel when, only two or three hours after giving birth, they are subjected to penetration by the males in their enclosure, even if they resist or attempt to refuse. For breeders, this has to do with utilizing the postpartum estrus period and maximizing use of the animal. I wanted to think about the emotional toll of having your pups taken away from you continuously or to consider the impact—physical and emotional—on *primerizas*, or "first-timers," those young females, sometimes as young as five days old, taken from their mothers and siblings and placed in a separate enclosure to be mounted by an adult, sexually mature, male.

Female cuyes usually mature sexually at two months of age, and yet breeders in Peru will wait *at most* until the animals are twenty-one days old to breed them. When I asked the owner of a breeding farm in Lima how often and how early females were bred, his reply was illuminating and disturbing: "Waiting five days or [until the female guinea pig weighs approximately] five hundred grams would be like impregnating a twelve-year-old girl. Waiting ten days or six hundred grams is like getting a fourteen-year-old pregnant. But waiting twenty days or until they weigh eight hundred or nine hundred grams is like an eighteen-year-old being pregnant. We wait twenty-one days because then they are stronger and ready to be mothers." This farm owner also makes a living by offering monthly cuy production workshops, by teaching online cuy production courses, and organizing seminars and conferences to enable cuy production at regional and national levels. In his discussions, and in almost all other discussions I heard from producers about breeding, the recommendation was usually to begin breeding animals at fourteen to twenty-one days. Researchers, such as those at the INIA, point out that at best, females mature sexually at six to seven weeks, but they are working on the modification of guinea pig genetics to lessen the time from birth to sexual maturity, much as they are successfully lessening the time from birth to kill weight.[10] Researchers also point out that social factors, such as placing the young female in an enclosure with a sexually mature male, can "help" her reach estrus earlier.

I was thinking about all this one afternoon in Lima, and as I searched for my notes from my visit to the breeding farm several years back, I came across some writing that I started working on after my son was born. It was a journal of sorts, something I thought I might be able to share with him later in his life. That is where I found the entry with which I begin this section. And it filled me with sadness, my ability to express this overwhelming emotional attachment to this small creature, to think through the trauma of that moment of birth and my inability to grasp or convey what I had witnessed at the farm, to convey the experiences of those caged beings subjected to constant manipulation and human intervention.

I took a walk to take a break, hoping to clear my head and perhaps come up with a way to write about the lived experiences of these animals without projecting my own emotions onto them. I walked from my hotel in Miraflores (an upscale, tourist-friendly neighborhood) to El Parque del Amor, a park with stunning views of Lima's coast, the ocean seemingly stretching forever. As I walked, I thought back to the guinea pig who had been tossed out of her enclosure and left to die in the sweltering heat of a Lima summer. What was she thinking? Was she feeling pain? Where? I remembered how I felt while I was there. I was seven months pregnant as I walked through the enclosures looking at the hundreds of guinea pigs housed there. And I was in constant pain. An old scar on my stomach stretched as my belly expanded, causing excruciating pain that moved from my stomach to my lower back, making it hard to sit or stand or lie down. I was also thirsty all the time, my hands and feet were swollen, and the heat of that summer felt unbearable. I remember noticing that the cuyes had no water. When I asked the farm's owner about this, he told me that they did not need water because they got the necessary fluids from the roughage they were given as part of their diets. Researchers, however, have made clear that water is important, especially for pregnant females and especially in contexts of intensified production.

I also thought about the other females and their pups who had shared the enclosure with her. I remember them scurrying to one corner, huddling close together, and vocalizing intently as the farm's owner reached in to grab their mate. Anxiety, fear, sadness. Those might have been the meanings behind the sounds of I heard. Or the sounds made by mothers when separated from their pups. Scientists have studied communication in guinea pigs, and their findings confirm what we might have imagined: the mother-infant bond among cuyes is strong; infants call out in distress when separated from their mothers, and mothers show visible signs of grief and anxiety when separated from their pups (Kober, Trillmich, and Naguib 2007). What I did not know until I read some of these studies is that this stress is communicated not only audibly but also through scent and body language (Wagner 1976).

How do guinea pigs experience production? Following the work of many scholars who write critically and carefully about the experiences of animals used in industrial agriculture, we can safely say that at various points during the production process, guinea pigs feel stress and terror, pain and fear. Cuyes are social animals with a keen sense of smell and hearing who recognize and respond to their caretakers. They are easily stressed by disruptions, one reason why a leading guinea pig researcher emphasizes the importance of delegating specific groups of cuyes to specific individual caretakers in order to avoid "unnecessary stress" that translates into a loss in profit. Stress has been known to lead to miscarriage and heart attacks in cuyes. The intensification of production increasingly means moving guinea pigs out of enclosures with dirt floors, and toward cages, often stacked on top of one another. Producers openly discuss the pros and cons of this, as wire cages can lead to fractured paws or severed toes. But keeping too many cuyes in a dirt enclosure without proper hygiene can also lead to infection of the teats in females or of penises in males.

I know all of this, and I have read many scientific studies about cuy behavior; and yet I still feel unable to properly write about the phenomenology of guinea pigs subjected to industrialized production.[11] I have been inspired by others who use fiction to try to grasp experience (Varzi 2020), and I considered using speculative fiction to imagine the experiences of female guinea pigs used in production. That was not working, but it was through that process of thinking with fiction and about representation that I remembered Lisa Stevenson's work. It was reading Stevenson and sitting with her writing about "looking away" and "seeing with our eyes closed" as a way of deepening our understanding of another being that opened up a possible path. Looking away, closing my eyes now, I can see her. And following Tina Campt, I can also listen to the image of her in my mind. I can try to attune myself toward the "quiet frequencies of possibility" in my affective engagement with her. She is not just the guinea pig tossed out who produced a torrent of feeling in me and pushed me to question my research and about whom I have been writing for several years. She is not just a representative of the hundreds of other guinea pigs in that breeding farm at that moment in February 2012. As Dominique Lestel, Jeffrey Bussolini, and Matthew Chrulew have put it, we should try to move "away from thinking species in general in order to think instead the singularity of animals" (2014, 126).

All these years I have been writing about that guinea pig but had stopped visualizing her, feeling her. Today, sitting in my office at the University of Washington in Seattle, I closed my eyes and thought back to that moment. And I saw, heard, and felt her again. I remembered that affective encounter powerfully. Her fur was white with caramel-colored patches. She was round but not as large as the other pregnant females around her. Perhaps this would have been her first time giving birth. I remember her face. She was beautiful, her black eyes striking against the white and brown markings on her face. And then I remembered, too, that she looked at me. After she was tossed out, as she lay on the ground, as the farm's owner put his hand on my back and moved me away from her, I turned back once, and she looked at me. She looked right at me, before I turned away. And I realized that it was perhaps that look that shook me. Maybe it was not just the fact that she was caged and exploited and destined to be used until she was no longer profitable. Maybe it was not the roughness with which she was picked up, looked over, and tossed away. Maybe it was the fact that despite that violent encounter, she looked back; she insisted on her singularity; she refused to be forgotten.

NOTES

Parts of this chapter draw from García 2021.

1 Indeed, Stevenson cites Campt in her work.

2 This periodization is problematic. Elsewhere I complicate the designation of Peru as "postconflict," particularly as it obscures the multilayered ways in which the violence "of the past" lives on today in brutal ways, especially in the lives and bodies of those who are most marginalized in the country.

3 I develop this idea more fully in "Killing Kin/Haunting Life: Towards Indigenous Vocabularies of Loss and Repair" (García, forthcoming).

4 This producer was also very excited about the development of products such as "cuy jerky" and cuy *enlatado* (canned guinea pig). A more recent development in this vein is "guinea pig ice cream," developed in Ecuador and apparently quite popular (Castrodale 2019).

5 The INIA's approach is more complicated than this calculation might reflect. While there is much talk about the importance of supporting and empowering women in communities, this vision of empowerment perpetuates heteronormative and patriarchal understandings of the role of women in society. As one technician told me, "Women are empowered when they are better able to care for their families, support their husbands and provide for their children."

6 Readers may already notice and feel the entanglements of gender, race, and Indigeneity. The developmentalist dreams of modernity are always linked to anxieties around race and Indigeneity and embedded within colonial formations that include heteronormative understandings of family.

7 There are similar efforts at work in US pork production (Blanchette 2020).

8 There is much work on the gendered commodification of female animals in industrial animal agriculture, such as the genetic modification of cow bodies to maximize milk production, the captivity endured by "laying" hens who sit in darkness without room to stretch out their wings or turn around, and the plight of sows who are forced into metal gestation crates for birthing and beyond. This commodification also includes continuous sexual violence against animal bodies, such as forced impregnation, as well as the continuous separation of mothers and their offspring, leading to significant emotional trauma. But male animals too are subjected to brutality in this industrial context, where male chicks are killed immediately after birth, sometimes tossed into woodchippers while still alive; bulls are forcibly ejaculated to collect their semen (for artificial insemination), often by inserting electric prods into their anus to shock the system; and male calves are turned into veal, tied in place, and allowed extremely limited movement in order to keep their meat tender. See Adams and Donovan 1995; Gaard 1993, 2013; King 2017; and Singer 2002.

9 Interestingly, many of these examples also reflect traces of animal agency and point to the recognition of it by researchers and producers. For example, there was one slide that explicitly addressed animal preferences: "What does the animal

ask? Because animals also ask. He asks for good nutrition, a clean home, and that he be taken care of." But then there were other ways of describing animal preferences in the context of production: "The animal asks that he be demanded to produce without putting his life at risk."

10 This was explicitly discussed in the cuy production workshop I attended in 2016. See also Trillmich et al. 2006. The normal life span of a guinea pig is six to seven years, but they are usually killed at two to two and a half months.

11 As feminist theorists have long noted, though, we should not need to understand nonhuman animal sentience or emotional capacities in order to know that they have a desire to live and not be harmed (Donovan 2006; Haraway 2007).

REFERENCES

Adams, Carol. (1990) 2015. *The Sexual Politics of Meat: A Feminist-Vegetarian Critical Theory*. New York: Bloomsbury.

———. 2003. *The Pornography of Meat*. New York: Continuum.

Adams, Carol, and Josephine Donovan, eds. 1995. *Animals and Women: Feminist Theoretical Explorations*. Durham, NC: Duke University Press.

Archetti, Eduardo. 1997. *Guinea Pigs: Food, Symbol and Conflict of Knowledge in Ecuador*. New York: Bloomsbury.

Blanchette, Alexander. 2020. *Porkopolis: American Animality, Standardized Life, and the "Factory" Farm*. Durham, NC: Duke University Press.

Campt, Tina. 2017. *Listening to Images*. Durham, NC: Duke University Press.

Cassidy, Rebecca. 2002. *The Sport of Kings: Kinship, Class and Thoroughbred Breeding in Newmarket*. Cambridge: Cambridge University Press.

Castrodale, Jelisa. 2019. "Ecuadorean Ice Cream Vendor's New Best-Seller Is Made from Guinea Pigs." *Vice*, October 9, 2019. www.vice.com

CVR. 2004. *Hatun Willakuy: Versión Abreviada del Informe Final de la Comisión de la Verdad y Reconciliación, Perú*. Lima: Corporación Gráfica.

Davis, Karen. 1995. "Thinking like a Chicken: Farm Animals and the Feminine Connection." In *Animals and Women: Feminist Theoretical Explorations*, edited by Carol J. Adams and Josephine Donovan, 192–212. Durham, NC: Duke University Press.

Degregori, Carlos Iván. 2012. *How Difficult It Is to Be God: Shining Path's Politics of War in Peru, 1980–1999*. Madison: University of Wisconsin Press.

Donovan, Josephine. 2006. "Feminism and the Treatment of Animals: From Care to Dialogue." *Signs: Journal of Women in Culture and Society* 31 (2): 305–29.

Gaard, Greta. 1993. *Ecofeminism: Women, Animals, Nature*. Philadelphia: Temple University Press.

———. 2013. "Toward a Feminist Postcolonial Milk Studies." *American Quarterly* 65 (3): 595–618.

García, María Elena. 2019. "Death of a Guinea Pig: Grief and the Limits of Multispecies Ethnography in Peru." *Environmental Humanities* 11 (2): 351–72.

———. 2021. *Gastropolitics and the Specter of Race: Stories of Capital, Culture, and Coloniality*. Oakland: University of California Press.

———. Forthcoming. “Killing Kin/Haunting Life: Towards Indigenous Vocabularies of Loss and Repair.” In *Indigenous Research Design: Conscientization, Decoloniality, and Methodological Possibility*, edited by Elizabeth Sumida Huaman and Nathan D. Martin. Toronto: Canadian Scholars Women's Press.
Gillespie, Kathryn. 2013. “Sexualized Violence and the Gendered Commodification of the Animal Body in Pacific Northwest US Dairy Production.” *Gender, Place & Culture: A Journal of Feminist Geography* 21 (10): 1321–37.
———. 2018. *The Cow with Ear Tag #1389*. Chicago: University of Chicago Press.
Haraway, Donna. 2007. *When Species Meet*. Minnesota: University of Minnesota Press.
King, Barbara. 2017. *Personalities on the Plate: The Lives and Minds of Animals We Eat*. Chicago: University of Chicago Press.
Kirksey, Eben, and Stefan Helmreich. 2010. “The Emergence of Multispecies Ethnography.” *Cultural Anthropology* 25 (4): 545–76.
Kober, Melanie, Fritz Trillmich, and Marc Naguib. 2007. “Vocal Mother-Pup Communication in Guinea Pigs: Effects of Call Familiarity and Female Reproductive State.” *Animal Behaviour* 73 (5): 917–25.
Lestel, Dominique, Jeffrey Bussolini, and Matthew Chrulew. 2014. “The Phenomenology of Animal Life.” *Environmental Humanities* 5 (1): 125–48.
Morales, Edmundo. 1995. *The Guinea Pig: Healing, Food, and Ritual in the Andes*. Tucson: University of Arizona Press.
Quijano, Anibal. 2000. “Coloniality of Power, Eurocentrism, and Latin America.” *Nepantla: Views from South* 1 (3): 533–80.
Ritvo, Harriet. 1987. *The Animal Estate: The English and Other Creatures in the Victorian Age*. Cambridge, MA: Harvard University Press.
———. 1997. *The Platypus and the Mermaid and Other Figments of the Classifying Imagination*. Cambridge, MA: Harvard University Press.
Rodríguez, Luis Aliaga, et al. 2009. *Producción de Cuyes*. Lima: Fondo Editorial UCSS.
Singer, Peter. 2002. *Animal Liberation*. New York: Ecco.
Stern, Steve, ed. 1998. *Shining and Other Paths: War and Society in Peru, 1980–1995*. Durham, NC: Duke University Press.
Stevenson, Lisa. 2020. “Looking Away.” *Cultural Anthropology* 35 (1): 6–13.
Trillmich, Fritz, Claudia Laurien-Kehnen, A. Adrian, and S. Linke. 2006. “Age at Maturity in Cavies and Guinea-Pigs (*Cavia aperea* and *Cavia aperea* f. *porcellus*): Influence of Social Factors.” *Journal of Zoology* 268 (3): 285–94.
Varzi, Roxanne. 2020. “Ethnographic Fiction: The Space Between.” In *Writing Anthropology: Essays on Craft and Commitment*, edited by Carole McGranahan, 220–21. Durham, NC: Duke University Press.
Wagner, Joseph. 1976. *The Biology of the Guinea Pig*. New York: Academic Press.

2

Working toward Livable Lives through Reproductive Justice for Community Cats

KATJA M. GUENTHER

In the spring of 2022, I conducted observations at a nonprofit veterinary clinic in Los Angeles that provides one core service: spaying and neutering cats. The clinic facilitates the sterilization of over ten thousand cats each year, the vast majority of whom are community cats, or free-roaming, outdoor cats who have no identifiable human owner. Staff welcomed my interest in the clinic, and I was able to speak with workers as they completed their work checking cats into the clinic, preparing them for surgery, conducting the actual surgical procedures, and monitoring the cats while they recovered. The clinic director placed only one restriction on my observation: I was not to take photographs showing any aspect of abortive spays, or the sterilization of pregnant female cats. Abortive spays were, she explained to me, "too controversial," and she did not want members of the public who "don't understand" the challenges facing community cats reacting with hostility to the clinic. Having conducted research for years in the context of high-intake public animal sheltering (Guenther 2020), I was familiar with the controversy surrounding the sterilization of pregnant animals. But I had never had an opportunity to explore how people working with and advocating for companion animals made sense of sterilization broadly and abortive sterilization specifically.

In this chapter, I engage with the reproductive politics of community cat sterilization, including abortive sterilization. Animal reproduction is often central in analyses of human-animal relationships but typically in the context of humans seeking to control the process of procreation for purposes of profit or species maintenance (e.g., García, chap. 1 in this volume; Moore, chap. 9 in this volume; Ellis 2022; Gillespie 2018; Parreñas 2018). Here, I examine how humans control reproduction to *stop* the possibility of life. I place this analysis in a volume focused on animal death because there is a deep connection between the politics of reproduction and of death insofar as without reproduction, new life can not begin. Discourses and practices of population control, eugenics, and sterilization involve death through the prevention of life and, in some cases, the culling of those individuals seen as undesirable.[1] Community cat caregivers and the broader advocacy movement for community cats in the Los Angeles area approach community cat sterilization through the lens of reproductive justice, and I argue that an even greater emphasis on this framework in public-facing work could increase support for community cat sterilization and for the presence of community cats more broadly. This framework acknowledges that community cats are too often unable to flourish because of the environments to which humans have relegated them and that working to end community cat death in the long run requires facilitating the slowing or stopping of reproduction in the short term.

The reproductive justice framework, which emerged from women of color feminisms advancing a more inclusive conceptualization than the reproductive "choice" approach dominant within white US feminism, draws necessary attention to the structural (i.e., economic, political, social, etc.) conditions necessary for reproductive and sexual agency (Silliman et al. 2016). As defined by Loretta J. Ross and Rickie Solinger, the reproductive justice framework "has three primary principles: (1) the right *not* to have a child; (2) the right to *have* a child; and (3) the right to *parent* children in safe and healthy environments. In addition, reproductive justice demands sexual autonomy and gender freedom for every human being. At the heart of reproductive justice is this claim: all fertile persons and persons who reproduce and become parents require a safe and dignified context for these most fundamental human experiences" (2017, 9). A reproductive justice approach also engages with intersectional feminism, emphasizing how class, race, gender, and other axes of inequality shape the opportunities that humans have for reproductive and sexual agency; as Marya Torrez notes, "Reproductive justice is at its core intersectional, and it focuses on the dignity of all individuals" (2014, 278).

The reproductive justice framework, however, is anthropocentric in that it considers human experience; note the repeated references to humans and persons in the preceding quotation from Ross and Solinger (for a detailed discussion, see also Gaard 2010). Here, I discuss how the reproductive justice framework can be fruitful in conceptualizing animal reproduction and show how community cat advocates are already often deploying it. Borrowing frameworks from any one group—whether a species group or a subgroup within a species—and applying it onto another group always runs risks of oversimplification and inappropriate parallels. But we can also sometimes carefully borrow what is helpful from a concept or framework developed in one specific context and use it as a jumping-off point for thinking about another context, such as about a different group at another moment in history. The reproductive justice framework is helpful for thinking about community cat sterilization because it moves beyond an individual concept of choice to engage more deeply about what is dignified and empowering and, coupled with a multispecies orientation, creates space for carving pathways toward lifeworlds that are just for humans and other-than-human animals. Further, I see important pathways in which reproductive justice for animals feeds back to support reproductive justice for humans.

In this chapter, I analyze the interconnections of discourses and practices among humans involved in preventing or stopping new life and show how this stoppage is needed to affirm existing animal life and enable it to flourish. Sterilization is an intervention carried out in the purported pursuit of better lives for community cats, even as it denies the cats the ability to reproduce across generations (of course, for individual cats, sterilization also means that the cats cannot have reproductive sex and, in the case of female cats, cannot experience mothering). The key strategy that community cat caregivers in the Los Angeles area use to try to provide these cats with healthier and better lives is to trap, neuter, return (TNR) them. As its name suggests, TNR involves a human trapping a community cat, bringing the cat to a clinic to be sterilized (spayed or neutered), and then returning that cat to the location at which it was trapped.

In reference to canine sterilization, Krithika Srinivasan notes, "Castrating or removing the ovaries and uterus of an otherwise healthy animal is certainly a biopolitical act in that it intervenes in basic life processes—sexuality and reproduction—on the basis of a set of truth discourses about the regulation of the wellbeing of dog individuals and populations" (2013, 113). In what follows, I examine the practice of TNR and its attendant truth discourses, with particular attention to what Srinivasan calls "agential subjectification." Unlike humans, animals do not generally understand themselves as subjects of the state or other institutions, and they consequently do not self-regulate in the same ways as humans. However, "where self-reflexive subjectification, i.e., subjectification at *the site of the target(s) of intervention*, is not evident, biopolitical techniques can operate by means of subjectification at another *site*: the site of *the agent of intervention*" (Srinivasan 2013, 114–15; emphases in original). Agential subjectification thus refers to how humans internalize dominant discourses and practices pertaining to other-than-human animals, which become a basis for action they undertake on the bodies of animals.

I support TNR, which as I show here has benefits for cats and other animals. My goal is not to question TNR as a practice but rather to analyze the discourses around TNR to make more visible that which is implied there and to talk openly about that which is elided, in the hopes of less stigmatized and more open conversations about TNR in the future. Stopping the development of life through TNR not only helps avoid future suffering for animals yet to be born but, as the caregivers I met discuss, also brings renewed life to community cats who are spayed or neutered. Building on Carly Thomsen's (2013) framework for celebrating abortion, I promote a practice of celebrating sterilization and abortive spays for community cats within a broader framework of reproductive and multispecies justice.

Caring for Community Cats in Los Angeles

Community cats are free-roaming animals who live within a specific territory; their colonies can include just a single individual or dozens of cats. In Los Angeles, community cat colonies are widespread in industrial and commercial areas, as well as in lower-income residential areas. Contra some other nations, like Australia, which have developed legal frameworks for managing community cat populations, Los Angeles is quite typical in the United States with regard to not having any prevailing legal or policy framework for addressing community cat populations. Local animal-control agencies across the US typically provide few, if any, services to these animals. Given the lack of governmental interest in these cats, it is not surprising that there has never been a census of community cats in Los Angeles; a population estimate by the City of Los Angeles Animal Services in 2019 (as part of a lawsuit after the city *did* attempt to introduce some regulation regarding community cats) suggests that roughly 340,000 community cats live in the City of Los Angeles (City of Los Angeles 2020). This estimate excludes the population of community cats in the rest of Los Angeles County (including populous areas like Santa Monica, the San Fernando Valley, and the San Gabriel Valley) and in the adjacent counties of Orange, Ventura, and Riverside. When I asked one of the caregivers I spoke with about her sense of the size of the population of community cats in the Los Angeles metropolitan area, she assessed, "Feral cats are *everywhere* in Los Angeles."

In the analysis that follows, I focus on the narratives and self-described practices of women who care for community cats in the Los Angeles metropolitan area, which includes both the City of Los Angeles and proximal urban and suburban communities that form their own municipalities (i.e., the City of Compton, the City of Torrance, the City of El Monte), as well as on the discourses circulating among community cat advocates. As community cat caregivers, women (and a handful of men) take on one or more of four primary roles vis-à-vis community cats: they trap, sterilize, and return community cats in an effort to reduce the future population of such cats; they feed community cats in colonies and usually also provide some other basic health care to these cats, such as flea control or euthanasia in the event of serious injury or illness; they remove young kittens and sometimes adult cats who are or could be friendly to humans from community cat colonies, foster them, and rehome them; and they communicate directly with members of their communities and/or elected and appointed officials about the need for care for community cats.

I conducted in-depth interviews with twenty-eight community cat caregivers. Because I began this research during the COVID-19 pandemic and had to negotiate the waves of rising and falling infection rates, changing social norms around meeting in-person, and my own health, I completed eleven of these interviews via Zoom. During interviews, which typically lasted around two hours but occasionally stretched as long as four hours, caregivers and I spoke about a range of topics, including how they became involved with community cat caregiving, their feelings about their work with community cats, the details of their actual practices, and more. Interviews were transcribed using voice-recognition software, and then a research assistant or I checked and edited those transcripts to align with the recordings. I engaged in inductive coding, using the qualitative software analysis program NVivo to help me sort and organize the raw material and the coding schemes.

The women who participated in interviews were primarily in middle or late middle age, ranging in age from twenty-three to sixty-four, with an average age of forty-seven (one respondent who declined to provide her age is excluded from this average; she appeared to be sixty-five to seventy-five years old). I did not exclude men but have only two men respondents, as men are underrepresented among community cat caregivers. Thirteen of the participants self-identified as white, eight as Latina or Hispanic, six as Asian American, and one as white-passing Middle Eastern. Eight of the women and one of the men are immigrants to the United States. Participants' apparent class status ranged from poor to upper-middle class, and the stratification among them was noticeable: many clearly indicated that they were living paycheck to paycheck or were renting basic or even substandard housing in lower-income neighborhoods, while a handful owned homes in affluent neighborhoods and communicated that they are financially secure. All but one of the caregivers I spoke with noted that caring for community cats is something that affluent women do not tend to do because they are less likely to come into contact with community cats since these cats are not present in wealthier neighborhoods and because working with community cats is dirty and often dangerous work that is unappealing to wealthier women, who are more likely to focus on rescuing dogs from shelters. As one caregiver, a white woman who did not appear to be affluent and who was the highest-volume trapper I met, told me about the apparent class divide in Los Angeles with regard to community cat caregiving, "Caring for cats is dirty work. Cats are scary. They smell. They're awful. [My car] smells like mackerel and cat pee. Rich white ladies don't want to do that; there is no glory."

Contra popular perceptions of "crazy cat ladies" as women who live without other humans and with many cats (Holmberg 2015; Probyn-

Rapsey 2019), sixteen of the participants were married or lived with partners; these marriage rates are roughly on par with national data. Participants did largely cohabit with cats, ranging in number from one cat to about sixty cats; most had between two and seven cats whom they considered personal companions (as opposed to animals in their temporary care). Those women who cohabited with more than seven cats were always doing so on a short-term basis, providing care as a foster guardian while the cats recovered from an illness or injury and/or awaited adoption placement into a permanent home. Two respondents had no cats whom they considered their personal companions but regularly foster between four and sixteen cats or kittens.

In addition to interviews, I joined two caregivers on their "rounds," accompanying them as they completed the work of caring for community cats in multiple colonies, and I met members of a colony whom a third caregiver feeds. Riding along during colony care gave me an opportunity to meet many community cats, observe them and their interactions with caregivers, and engage in additional conversation with the caregivers about the cats and their work with cats. I spent time visiting two colonies more regularly to observe how the cats spent their time and interacted with each other and the environment. I also was able to observe five caregivers who foster cats as they engaged in caring for their foster cats. I completed training in how to do TNR through a nonprofit organization promoting TNR, although I did not trap any cats directly. Finally, I observed routine operations at a high-volume, low-cost spay/neuter clinic where 85 percent of patients are community cats. During this time, I was also able to speak with veterinary and general staff about their activities. Across these various research experiences, I had extensive exposure to the discourses and practices of community cat sterilization.

Controlling Feline Reproduction through Sterilization

Forced sterilization of animals rarely enters conversations about reproductive justice or freedom or about biopolitics (Foucault 1978), a widely utilized Foucauldian approach that refers to how the organization of life emerged as a political problem in Western societies and resulted in the development of new mechanisms to manage human life (but for examples of animal studies scholarship that engages with reproductive justice, see Gaard 2010; and Srinivasan 2013). Reflecting humans' conviction of our own right to control animals' bodies and determine animals' best interests, humans freely promote sterilization among companion animals, just as we promote forced reproduction among animals farmed for flesh and other bodily products. Captive animals have constrained opportunities to participate in decisions that humans make about their reproduction, and humans also routinely interfere in the reproduction of free-roaming animals, such as by sterilizing community cats. In the context of community cat care, the humans who engage in TNR are the agents of subjectification as they respond to dominant discourses about community cat health and well-being by enacting practices stemming from the dominant discourse onto cats (i.e., sterilization is in cats' best interest, so caregivers sterilize cats).

The human relationship with domesticated animals is ultimately one of domination, and control over animal reproduction is central to human domination of many species and specific members of species, including farmed animals, zoo animals, animals who are part of conservation programs, and companion animals. Humans have intervened in companion animal reproduction for centuries, with feline domestication and breeding dating back as far as the seventh century BC. Early strategies for human management of domesticated and companion animals, including cats, involved the killing of unwanted or undesirable offspring at or near the time of birth, with drowning documented as a particularly popular method in much of the world, including the United States. Surgical sterilization began in the late nineteenth century but was not endorsed or propagated until the 1930s and did not experience a takeoff in the United States until decades later.

Today, 85 percent of domestic (or house) cats in the United States are spayed or neutered (Humane Society of the United States 2022). Still, globally, stray and community cats outnumber house cats two to one, and while there is no data on sterilization of community cats globally, that rate is probably a small fraction of what it is for house cats. The sterilization of community cats is discursively constructed as necessary because cats would otherwise be too numerous. Since humans, at least in the US, apparently do not want to be part of a lifeworld in which cats are present on streets and in homes in large numbers, humans sterilize cats. Sterilization is then framed as being in the best interest of cats: cats in this framing need humans to intervene in their reproduction to keep the human-cat relationship tenable.

Among community cat caregivers I met, as well as within the broader landscape of companion animal welfare in Los Angeles, sterilization of companion animals is promoted as something beneficial to individual animals and to the category of companion animals as a whole. This reflects broader trends: the work of spaying and neutering companion animals is generally seen in the United States as a good deed and what responsible guardians to companion animals do. The companion animal welfare industry promotes the idea that responsible guardians to companion animals sterilize them and that only so-called responsible breeders of pure-bred animals allow their animals to reproduce through carefully planned reproduction. Advocates maintain that spaying and neutering companion animals helps reduce the population of unwanted companion animals and, by extension, the population of companion animals who are unhoused or who ultimately die, whether at the hands of a shelter worker or in a traffic collision, because they are unhoused.

Still, in spite of the positive discourse around the practice, spaying and neutering companion animals remains contested terrain. Community cat caregivers I met routinely encountered human members of the communities where they were engaging in TNR (or trying to) who resisted TNR. Caregivers told me that these resisters cited that sterilization is "disrupting nature," "interfering with God's will," or, by providing care to community cats, supporting their continued presence (as opposed to, for example, culling them or relocating them). The community cat caregivers I met all reported both being accustomed to and frustrated by their encounters with people who hold these views, often attributing their resistance to "cultural" or "old world" (i.e., preimmigration) values, and sought to educate people who do not support TNR whenever possible or, when not possible, to carry out their TNR work anyway. While encounters with resisters to TNR often seemed to make the work of community cat caregivers more difficult, it did not shift their own powerful commitment to TNR as a humane and appropriate way to reduce suffering among community cats.

Yet, subjecting nonconsenting beings to reproductive sterilization is also a form of violence. Although not part of the dominant discourse around spaying and neutering of companion animals, the violent and traumatic aspects of the TNR experience for cats are recognized by caregivers, who note that being in a trap is stressful and scary and that the experience of spending twenty-four to forty-eight hours in captivity is disorienting and taxing for community cats. Several caregivers openly empathized with trapped community cats, observing that a cat's TNR experience is "probably one of the worst days of their lives."

The coherence of institutional and individual support for sterilization was notable as I carried out my fieldwork. That is, even when community cat caregivers acknowledged the violence of the TNR experience, they also maintained that it is the morally "right" thing to do and in the cats' best interests. While I sometimes heard criticisms of a specific spay/neuter clinic, I never encountered anyone who adopted the position that community cats should be killed (which is the position of People for the Ethical Treatment of Animals, for instance) or that they should not be sterilized.

In fact, I found that talking about the spaying and neutering of community cats as coerced or violent remains taboo among community cat caregivers, who instead insist that sterilization is the only path forward to reduce and ultimately eliminate the suffering of community cats. While caregivers acknowledged the stressful and traumatic aspects of TNR for cats, they were clear that they do not discuss this with members of the public or often even with other community cat caregivers who they know. The violence of sterilization thus exists as a hidden subnarrative within the far more powerful and audible discourse promoting sterilization.

The reticence both among caregivers represented in this research and within the broader companion animal welfare movement to engage critically with sterilization of companion animals as a form of violence probably stems from multiple, interrelated issues. First, widespread and targeted spaying and neutering have had many positive consequences for companion animals, including shrinking the population of unwanted and free-roaming companion animals and reducing intakes and kill rates at animal welfare shelters (Kustritz 2012). Analyzing sterilization discourses and practices may be seen as threatening or even reversing these gains. Second, and relatedly, the companion animal welfare industry has successfully framed spaying and neutering as the right thing to do and as what all responsible human guardians to companion animals should do. Engaging critically with sterilization thus is swimming against the stream. It could also be seen as enabling people who are uncomfortable with sterilization—people with whom community cat caregivers routinely have to negotiate when they want to trap cats on private property and are told that they are interfering in nature or God's will and/or that they are enabling the continued presence of a pest animal. Third, companion animal welfare advocates are not inherently free of the anthropocentric views that are dominant in the broader society and that justify human control over animal reproduction generally. Finally, in regard to abortive spays specifically, the prevailing discourse provides limited opportunities for bringing animal concerns into discussions of reproductive rights or justice, and the controversial nature of abortion nationally in the US may inhibit open conversation among community cat caregivers (as the instruction that I not document abortive spays photographically for fear of unwanted public attention suggests).

Many advocates for spay/neuter recognize the touchiness of feline abortion in particular. As I mentioned at the opening of this chapter, when I visited a high-volume spay/neuter clinic, I asked if, in addition to field notes, I could take photos to help me document what I was observing. The clinic director was happy to give me free rein in the clinic with my camera but asked that I not take any photos involving abortions or aborted fetuses because, she said, "people don't understand." Indeed, while almost all of the participants in this research support aborting feline embryos and fetuses during a spay surgery, they also recognized that the issue is contentious and that some people would accuse them of hating cats, hating animals, "murdering" kittens, or just being all-around awful people.

At the same time, community cat caregivers are particularly enthusiastic about trapping cats who they suspect are pregnant. Such animals are a high priority because time is of the essence: if the cat is not abortively spayed before the kittens are born, there will be more kittens for whom the human caregiver must try to find rescue and/or sterilize, thus straining already-very-limited resources further. Many respondents told me about the particular dedication they bring to trapping pregnant female cats, hoping to intervene in the reproductive cycle before they give birth. Over and over again, I heard the sentiment that "the last thing we need is more kittens." Bethany, a twenty-five-year-old Latina woman who traps cats several nights a week and has built a substantial social media presence around her cat-related advocacy, relayed a common sentiment among respondents: "When we see a cat that's already pregnant, our main priority is to trap her so we can terminate her pregnancy."

What critics of abortive spays fail to understand, according to community cat caregivers, is the sheer volume of kittens they must contend with already. Female cats can begin reproducing as young as at four months of age and can get pregnant throughout their lives. Domestic cats typically have litters of three to five kittens but can give birth to a dozen. Although "kitten season" extends well beyond spring in the temperate climate of Los Angeles, the months of March through May see the highest rates of pregnancy among community cats, and some cats will have more than one litter each year. Trappers are more likely to trap female rather than male cats in the spring because they are pregnant and hungry and thus more willing to enter baited traps in their search for food. The clinic aborts upward of two hundred feline embryos and fetuses a day in the spring. In one day of clinic observation in April 2022, only one single female cat who came into the surgery suite for spay while I was observing was *not* pregnant. Caregivers not only do the math—they see the consequences of unchecked fertility in the colonies where they care. Because of clinic closures during the COVID-19 pandemic, the 2020 kitten season in particular went unchecked, and caregivers consistently reported a fast rate of growth in the colonies they care for during this time.

In the context of spaying a community cat, veterinarians will generally abort embryos and fetuses at any stage of pregnancy. The gestation period for domesticated cats is about sixty-five days. Fetal heartbeats are typically detectable about seventeen days after conception, but the heart becomes visible on ultrasound only after fifty days (over three-quarters of the way through gestation). Birth before sixty or sixty-one days markedly increases the likelihood that one or more kittens will not survive. The veterinarians I observed do not attempt to assess the stage of pregnancy: the clinic's practice is to abort and spay as long as the fetuses are still in utero (some pregnant cats give birth in their traps or carriers even while at the clinic, and their kittens will be cared for and adopted out).

Although abortive spay is standard practice among community cat caregivers and in spay/neuter clinics, even some TNR advocates and practitioners are uneasy about abortive spays. Kendall, a thirty-five-year-old white woman who has been engaged in TNR for over five years, told me that when she started doing TNR, she could not knowingly take pregnant cats whose pregnancies appeared to be advanced to be spayed. She even lied to colleagues in her TNR network about the cats' fates, giving at least one pregnant cat to someone outside the network to allow the cat to give birth. Staunchly supportive of reproductive rights for humans, Kendall during our conversation seemed confused by her own reaction to aborting feline fetuses. As we talked it through, she attributed her resistance to aborting feline fetuses to her regular fostering of neonatal kittens:

> I was fostering [kittens] a lot at that period [when I was hiding pregnant mothers]. And I was getting them pretty young, you know, four weeks, three weeks, whatever. . . . A lot of times, the pregnant cats that we get are very close to having kittens. That's when it's really hard for me, if you can see them in the belly. . . . There are times where I'm like, "I'm, I'm not gonna do it." You know, it's *that* close. . . . And I think it is just my experience with baby kittens and having as much [experience with new kittens] as I do and just not being able to wrap my head around that. Because it's hard. . . . We've had them have babies in the trap the night before [the sterilization surgery]. And I, being the jerk that I am, I'm like, "Oh, I'm so happy that that happened. And we didn't have to do that [abortive spay]." I would never say that to certain people at the rescue because they would want to punch me.

Kendall attributes her discomfort around abortive spays to her involvement in caring for very young kittens. She sees the continuity between the life-forms of an advanced fetus and a newborn kitten. She also recognizes that her views are so unpopular that her fellow trappers may want to physically assault her if she said she was relieved that a cat gave birth en route to or at the clinic, before an abortive spay could be completed. Kendall thus deviates from the agential subjectification in that she questions the practice of abortive sterilization.

Kendall's comments also draw attention to how life and death are themselves socially constructed: when so-called life begins in the reproductive process is particularly contested. Many who oppose abortion and abortion rights for humans maintain that "life" begins at the moment of conception and/or well before fetal viability outside the womb, whereas abortion-rights supporters generally hold that life begins at viability outside the womb. In the context of community cats, it is also important to note the argument that human caregivers make: fetal felines born on the street are not really "viable" even *after* being born because the risks to their health and well-being are so great. They routinely die of malnutrition, opportunistic infections and diseases, accidents, and violence. By some estimates, only a quarter of kittens born on the street in the United States will survive to reach six months of age (Humane Society of the United States 2023). Just as the reproductive justice framework for humans centers the difficulty that many children and their caregivers in marginalized and structurally disadvantaged communities face, so, too, does the discourse around community cats incorporate the fact that community cats' lives cannot flourish in current conditions (a point to which I return in the next section).

To better understand the practice of abortive sterilization, I asked the veterinarians about their techniques while they engaged in the abortive spays of dozens of cats, many of them barely adult cats themselves. I could see the fetal kittens being removed from the uterus. Left inside their connected gestational sacs, the removed flesh did not look like anything I recognized as a kitten or really as anything I recognized at all: the best description I can come up with is that the aborted fetuses look like a chain of uncooked sausages. (Veterinarians often call them "bubbles"; a trapper I met who used to work in a clinic and has seen many abortive spays refers to the fetal kittens in their sacs as "balloons.") The veterinarians tied off the fetal sacs with clamps and then placed them in a metal bucket, where they would asphyxiate. When the bucket was close to full, the operating-room staff member would dump them into a trash bag, which subsequently went into a freezer to wait for a pickup by the rendering plant.

As I reflected on the clinic director's instruction to me not to photograph abortive spays, I wondered if making these surgeries more visible would actually *increase* support for them. I thought, too, of how antiabortion activists use misleading imagery to try to garner support for restrictions on human abortions and how rarely we see images that represent the most common types of human abortions in the US (Bliss, Fleischman, and Gomez 2023). Perhaps increased visibility, rather than secrecy, would garner support for abortive sterilization.

One of the veterinarians explained to me that she believed this method of abortive spay was the most humane, with the other veterinarian nodding in agreement. An alternate approach is to cut open each gestational sac and euthanize the fetal kitten, if alive, with an injection. But even kittens who are at the very end of the gestation period and are viable will have difficulty trying to breathe inside the sac. The veterinarians at the clinic agreed that opening a fetal sac so that the kitten would take their first breaths, only then to lethally inject the kitten, seemed more stressful to the kitten than simply allowing the kitten to asphyxiate inside the sac, especially as the fetuses are already sedated via the medication that the pregnant cat receives for the surgery. The veterinarians further noted that opening the sac to euthanize the kittens would substantially increase the emotional difficulty that veterinarians in a spay/neuter clinic experience. "We all love kittens," one of the veterinarians explained as she sewed up an incision after completing a spay on a petite tabby cat. "They're just lumps in a sac right now, and that makes it easier to digest."

As I watched dozens and dozens of female cats be abortively spayed, I found that my empathy lay with the cats undergoing surgery. Their tender vulnerability as their anesthetized bodies lay limply across the surgical trays designed to keep them straight and their bare stomachs propped slightly up touched me. I reflected on how caregivers perceived the experience of TNR as stressful for the cats but also noted how these hours sedated at the clinic could be among the most relaxed, peaceful, and cared-for hours in their lives as street cats. The staff handled their bodies efficiently but thoughtfully, sometimes pausing to gaze on a cat's face or to stroke their fur. I could feel the elision between harm and care, the slipperiness leaving me with the feeling that the moment of sterilization, abortive and nonabortive, both ending the possibility of new community cat life, is a moment of great care.

Reducing Suffering

The principle of providing care and reducing suffering is the central guiding motivation for community cat caregivers. Yvonne, a forty-seven-year-old Mexican American woman who cares for multiple colonies of cats in her lower-income urban neighborhood, described the life of community cats as organized around bare survival and filled with suffering:

> If they're lucky enough to make it out of kittenhood, all it is is a constant battle to survive. That's what it feels like just from watching them out there. They're trying to stay clear of cars, humans, dogs, other cats. And if they're intact, you know, all while either raising babies or trying to make babies. . . . I think it's one of the most inhumane things to ever do or allow to happen to any living creature. . . . It's one of the saddest existences, I think. I've seen them with their ears just bitten, torn to shreds. You know, some of them who we've trapped have had these gashes on their faces from cat fights. I've seen some of them limping, either as a result of being bitten on the paw or abscesses.

Like other caregivers I spoke with, Yvonne sees the toll that living on the streets takes on free-roaming cats: they are routinely injured, sick, and struggling with parasitic infections like flea infestation and mange.

Suffering is a pathway to death that community cat caregivers are attempting to disrupt. Community cat caregivers identify their purpose as to reduce some of this suffering, to create a higher quality of life for these animals, and to reduce the cats' risk of painful and premature death. They feel they cannot control all aspects of how the cats live or the challenges they face; so they do what they can to meet basic needs that these cats have for food and water, and they try to intervene when they see serious health issues.

TNR is central to the goal of reducing suffering in two ways. First, at the population level, TNR is currently the only viable strategy in the US for maintaining or reducing the size of the community cat population overall (chemical birth control is used on a shorter-term basis in other nations but is not approved for use in the US). Because community cat caregivers see the lives of community cats as primarily lives of suffering, preventing more cats from being born also means preventing future suffering. Second, TNR has noticeably positive effects for the specific cat who is sterilized and for any community of cats or humans of which that cat is a part. Community cat caregivers consistently reported that male cats fought less with other cats—a major source of injury—once they were neutered. This means that they are also quieter and less likely to disturb humans. Noises related to mating, which can also be disruptive to humans, abate. Caregivers report that neutered cats have less desire to roam, possibly reducing their risk of car strikes or running into unfamiliar dangers. They become overall "more mellow," as one caregiver described the effects of neutering. Female cats who are spayed also no longer have the stress and strain of mating, pregnancy, or postnatal kitten care (again also reducing noise and other behaviors that humans find problematic). They are able to focus on feeding and caring for themselves, rather than attempting to do this for their kittens.

Ginny, a thirty-four-year-old white woman who has been engaged in TNR since adolescence and who could be described as a second-generation community cat caregiver since her parents first got her into this work, reflects on how spay/neuter benefits the quality of life for cats and saves them from the violence of repeated reproduction. TNR in this vision is about giving life—taking animals from a state that we might think of as a bare life and making it one in which animals experience more joy. Here, she describes what she observes in community cats who are trapped and returned to well-managed colonies with a regular feeder:

> I love seeing how boy cats just melt into like these little marshmallows [after they are neutered], that they're . . . just all lumpy and happy. All they want to do is like hang out and lay in the sun. And the boys generally end up being more friendly and sweet [after neutering]. And I love watching girl cats especially because it's this, like—breaking out of this cycle of breeding where, like, for most of their lives, from, like, four months on, all they've done is, like, breed and have kittens. . . . And I'm seeing female cats after they've been spayed actually acting like kittens again. It is, like, the cutest thing. And just being able to have, like, a fun life where they don't have to be forced to breed all the time. Or male cats, when they're not fixed, they'll actually sometimes come in and kill a litter of kittens to force the female back into heat. And so it's just, like, breaking them out of that cycle of tragedy is so awesome.

Ginny draws attention to the multiple positive effects of sterilization for cats of both sexes and sees breaking a cycle of community cat suffering as a rewarding part of her labor.

Notably, many caregivers I encountered viewed feline sexuality as itself violent and female cats as victims of sexual violence. Many used the term "rape" to refer to community cat sex and described how interrupting the reproductive cycle specifically benefits female community cats. Ashley, a thirty-year-old white woman with extensive TNR experience, said, "It's nice when you do release them [after sterilization], and you see them run off and rejoin their friends or whatever. And you're like, 'Oh, you're happy. Your life is better now.' And then you're also just thinking, like, 'Oh, you're not going to fight, and you're not gonna get cat raped, and you're not going to have babies, and you're just gonna go have a cool life where you enjoy yourself.' And I got to be a part of that." Unlike in other animal rescue scenarios, in which human rescuers of animals "save" animals from what they see as terrible living situations and position themselves as saviors (Weaver 2021), community cat caregivers routinely return animals to what they see as suboptimal living conditions on the streets and do not tend to describe themselves in savior-like terms. But, like Ashley, they do feel particularly grateful for being able to disrupt reproduction and often characterize their work as "sparing" female cats from the victimization of tomcats and as sparing tomcats from conflict and violence with other toms.

The Future Lives of Community Cats

Community cat sterilization is a violence in that the cats' bodies are subjected to an irreversible and invasive surgical intervention to which they cannot fully consent, ending the possibility of life for future colony cats in order to eliminate their future suffering and to reduce the likelihood of future suffering among other cats (including their potential offspring but also other colony cats with whom they might struggle for territory, food, mating opportunities, etc.). "This, then, is the kind of subjectification that biopower is widely associated with, where care and harm are knotted up together" (Srinivasan 2013, 115). TNR ends the possibility of some forms of life reproducing while enhancing possibilities for other lives to improve.

Its propagators—community cat advocates and all those who are engaged in TNR—act as agents of subjectification, carrying out the practices associated with resolving the discursive claim that community cats' unsterilized lives are lives of suffering and that their bodies require human intervention.

Poststerilization flourishing is not central in the public-facing discourse about the sterilization of community cats, perhaps because the happiness of community cats is not generally a public concern. Yet, integrating attention to the positive effects of sterilization could help to counter negative feelings that some people hold about sterilization and abortive spays and even about community cats more generally insofar as the stories of their poststerilization lives are joyful and even touching. Attention to the happiness of community cats after sterilization undermines concerns that sterilization, and especially abortive spays, are life ending or an overextension of human control over animal bodies. Recognizing and centering this happiness also aligns with the commitment in reproductive justice and multispecies democracy frameworks to include the concerns of those whose reproduction is affected by choices being made for them. Community cats may enjoy sex and/or mothering, both of which become impossible after sterilization. Yet, they also appreciate other activities that increase after sterilization.

Conceptualizing reproductive justice for community cats allows us to engage more deeply with thinking about sterilization and abortive spays of community cats as an opportunity both to help individual animals thrive and to reduce suffering of future community cats. Ultimately, a central goal of reproductive justice for community cats must be the creation of conditions that *are* favorable to their reproduction, such as safe, stable environments with access to food, water, and veterinary care. It is possible to forge pathways that facilitate the flourishing of community cat colonies through the creation of conditions that enable them to thrive. Efforts at reshaping cities and communities to be safer spaces for community cats run parallel to the shorter-term and, at this juncture, emergency tactics that community cat caregivers use to minimize suffering and reduce premature and painful death.

One strategy that is currently not being widely pursued in the Los Angeles area but that offers a less invasive and violent way of addressing community cat reproduction is birth control. Currently, oral birth control is used on cats in many parts of the world but has faced obstacles to widespread use in the United States. Megestrol acetate is safe to use on a temporary basis of up to eight months, as a way to prevent pregnancy while cats await a space in a clinic to become available (Greenberg et al. 2013). In places like Los Angeles, where the demand for sterilization surgeries for community cats far outweighs the availability, temporary oral birth control will help reduce community cat populations. Permanent (or even very long-term) chemical sterilization is not yet available, but its ultimate development would offer a less traumatic intervention for community cats.

Los Angeles, like so many cities, is an anthropocentric urban and suburban environment in which animals of all kinds are primarily seen through a management lens. Policy makers and policy machinations, including animal control, transit and road development, housing development, and parks and recreation, seek to manage animals in ways that minimize the public perception of inhumane treatment of animals and that reduce health and safety risks to humans. Only within limited frameworks are animals' concerns taken into account. Happy, healthy cat colonies could exist by meeting their basic needs for food, water, shelter, and veterinary care; providing them with safe physical spaces that are free from cars or other threats and where the risk they pose to other species (i.e., birds) as hunters is minimized; and promoting appreciation for them as part of the lifeworld of the city. Like other animals in the urban landscape (Wolch 2002), such as community cats' much larger and more famous brethren, the local celebrity mountain lion P-22, who was euthanized in December 2022, community cats can be a source of wonder, a disruption of humancentric activity and thinking, and a partner in multispecies connection.

NOTES

I extend my gratitude to Tempest Won for their research assistance.

1 Discussing sterilization, and especially abortive spaying, in the context of death is not to suggest that anyone is being murdered, a common claim in the anti-abortion-rights movement about what abortionists do. Who is murderable is itself socially defined (Kim 2017), and at present, embryonic and fetal animals are not murderable in our society; quite the contrary, animals as a group are generally

killable, albeit with some variation across species and even across individuals within a species.

REFERENCES

Bliss, Erika, Joan Fleischman, and Michele Gomez. 2023. "Early Abortion Looks Nothing like You've Been Told." *New York Times*, January 22, 2023. www.nytimes.com.
City of Los Angeles. 2020. *Citywide Cat Program: Final Environmental Impact Report*. SCH#201310. Los Angeles: City of Los Angeles.
Ellis, Colter. 2022. "Breeding, Calving, and Trafficking in Conventional Beef Production." *Society & Animals* 30 (2): 1–19.
Foucault, Michel. 1978. *The History of Sexuality*. New York: Pantheon.
Gaard, Greta. 2010. "Reproductive Technology, or Reproductive Justice? An Ecofeminist, Environmental Justice Perspective on the Rhetoric of Choice." *Ethics and the Environment* 15 (2): 103–29.
Gillespie, Kathryn. 2018. *The Cow with Ear Tag #1389*. Chicago: University of Chicago Press.
Greenberg, Michael, Dennis Lawler, Stephen Zawistowski, and Wolfgang Jöchle. 2013. "Low-Dose Megestrol Acetate Revisited: A Viable Adjunct to Surgical Sterilization in Free Roaming Cats?" *Veterinary Journal* 196 (3): 304–8.
Guenther, Katja M. 2020. *The Lives and Deaths of Shelter Animals*. Stanford, CA: Stanford University Press.
Holmberg, Tara. 2015. *Urban Animals: Crowding in Zoocities*. New York: Routledge.
Humane Society of the United States. 2022. "Pets by the Numbers." Accessed March 21, 2022. www.animalsheltering.org.
———. 2023. "Outdoor Cats FAQ." Accessed January 26, 2023. www.humanesociety.org.
Kim, Claire Jean. 2017. "Murder and Mattering in Harambe's House." *Politics and Animals* 3 (2): 37–51.
Kustritz, MV Root. 2012. "Effects of Surgical Sterilization on Canine and Feline Health and on Society." *Reproduction in Domestic Animals* 47 (Suppl. 4): 214–22.
Parreñas, Juno Salazar. 2018. *Decolonizing Extinction: The Work of Care in Orangutan Rehabilitation*. Durham, NC: Duke University Press.
Probyn-Rapsey, Fiona. 2019. "The 'Crazy Cat Lady.'" In *Animaladies: Gender, Animals, and Madness*, edited by Lori Gruen and Fiona Probyn-Rapsey, 175–86. New York: Bloomsbury.
Ross, Loretta, and Rickie Solinger. 2017. *Reproductive Justice: An Introduction*. Berkeley: University of California Press.
Silliman, Jael, Marlene Gerber Fried, Loretta Ross, and Elena Gutiérrez. 2016. *Undivided Rights: Women of Color Organize for Reproductive Justice*. Chicago: Haymarket.
Srinivasan, Krithika. 2013. "The Biopolitics of Animal Being and Welfare: Dog Control and Care in the UK and India." *Transactions of the Institute of British Geographers* 38:106–19.

Thomsen, Carly. 2013. "From Refusing Stigmatization toward Celebration: New Directions for Reproductive Justice." *Feminist Studies* 39 (1): 149–58.

Torrez, Marya. 2014. "Combatting Reproductive Oppression: Why Reproductive Justice Cannot Stop at the Species Border." *Cardozo Journal of Law & Gender* 20:265–306.

Weaver, Harlan. 2021. *Bad Dog: Pit Bull Politics and Multispecies Justice*. Seattle: University of Washington Press.

Wolch, Jennifer. 2002. "Anima Urbis." *Progress in Human Geography* 26 (6): 721–42.

3

Roadkill, or the Logic of Sacrifice

MATTHEW CALARCO

Obstructions

In *Eclipse of Reason*, Max Horkheimer offers a remarkable anecdote to illustrate what he labels "modern insensitivity to nature" (2004, 71). In his discussion of the logic of domination as applied to the natural world, Horkheimer mentions how the landing of planes in Africa at the time (landings that presumably occurred in a region that had not had previous substantial air-travel infrastructure in place) was seen as often being "hampered by herds of elephants and other beasts" (71). That the air-travel infrastructure and landings were at odds with the welfare of elephants and other animals did not, Horkheimer suggests, lead to a rethinking or curbing of such practices; instead, the animals themselves were viewed as constituting the problem. In this situation, animals were, in Horkheimer's words, "considered simply as obstructers of traffic" (71), and their lives and deaths were understood to have no significance or importance in their own right.

Horkheimer links this insensitivity to the lives and deaths of animals to a "pragmatic attitude" (2004, 71) that he argues is operative throughout the history of Western thought and culture up to the present. My aim in this chapter is to probe further into this "pragmatic attitude," specifically in relation to the problem of roadkill. I do so through an examination of what I call a *logic of sacrifice*. I explicate this logic by way of an engagement with the work of Judith Butler, Donna Haraway, and Jacques Derrida, all of whom are concerned to demonstrate that the dominant social order is predicated on the structural exclusion of certain beings from the circle of social and normative consideration. Extending these analyses, I seek to explore how this logic of sacrifice functions in the context of modern systems of mobility to frame animals as beings who can be routinely sacrificed in the service of the established social order. I then consider possible critical responses and alternatives to this logic under three different rubrics: liberal humanism, zoo-pessimism, and inhumanism. I close the chapter by examining how certain contemporary roadkill artists endeavor to challenge the logic of sacrifice and how their work aligns with key elements of the inhumanist perspective.

The Logic of Sacrifice

Judith Butler's *Frames of War* (2009) is the locus classicus for the fecund contemporary dialogue that has grown up around the concept of *grievability*. In this text, Butler develops a richly layered notion of grievability in view of discerning how some beings are framed as mattering while others are made not to matter—which is to say, how some beings bear social significance while others lack it (a theme that will be familiar to readers through contemporary political struggles such as Black Lives Matter and other struggles for social recognition and mattering). She suggests that one way to understand a particular being's social significance and standing is to consider whether it is "grievable" by the dominant standards of a given social order. To be grievable on this account is to have a death that is considered worthy of mourning, a death that has some significance and that is marked as mattering in various ways by the moral community. So, in response to the death of human beings who are seen as grievable, a community might participate in certain funeral rites, orations, days of remembrance, and other such ceremonies that mark that person as mattering. Butler suggests that grievability of this sort is "a presupposition for [a] *life* that matters" and "a condition of a life's emergence and sustenance" (2009, 14–15). Thus, for a life to be livable, the death of that life must at the same time be framed as grievable. Butler writes, "Without grievability, there is no life, or, rather, there is something living that is other than life. Instead, 'there is a life that will never have been lived,' sustained by no regard, no testimony, and ungrieved when lost. Grievability precedes and makes possible the apprehension of the living being as living" (15). That there are lives that amount to something less than and "other than life" speaks to the fact the grievability is differentially allocated by the established order (182). Among those who are included in the moral community, grievability is dispensed in varying degrees; and for those who are excluded from consideration, grievability is often entirely denied. In line with the concerns of the present chapter, Butler clearly recognizes that the complex borderlines of grievability run in concert with the contours of the subject position of the human (76). Those who are genuinely grievable, Butler suggests, are those deemed to be fully and properly human; and the degree to which a given being is understood to participate in and depart from that subject position functions to determine the relative worth of its life and death.

So, how to name and think more carefully about those beings who are *denied* grievability? Butler uses the term "lose-able" for this task, a term that speaks to the logic of sacrifice that I will be elaborating in what follows. In referring to beings and groups who have been exiled from the circle of social consideration, Butler notes, "Such populations are 'lose-able,' or can be forfeited, precisely because they are framed as being already lost or forfeited; they are cast as threats to human life as we know it rather than as living populations in need of protection from illegitimate state violence, famine, or pandemics. Consequently, when such lives are lost they are not grievable, since, in the twisted logic that rationalizes their death, the loss of such populations is deemed necessary to protect the lives of 'the living'" (2009, 31). The sociologist David Redmalm offers a helpful rubric for understanding how beings become lose-able in the sense articulated by Butler. On Redmalm's account, the individual deemed not worthy of grieving must be desingularized and "framed as replaceable" (2015, 23). In addition, the death of a lose-able individual must be characterized as having no transformative force and as belonging to a predictable and insignificant course of events. Finally, the lose-able individual's death is characterized as one that is not shared by those who matter. Their mortality and finitude do not denote "a common state of precariousness" (23) but belong to a different order of death from which members of the dominant social order are believed to be exempt.

In a gesture that resonates with our central concern here, Redmalm goes on to take up the question of how people mourn animal pets. As he notes, in the ambiguous and fraught process of grieving for pets, the grieving person is trying in some way to shift the status of that individual pet from being lose-able to being grievable against the backdrop of social conditions where grievability is largely coterminous with the human (Redmalm 2015, 23; for further reflections on this point, see also Guenther 2020). Although Butler herself does not focus in detail on the grievability and lose-ability of pets or animals more generally, she is nevertheless cognizant that her discourse on grief has the potential to contest the anthropocentrism of dominant attitudes toward animals and other beings who circulate on and outside the margins of the human. In this vein, Butler does not rest content with the facile assumption that the differential allocation of grievability can be solved by an appeal to straightforwardly humanist premises or to a common human nature, for such gestures simply reinforce anthropocentric dogmas. Thus, in reflecting on the limits of a universalist humanism in thinking about grievability, Butler asks,

> How does one object to human suffering without perpetuating a form of anthropocentrism that has so readily been used for destructive purposes? Do I need to make plain in what I consider the human to consist? I propose that we consider the way "the human" works as a differential norm: Let us think of the human as a value and a morphology that may be allocated and retracted, aggrandized, personified, degraded and disavowed, elevated and affirmed. The norm continues to produce the nearly impossible paradox of a human who is no human, or of the human who effaces the human as it is otherwise known. Wherever there is the human, there is the inhuman. (2009, 76)

I shall return to the concept of the inhuman later in the chapter. For the moment, though, I want to suggest that, despite Butler's awareness of the problems associated with naïve anthropocentrism, there are certain limits to her approach when it is applied directly to road-killed animals. For there is a significant difference between (1) attending to the general ways in which the concept of the human produces a "constitutive outside" of dehumanized and subhumanized others (which is characteristic of Butler's approach) and (2) understanding the specific ways in which discourses and practices related to the grievability and lose-ability of life and death produce and normalize the routine sacrifice of roadkill (which is part of our task in this chapter). Although these two projects are necessarily related, there is precious little direct attention to animals themselves (whether living or dead) in Butler's work or to the sorts of questions posed by Redmalm and other animal studies scholars about the relative lose-ability and grievability of animals (Stanescu 2012). In order to address this limitation, it will be helpful to examine how Donna Haraway and Jacques Derrida—two authors who have written at length on animals themselves—frame the question of animal life and death in relation to the established anthropocentric order.

For Haraway (2008), the question concerning animal mattering is one of whether animals are made *killable*, which is to say, whether they can be killed with moral impunity and whether they are understood ontologically as being no more than entities to be used and discarded. The notion of killability is essential for understanding Haraway's approach, for she is keen to distance herself from certain animal rights and animal liberation frameworks that (on her account) try to remove animals *tout court* from the realms of death, predation, and other modes of violence. Haraway's thought presumes, by contrast, that life is inherently violent and involves ubiquitous killing and consumption. There is, she argues, no way to avoid these interlaced cycles of life and death, of giving birth and bringing death. So, rather than seeking to establish bulwarks that protect animals from any and all forms of violence and death, Haraway argues instead that we need to guard against "exterminism" and reducing animals and others to the realm of beings that are "merely" killable (2008, 78–80). In Haraway's words, "it is not killing that gets us into exterminism, but making beings killable" (80). If, then, we are not entirely able to avoid killing, the problem becomes one of learning to "live responsibly within the multiplicitous necessity and labor of killing, so as to be in the open, in quest of the capacity to respond in relentless historical, nonteleological, multispecies contingency. Perhaps the commandment ["Thou shalt not kill"] should read, 'Thou shalt not make killable'" (80). Haraway's point about the "necessity and labor of killing" is apt and one that is all too easy to disavow, especially when considering the case of roadkill, where the temptation might be to try effectively to eliminate roadkill entirely through certain activist and policy measures. But animals who are not killed by cars will, of course, be killed or die in some other way—indeed, in a way that might be worse than death by car, plane, or train. Moreover, road-killed animals themselves are often taken up within the trophic chains of other animals and thereby rendered significant bodies in a different set of multispecies relations. So, our analysis of roadkill should bear in mind Haraway's point about the necessity of killing and the unanticipated fates of roadkill as we develop our analysis.

I would suggest, though, that Haraway's approach to killability—for all its strengths—is nevertheless problematic inasmuch as it tends to allow the irreducibility of violence and the necessity of killing to occlude the possibility of making radical changes in certain behaviors and institutions that can partially ameliorate useless suffering and unnecessary killing. Thus, Haraway will consider the possibility of eating meat that has been raised under better welfare conditions or improving the conditions of experimental animals, but she tends to dismiss veganism or the abolition of invasive animal experimentation as naïve ideals that turn farmed and experimental animals into living museum pieces (Williams 2010; Franklin 2017). Her stance seems to presume that if these animals are not farmed for food or used for the advancement of science, they will not have a life worth living. Better, then, she argues to maintain these relations that involve killing but that also allow for the ongoing possibility of living. We could insist in response that to struggle to free animals from such forms of confinement and commodification and toward other potentialities is not so much a matter of denying their finitude or mortality or keeping them protected from violence and on display in a museum but an attempt to free animals for a more worthwhile life—and death. The same is true of the struggle to reduce the number of road-killed animals. The point of such work is not somehow to remove animals from the condition of being mortal but to recognize and challenge the multiple ways in which modern systems of mobility cause useless suffering and countless deaths, actions that create tears in the fabric of life and relation that tend to rip and contribute to other unnecessary cuts and crises (from habitat fragmentation to defaunation and beyond).

What goes missing, then, from Haraway's analysis of many (but certainly not all) human-animal relations is that the established order is susceptible in some cases to being fundamentally contested and radically changed in the direction of maximal respect for animals. Moreover, it should be noted that the making killable of animal life that Haraway seeks to contest is not an unfortunate side effect of many human-animal relations but is functionally and structurally integral to many of those relations and their institutional settings—which means that contesting the killability of animals often means working fundamentally to curtail and even abolish certain practices. In institutions like factory farming and invasive experimentation, animals are ontologically framed as equipment and commodities to be reared and killed for human use; and this frame remains in place even in "free-range" and "green" alternatives to factory farming and in the supposedly "less cruel" alternatives to invasive experimentation (which Haraway tends to favor). Contemporary systems of mobility are no different. The ongoing sacrifice of animals, the fragmentation of animal habitat, the degradation of ecosystems, and myriad other problems that attend the institution and maintenance of circuits of mobility are not accidents of the system but are essential parts of its design; and many of the "solutions" that seek to address roadkill and other harms to the more-than-human world do nothing to challenge the fundamental assumptions that undergird that system.

We are led to conclude, then, that the lose-ability and killability of animal life—what we might call a generalized animacide—characteristic of many contemporary modes of human-animal interactions are ultimately predicated on the *sacrifice* of animal life. By sacrifice here, I have in mind not so much the killing of animals for religious or ritual purposes but rather the destruction or surrender of something for the sake of something else. Phrased in the simplest terms, we could thus say that animals and more-than-human others of many kinds are routinely sacrificed to (that is, destroyed for the sake of, surrendered to) the dominant way of life. This way of life—animated by its anthropocentric, hypermobile soul (Freund and Martin 2007)—takes itself to be nonnegotiable. It allows for minor reforms at the structural level and sometimes seeks to cloak the cruelty of its veneer to some degree, but as a matter of principle, it structurally leaves open a space for what Jacques Derrida refers to as the "noncriminal putting to death" of animal life (Derrida and Nancy 1991, 112). This is why Derrida can write, in a way that complements Haraway's insights but simultaneously departs from them, that the commandment "Thou shalt not kill" is never extended by the dominant culture to the "living in general" (112).

In this way, Derrida—much like Haraway—underscores the fact that animals are rendered killable by the established order. Derrida emphasizes, however, the inverse point as well—namely, that such killability presupposes a group of beings (those individuals who are taken to be paradigm instances of the human) who render others killable but who exempt themselves from being killable. Derrida refers to this gesture of designating others as killable while exempting oneself and one's confederates from this fate as a "sacrificial structure" (Derrida and Nancy 1991, 112). He suggests that even the most insightful critics of traditional humanism rarely, if ever, call this sacrificial structure into question—which is to say, these critics of humanism fail to "*sacrifice sacrifice*" and thereby remain dogmatically committed to a certain anthropocentrism (112). Following Derrida, we can observe that, despite the proliferation of criticisms of and alternatives to humanism in our own time—from antihumanism to transhumanism to posthumanism—this logic of sacrifice still forms the invisible contours of thought and practice. The standard alternatives to humanism might include a consideration of reforms to this logic, but the logic itself and the broader anthropocentric order to which it belongs lie largely beyond the range of critique.

Liberal Humanism, Zoo-Pessimism, Inhumanism

The discourses I have examined thus far in this chapter concerning lose-ability, kill-ability, and sacrifice-ability all highlight a structural problem with the dominant social order: namely, that it functions to obscure, minimize, and ultimately justify the sacrifice of countless lives—both human and more-than-human—in the service of constituting and sustaining the dominant way of life. In relation to roadkill in particular, this logic is deployed to justify the ever-increasing presence of automobiles on our roads, the ever-increasing expansion of roads and other circuits of mobility, and the minimizing of the violence, harm, and disruption of subjective, social, and ecological relations that circulate among human and more-than-human lives. Now, even if it is clear that the field of animal studies is premised on a general rejection of the marginalization and sacrificeability of animal life, it is far less clear what such a rejection involves or what an actualizable alternative to this logic might be. Let us, then, sketch a series of possible responses to the logic of sacrificeability from a generally pro-animal perspective and do so specifically in view of the problem of how to address the problem of roadkill. Here, I consider three different approaches under the rubrics of liberal humanism, zoo-pessimism, and inhumanism.

Consider, first, a *liberal humanist* approach to the problem of sacrificeability. For the liberal humanist, the overarching aim of politics and normative theory is to recast who does and does not count, using the human as the measure. Typically, liberal humanism has limited itself to extending consideration to human beings who have previously been excluded from consideration (people of color, women, people of alternative sexual orientations, and so on); but, as pro-animal advocates have pointed out, there is no reason to restrict such extensionist logic to paradigm members of the biological species of human beings. If the primary criteria for inclusion in the liberal political sphere are subjectivity, consciousness, sentience, autonomy, or other such characteristics, then what it means to be "human" in the political and normative sense is not coterminous with the biological species *Homo sapiens*—for we find these traits to a greater or lesser degree, pro-animal advocates argue, among animal species of various sorts. Consequently, the reasoning goes, animals displaying these characteristics can be excluded from consideration only by illogical and unjust means. For the pro-animal advocate, the lives and deaths of animals should be seen as having just as much worth and being just as grievable as those of human beings. Human rights, on this account, are thus not exclusively human but belong to a variety of animals as well (Cavalieri 2001). Just as rights are intended to provide (relatively) absolute bulwarks against violations of life, bodily integrity, and autonomy for human beings, giving animals similar rights (it is argued) will prevent them from suffering similar forms of violence.

If we consider roadkill from this perspective, we would assume that critical analysis of systems of mobility would figure centrally in the animal rights discourse that issues from liberal humanist commitments. For, even under the most conservative estimates, roadkill is a significant cause of animal injury and death in many advanced industrial societies (the standard number cited in the literature is that some one million animals are killed per day by car in the United States alone, and this figure does not include rail or air or marine traffic; Seiler and Helldin 2006). Yet, a relative silence reigns around the issue of roadkill in mainstream forms of pro-animal discourse and activism influenced by liberal humanism. Where we might expect calls for a radical reduction in driving and a complete reconsideration of urban and rural mobility infrastructure, we tend to find among mainstream animal rights and welfare organizations little more than tepid endorsements of wildlife crossings, lower speed limits for vehicles, and similar reforms.

One of the reasons for this relative silence might be that there is no meaningful consumer-based solution to the problem of roadkill. As just noted, the guiding ideal behind liberal humanist versions of animal politics is that animals should, for the most part, be lifted "up" out of the realm of sacrificeability and be provided the same kinds of strict protections that paradigm instances of "the human" are understood to bear. The chief strategy for achieving this goal in mainstream animal advocacy circles has generally been consumerist in orientation—which is to say, mainstream animal politics is often premised on having individuals purchase and consume alternative products that avoid using animals in instrumental ways. So, rather than eating animal-based meat, we are encouraged to consume plant-based meat alternatives; rather than purchasing cosmetics tested on animals, we are counseled to buy "cruelty-free" products; and so on. To be sure, there are certain practices from which we are encouraged to abstain *tout court* (for example, the exploitation of animals in the pet and entertainment industries); but the central message of mainstream animal rights and animal welfare organizations is that no fundamental changes are required in our present (which is to say, consumerist) way of life in order for animals to be granted full ethical and legal standing. It is assumed that we can, for the most part, purchase our way out of injustice.

As Dennis Soron (2008) has persuasively argued, however, the kinds of ethico-political intervention required for addressing the problem of roadkill are rather different from these sorts of strategies and tactics. While it might be possible to limit and almost eliminate the direct consumption of animal products from one's diet, there is no similar abstention possible in regard to the use of structures of mobility for most individuals, as these circuits and modes of transport permeate every aspect of our lives, in both direct and indirect forms. Nor are there any simple, ready-made consumer substitutes (such as, say, a "cruelty-free" automobile) that avoid the harms done to animals by our hypermobile way of life (although there are certainly *better* modes of mobility possible than the modes currently dominant). In short, addressing the issue of roadkill entails a full reconsideration of dominant structures of mobility across a variety of registers, a reconsideration that cannot help but to call fundamentally into question our consumerist and hypermobile form of life. Of course, most mainstream activists, theorists, and organizations do not want to preach this sort of message, for fear of being seen as fringe or unpragmatic. While such hesitance is understandable, the fact remains that we have collectively built a mobility infrastructure and form of life that can only be made (even partially) just by being (for the most part) dismantled and reconstituted from the ground up.

It could be suggested that another reason the liberal humanist approach runs into an intractable limit with regard to roadkill is because it starts from an overly optimistic assessment of the potential for reform of human-animal relations within the current social order. Rather than assuming that animals can be fitted over time into the dominant normative (ethical, legal, and political) order, it might be more fairly concluded (the critic could suggest) that the established order cannot be genuinely reformed with regard to animals. Animals enter this order in various ways: as pets, meat, laborers, clothing, pests, entertainment, resources—in short, as usable, losable, killable, and sacrificeable—but never as beings who exist in and for themselves, as independent of the (lack of) meaning granted to them by the dominant human culture, and almost never as beings with their own significant worlds, relations, lives, and deaths. Our systems of mobility, it could be argued, cannot be reformed in such a way as to recognize the singularity and alterity of animals without failing to exist; rather, the very nature of those systems is founded on the desingularization of animal life and requires its ongoing sacrifice for continued operation and expansion.

Forthright recognition of this dominant anthropocentric ontologic concerning animal being might lead us to a different, less optimistic conclusion about addressing the general sacrificeability of animals within the current coordinates of the status quo. Let us refer to an approach based on such recognition as *zoo-pessimism*. For the zoo-pessimist, it is necessary to begin with the admission that animals—contra the liberal humanist approach—are never going to be raised up fully into the sphere of the human, are never going to be granted human rights, and will always be seen as subhuman or less-than-human within the current social order. In the dominant cultural context, animal life is and remains fundamentally lose-able, even if the death of the occasional individual animal (typically, a charismatic animal) might be considered grievable. Animals are and always will be framed, the zoo-pessimist argues, in such a way as to render them killable by human subjects with impunity. Animals are and will continue to be sacrificed by the billions so that our way of life can be maintained. With regard to roadkill in particular, the pessimist would counsel against the naïve belief that mobility infrastructure will ever be fundamentally transformed in a pro-animal direction by the dominant culture. At best, roadkill numbers might be lowered through reducing speed limits and constructing wildlife crossings, but the telos of such policy and practical initiatives is and always will be human well-being, whether in view of improving the welfare of human drivers who might be injured in human-animal collisions or in the form of maintaining the enjoyment that human beings gain from having ongoing access to wilderness areas richly populated by fauna.

The zoo-pessimist is thus likely to see animal welfare issues in general and the problem of roadkill in particular as intractable problems and as a cause for despair. The minor reforms to mobility infrastructure and the expansion of wildlife crossings and other such strategies celebrated by mainstream pro-animal organizations are bound to appear to the zoo-pessimist as mere Band-Aids applied to a massive and persistent wound. Moreover, the zoo-pessimist would be disinclined to believe that other, better solutions to the problem of roadkill are possible on the collective level. The social order, it will be argued, is founded on anti-animal, anthropocentric premises that cannot be easily displaced. The best that can be hoped for is that conscientious individuals might adopt an ethic of limiting or eliminating driving and will try to remove themselves from the dominant circuits of mobility as much as is reasonably possible. We are caught up in a set of structures, the zoo-pessimist maintains, that has taken on a life of its own; and there is limited agency possible under such conditions, either for human beings or for animals. The zoo-pessimist might also remind us that hypermobility is only the latest manifestation of an anthropocentrism that has persisted in Western and many other cultures for millennia. Horkheimer's comments on pragmatic attitudes toward animals apply to ages much earlier than our own. Animals have long been viewed as "mere obstructers of traffic" in one way or another. The only genuine hope for a better life for animals, it might be maintained, is the decay and eventual death of large-scale human societies.

If we assess the relative probity of the liberal humanist and zoo-pessimist analyses of the situation concerning the sacrificeability of animals and roadkill, I would suggest that zoo-pessimism is much nearer the mark about the prospects for fundamental change within the coordinates of the established order. The oft-repeated dogma among theorists and activists that we can gradually reform our way to genuine rights for animals within present economic and legal frameworks is clearly no longer tenable, given the meager success this strategy has had over the past several decades. In saying this, I am not suggesting of course that all such efforts at achieving rights or reform are pointless, only that we would be naïve to believe that animals can somehow be fitted over time in a full and genuine way into the liberal humanist social and political order. The zoo-pessimist is right, I think, to be skeptical of this optimistic vision. To extend rights to animals and to fundamentally change the hypermobility of the dominant culture cannot be accomplished within the wineskins of the present order; the implementation of such changes would certainly cause those skins to burst—or, to stay with the metaphor, require an entirely different sort of skins.

Now, if zoo-pessimism is helpful for pinpointing the limitations of the optimistic reformism of the liberal humanist approach, it nevertheless bears a serious, critical limitation of its own. In particular, zoo-pessimism shares with liberal humanism a totalizing view of the established anthropocentric order. For, even though it is crucial to mark the ways in which the dominant ontological order recurrently and differentially excludes those beings who are deemed to be other-than-human, it is equally essential to attend to the ways in which meaning, value, and relation circulate through, around, and outside those zones. The established order is but one (admittedly powerful and consequential) order among many. If there is any hope of shrinking the impact of the dominant order (for seeking its utter elimination in the near future would be naïve), such a gesture must ground itself in recognition of and affirmation of the rich variety of outsides to that order that are already present.

Let us name an approach grounded on the recognition and affirmation of such outsides to the dominant order *inhumanism*. Beyond liberal humanism (which seeks to raise up animals into the protected realm of the human) and beyond zoo-pessimism (which seeks to demonstrate the dead end of pursuing liberal humanist solutions for animal issues), the inhumanist approach proceeds from the premise that the other worlds, values, relations, and ways of being that constitute genuine alternatives to anthropocentrism are already to some extent present and make their presence known in a variety of ways. The task we face, according to inhumanism, is not so much creating such alternatives from scratch as attending to presences that are not necessarily intelligible in the terms offered by the established order while simultaneously attenuating that order's realm of influence. In other words, the goal envisioned by the inhumanist approach is one of learning to perceive, think, attend to, and value life and death in a fundamentally nonanthropocentric manner.

The most proximate source of this sense of the term "inhumanism" derives from the poet Robinson Jeffers, who uses it to name the underlying philosophical vision animating his work. Jeffers's mature poetry is aimed throughout at encouraging readers to "turn outward" (Jeffers 1989: 418) and move beyond the human narcissism characteristic of so much of contemporary culture. For Jeffers, narcissism and anthropocentrism constitute the chief sources of our contemporary psychological, social, and ecological ills. Although Jeffers describes his ideas about inhumanism as being philosophical in content, his presentation of those ideas is resolutely poetic and artistic in form. Jeffers's decision to opt for writing poetry over prose (by the latter term, he intends to denote not all nonpoetic writing but rather the idle chatter of everyday discourse) is deliberate and strategic (Jeffers 2000: 391). He finds in poetry the kinds of movement and structure that emulate the rhythms (bodily, tidal, seasonal, planetary, cosmic, and so on) of the inhuman reality and beauty toward which he believes we should turn (Jeffers 2009: 685). Thus, Jeffers's poetry not only calls for a turning outward of our loyalties and loves but also enacts this turn in the very form of its verse.

In line with Jeffers's poetic and philosophical vision, the inhumanist approach I describe here takes as its aim a fundamental conversion in our individual and collective subjective dispositions and aesthetic sensibilities. By "aesthetic," I have in mind the common use of the term as denoting the domains of beauty and the arts but also the etymological sense of *aisthēsis* as naming the general capacity for perception and discernment. In this sense, inhumanism is ultimately a matter of shifting one's attention and perception—and, ultimately, one's loyalties and loves—to the beauties and majesties of more-than-human registers of existence, which is to say, precisely to those ontological zones that have been delimited by the status quo as sacrificeable. Through inhumanist perception, the more-than-human world is glimpsed anew, viewed now as constituting a realm that precedes and exceeds the orbit of the human and its concerns.

Inhumanism offers a stark contrast to liberal humanism and its strategy of seeking to "raise up" animals into the subject position of the human. Inhumanism suggests that the path beyond sacrificeability is to be found in contesting the very notion that there *is* a sharp ontological or normative break between human and animal (or, for that matter, between the human and its variety of other "others"). For the inhumanist, the liberal humanist strategy employed by some pro-animal discourses that states that (certain) animals can be somehow aligned with human beings while leaving other (less human-like) animals and nonanimal entities in a sacrificeable realm is fundamentally objectionable. Indeed, the good news of inhumanism is that there are no inherently sacrificeable beings—that the very idea of creating a zone in which beings of any sort are to be seen as sacrificeable to an exclusively human order (or even an order that has been expanded to include sentient animals) is precisely the gesture that must be avoided. From the inhumanist perspective, the chief failure of the liberal humanist approach to animal justice is that it merely shifts the boundaries of sacrificeability and thereby ultimately remains committed to a sacrificial logic of establishing zones of inclusion and exclusion.

Inhumanism departs from zoo-pessimism as well in emphasizing the limits of the established anthropocentric order in terms of the presence and circulation of meaning and values and the constitution of worlds and relations. To be sure, an inhumanist approach has no interest in denying the significant presence and influence of anthropocentrism (a point that the zoo-pessimist is right to emphasize); yet, acknowledging the force of anthropocentrism need not lead to overlooking the fact that the world is far richer in meaning, relation, and value than the anthropocentric order can fathom. Recognizing and affirming this more-than-human excess is precisely what the inhumanist believes is necessary for moving beyond the logic of sacrifice and adopting an alternative sensibility, posture, and mode of perception.

The Art of Pulling the Emergency Brake

We can catch sight of key elements of this inhumanist sensibility in the remarkable expansion of interest in, and production of, roadkill art over the past two decades (for an in-depth overview of these developments, see Desmond 2016). Roadkill artists such as Bobby Neel Adams, Marian Drew, Viivi Häkkinen, Marcel Huijser, Joy Hunsberger, Emma Kisiel, L. A. Watson, and Kimberly Witham (to name just a handful of the artists who have inspired my reflections in what follows) have created artworks involving roadkill that attempt to draw attention to the forces—both social and subjective—that lead to the notion of animals as mere obstructers of traffic. These artworks strive to present road-killed animals to the viewer in ways that standard habits of modern systems of mobility preclude (Watson 2015). Road-killed animals that might, at most, be merely glimpsed as one speeds by on a country highway or suburban freeway are presented in these artworks so as to recall that animal's life and death, its vitality and mortality, its mangled limbs as much as its uncanny beauty. By remaining behind with and recalling us to the animals who have been struck and left for dead on our roadways, these artists effectively serve as agents of Walter Benjamin's "emergency brake" (2003, 402), seeking to slow and even jam the ever-more-rapid machine of hypermobility and redirect viewers onto another historical path.

These roadkill artists acknowledge that the practice of photographing, displaying, and re-presenting the bodies of dead animals is a controversial practice, especially given the increasingly callous use of animal bodies and materials by some contemporary artists (Aloi 2012; Watson 2015). Yet, the bulk of the artists I have mentioned earlier insist that their artistic employment of roadkill is intended to demonstrate and enact their deep respect for the animals in their art and not to denigrate or make light of the animals' fate. Thus, the artist Bobby Neal Adams describes the aim of his work as "paying homage to the creatures we are obliterating" through our driving practices (Minton 2018). Similarly, the artist Kimberly Witham acknowledges that her work displaying dead animals walks a fine line of acceptability and might be seen by some viewers as offensive. She emphasizes, though, that "showing reverence for the creatures pictured" is of utmost importance for her work (Ching and Ching 2017). The sentiments of veneration, love, and gratitude are expressed repeatedly by these roadkill artists and underscore their profound desire to render animals something other than, something more than, beings who are merely lose-able. By paying homage to the deaths of animals in their work, roadkill artists thus provide a performative enactment of a different kind of relation with the lives and deaths of animals beyond animacide.

At first glance, it might be tempting to interpret much of contemporary roadkill art as an instance of the liberal humanist sentiments we mentioned earlier. From this perspective, it might appear that roadkill art is an attempt to say that animal lives should be seen as being akin to human lives and as deserving the same respect and dignity. To be sure, something of this humanist sentiment is operative here. Nevertheless, many of these artists insist that what is at stake in their work is recalling human beings to their *mortality* and *finitude*, conditions that exceed the orbit of the human and that are shared with other animals (Häkkinen 2018; Kisiel 2014; Watson 2015; see also Marian Drew's remarks in Rosenberg 2013). They believe that we ignore the deaths of road-killed animals in much the same way that many of us try to hold our own vulnerability, fragility, and death at a distance. In effect, then, roadkill art of this sort is not asking us to affirm that human beings have a unique relation to death or that some animals might share a "human" understanding of death (which is the temptation of liberal humanist animal advocates). Rather, this art endeavors to displace us from our all-too-human perspectives on the carnage and death caused by our systems of mobility and to encourage us instead to inhabit a shared, indistinct, inhuman space wherein mortality and finitude circulate indiscriminately and without regard to any supposed human distinctives.

The viewer might be tempted, conversely, to see a distinctly melancholic affect running through much of contemporary roadkill art. There is a certain inevitability and intractability about the problem of roadkill that the artists seem to wish to bring to the surface, a reminder to the viewer that these deaths are the inevitable consequence of contemporary hypermobility. None of the artists I have mentioned present their work, after all, as being capable of *solving* the problem of roadkill, only drawing our attention to it. In this way, roadkill art might be read as being fundamentally pessimistic in nature and intent, as an act by the individual artist of paying one's respects to dead animals, while lamenting the inevitable violence of the established order. Such art does not aim at changing reality, it might be assumed, but rather serves as pessimistic confirmation of the ongoing violence and terror of anthropocentrism.

We should not dismiss too hastily the possibility that some roadkill art functions in precisely this pessimistic register. At the same time, the artists I have referred to here emphasize that their work is ultimately about helping viewers attend to and affirm the transformative *beauty* of animal life—and death. As uncomfortable as this truth might be, a certain beauty is often manifest even in dead animals (Huijser 2013). For many artists, encounters with roadkill are some of the only instances in which they have the opportunity to carefully examine and study—even hold—certain animals. In reframing road-killed animals not just as mattering but as manifesting beauty, these artists recall us to the mundane but nevertheless astonishing fact of animal embodiment. They redirect our attention to the sheer fact *that animals are there* and thereby seek to convert our gaze from all-too-human affairs and toward the overlooked lives, deaths, sufferings, and beauty of the animals littering our roads (Hunsberger, n.d.). Here, roadkill is temporarily displaced from a logic of sacrifice and allowed to circulate, however briefly, in another register of meaning—one that is inhuman and more-than-human, thereby bearing witness to the fact that the dominant anthropocentric circuits of everyday meaning are not exhaustive or exclusive.

Again, there should be no naïveté about the salvific role of such art in addressing the problem of roadkill (Watson 2015). None of the artists mentioned here would suggest that art alone suffices for actualizing the sorts of fundamental transformations needed to address the scope of the problems surrounding contemporary hypermobility and the production of roadkill. But what *is* being suggested by this work is that something like a conversion in our individual and collective subjectivity and modes of *aisthēsis*—a conversion away from the logic of sacrifice that structures our average, everyday lives and toward inhuman and more-than-human reality, value, meaning, and beauty—is a necessary step on the path toward building a genuinely nonanthropocentric way of life. How widely such a way of life might be adopted or whether such an aesthetic revolution at some scale is even possible are not questions for the artist. Instead, they are tasks to be assumed and forms of life to be invented in response to the inexhaustible gift of animal life-death.

NOTE

I wish to thank the Dean's Office at CSU Fullerton for financial support of this work.
The present chapter forms part of a larger work in progress titled *Altermobilities*.

REFERENCES

Aloi, Giovanni. 2012. *Art and Animals*. New York: I. B. Tauris.

Benjamin, Walter. 2003. "Paralipomena to 'On the Concept of History.'" In *Selected Writings*, vol. 4, *1938–1940*, edited by Howard Eiland and Michael W. Jennings, 389–400. Cambridge, MA: Harvard University Press.

Butler, Judith. 2009. *Frames of War: When Is Life Grievable?* Brooklyn, NY: Verso.

Cavalieri, Paola. 2001. *The Animal Question: Why Nonhuman Animals Deserve Human Rights*. Translated by Catherine Woollard. New York: Oxford University Press.

Ching, Darren, and Debra Klomp Ching. 2017. "Interview with Kimberly Witham." *at Length*. Accessed March 1, 2022. http://atlengthmag.com.

Derrida, Jacques, and Jean-Luc Nancy. 1991. "'Eating Well,' or the Calculation of the Subject: An Interview with Jacques Derrida." In *Who Comes after the Subject?*, edited by Eduardo Cadava, Peter Connor, and Jean-Luc Nancy, 96–119. New York: Routledge.

Desmond, Jane. 2016. *Displaying Death and Animating Life: Human-Animal Relations in Art, Science, and Everyday Life*. Chicago: University of Chicago Press.

Franklin, Sarah. 2017. "Staying with the Manifesto: An Interview with Donna Haraway." *Theory, Culture & Society* 34 (4): 49–63.

Freund, Peter, and George Martin. 2009. "The Social and Material Culture of Hyperautomobility: 'Hyperauto.'" *Bulletin of Science, Technology & Society* 29 (6): 476–82.

Guenther, Katja M. 2020. *The Lives and Deaths of Shelter Animals*. Stanford, CA: Stanford University Press.

Häkkinen, Viivi. 2018. "Artist's Statement from 'Forget Me Not.'" Muybridge's Horse, August 9, 2018. http://muybridgeshorse.com.

Haraway, Donna J. 2008. *When Species Meet*. Minneapolis: Minnesota University Press.

Horkheimer, Max. 2004. *Eclipse of Reason*. New York: Continuum.

Huijser, Marcel. 2013. "Road Ecology Blog: American Badger (*Taxidea taxus*) Killed by a Car, Montana, USA." Marcel Huijser Photography, November 12, 2013. www.marcelhuijserphotography.com.

Hunsberger, Joy. n.d. "Roadkill Manifesto." Joy Hunsberger's website. Accessed March 1, 2022. http://joyh.com.

Jeffers, Robinson. 1989. *The Collected Poetry of Robinson Jeffers*. Vol. 2, *1928–1938*. Edited by Tim Hunt. Stanford, CA: Stanford University Press.

———. 2000. *The Collected Poetry of Robinson Jeffers*. Vol. 4, *Poetry, 1903–1920, Prose, and Unpublished Writings*. Edited by Tim Hunt. Stanford, CA: Stanford University Press.

———. 2009. *The Collected Letters of Robinson Jeffers, with Selected Letters of Una Jeffers*. Vol. 1, *1890–1930*. Edited by James Karman. Stanford, CA: Stanford University Press.

Kisiel, Emma. 2014. "At Rest." Emma Kisiel's website. www.emmakisiel.com.

Minton, Eric. 2018. "Artful Decay: Bobby Neel Adams' Photography in Mourning." *Professional Photography*, August 2018. www.ppa.com.

Redmalm, David. 2015. "Pet Grief: When Is Non-human Life Grievable?" *Sociological Review* 63 (1): 19–35.

Rosenberg, David. 2013. "Making Roadkill Beautiful." *Slate*, February 27, 2013. https://slate.com.

Seiler, Andreas, and J.-O. Helldin. 2006. "Mortality in Wildlife Due to Transportation." In *The Ecology of Transportation: Managing Mobility for the Environment*, edited by John Davenport and Julia L. Davenport, 165–90. New York: Springer, 2006.

Soron, Dennis. 2008. "Road Kill: Commodity Fetishism and Structural Violence," *TOPIA: Canadian Journal of Cultural Studies* 18 (1): 107–25.

Stanescu, James. 2012. "Species Trouble: Judith Butler, Mourning, and the Precarious Lives of Animals." *Hypatia* 27 (3): 567–82.

Watson, L. A. 2015. "Remains to Be Seen: Photographing 'Road Kill' and *The Roadside Memorial Project*." In *Economies of Death: Economic Logics of Killable Life and Grievable Death*, edited by Patricia J. Lopez and Kathryn A. Gillespie, 137–59. New York: Routledge.

Williams, Jeffrey J. 2010. "Science Stories: An Interview with Donna J. Haraway." *Minnesota Review* 73–74:133–63.

PART II

During

4

Digidogs and the Science Fiction of Blackness

BÉNÉDICTE BOISSERON

"Have you ever seen a shoe that just . . . looks racist? That's how Crocs look," says Scaachi Koul (2021), a *BuzzFeed News* reporter. The author is being ironic in a piece about how to wear the popular plastic shoes Crocs. Because the crocodile shoes are often deemed ugly, the author humorously equates "ugly" with "racist" in a tongue-and-cheek allusion to the woke generation. While Koul indexes the word "racist" as a jack-of-all-trades Gen Z word, the question stands. Can shoes be racist? Obviously, shoes can hardly be said to be inherently racist or antiracist because they do not have agency. Koul toys here with a kind of absurdism reminiscent of the African American banter tradition of "Yo mama so ugly" jokes, in which the phrase "Yo mama is so ugly that . . ." is to be filled with a random statement. Likewise, Crocs are so ugly that they look racist.

All jokes aside, Koul's statement is a nod to a modern era known for its keen eye for the racially charged. This keen eye, however, begs the question as to where to draw the line. Can anything be deemed racist? Semantically speaking, nothing is off-limits when human agency is involved. One talks of a "racist shirt," since the shirt speaks for the deemed racist wearer or designer. Likewise, a policy can be racist, as it speaks to the human bias that shaped it. As Ibrahim X. Kendi says in *How to Be an Antiracist*, "a racist policy is any measure that produces or sustains racial inequity between racial groups" (2019, 18). Though racism does not always come in human shape, the human shape never looms far behind when it comes to racism.

Are robots racist? Ruha Benjamin raises the question in *Race after Technology* (2019). Yes, they can be, she answers, because their artificial intelligence or algorithm is designed by humans. And the commonly shared assumption of color-blindness in machines allows racism to seep even more insidiously and deeply into the fabric of our society. Benjamin refers to this assumption as the "New Jim Code," a key phrase in what she calls "race critical code studies." Even though an algorithm may sound scientifically based, the coding behind it is human made and hence potentially biased.

Benjamin coined the phrase the "New Jim Code" as an intertextual reference to Michelle Alexander's *The New Jim Crow* (2012). Alexander argues that our modern criminal justice system is a form of institutional racism not unlike Jim Crow, except that it presents itself with a veneer of color-blindness. Benjamin posits that the same is true with technology: the new is not necessarily all that different from the old, but it just presents better. The New Jim Code, like the New Jim Crow, hides its racist structure in plain sight. As Benjamin writes, the New Jim Code is based on "the employment of new technologies that reflect and reproduce existing inequities but that are promoted and perceived as more objective or progressive than the discriminatory systems of a previous era" (2019, 3). Technology can be a devil in disguise when its presumption of objectiveness obstructs its biased outcomes. Think, for example, as Benjamin suggests, of the result of a Google search on "Black women" that would prioritize sexualized or pornographic entries as a misogynoir-influenced algorithm; or a "pit bull" Google search that would give first choice to the word "aggressive" or any other allusions to the bad reputation of this canine phenotype. Algorithms have a mind of their own, but it is ultimately the mind of their design masters or users that speaks for them. Benjamin mentions a 1993 *New Yorker* cartoon by Peter Steiner showing a black dog typing on a computer with the line, "On the Internet, nobody knows you're a dog." But as Benjamin demonstrates very well in her book, the internet knows you are a dog, and it even knows you are a black dog.

That said, with technological progress, the traces of human agency behind artificial intelligence become less and less visible. Could there be a day when technology really gets a mind of its own? Could the human mind behind the machine fade away to the extent that the machine carries on without human agency? It is no coincidence that Donna Haraway followed her 1985 essay "A Cyborg Manifesto," with the publication of *The Companion Species Manifesto*, a 2003 essay on dogs. Because of dogs' trainability, they may feel like a Cartesian automaton that responds to humans' will, but their agency and sentience set them apart from the machine. Cyborgs and dogs combine "the human and the non-human, the organic and the technological" ([1985] 2016, 4), Haraway writes. Both have porous boundaries and exceed human control, and together they capture our imagination. Dogs combine the human and the nonhuman not only because of their privileged status as humans' best friends but also because there is a form of contamination, a DNA exchange, between humans and dogs due to, as Haraway points out, centuries of infectious co-companionship. Because of their proximity with humans and their blending with them, dogs are the ideal proxy that can carry on the human legacy potentially even beyond human existence. The future of cyborgness is therefore not the humanoid but the dog machine, a hybrid of canine, human, and technology. What I call the "cynobot"—a portmanteau of the Greek *cyno*, meaning "dog," and "robot"—is the epitome of cross-species and cross-genre resilience.

My book *Afro-Dog* (2018) briefly mentioned the long-term implications of using dogs to do the dirty work for humans, but this question has even more relevance in the context of cynobots. Like Benjamin's initial question about robots, one may wonder, are dogs racist? And based on history, there is no doubt that dogs can be racist by proxy. In the United States and the Americas, there is a long-standing tradition of using dogs against Indigenous people and Blacks to keep the subalterns in check. The Dominican friar Bartolomé de Las Casas was one of the first to report orchestrated dog attacks against the Indigenous people of the West Indies in the early stages of the Spanish colonization in his 1542 book *A Short Account of the Destruction of the Indies*. In 1845, former slave Frederick Douglass would describe a similar repressive tactic against runaway slaves in his memoir *Narrative of the Life of Frederick Douglass*. In a West Indian context, the Martinican author Patrick Chamoiseau in his 1997 novella *L'esclave vieil homme et le molosse* (*Slave Old Man*) offered a lyrical tale of the chase between the master's bloodhound and the fugitive slave, thereby cementing a brutal side of history that does not get much attention in historical archives. In the Jim Crow era, the dogs trained to discriminate against the racialized subject would get a name; they were called "white dogs." In Romain Gary's 1970 autofiction book *Chien blanc* (*White Dog*), the French author gave a closer look at the nature of the white dog, positing that, once the white dog was trained to be racist, the conditioning might not be reversible; the white dog might be irreversibly racist. As one of the African American characters says in Gary's book, "In the old days, they trained them [the dogs] to track down runaway slaves. Things have changed. We don't run away anymore. Now those dogs are used against us by scared cops" (1972, 19–20). The most well-known white dog in history is the Connor dog. Commissioner of Public Safety Bull Connor infamously ordered the police dogs to attack civil rights protestors in Birmingham, Alabama, in 1963. The dog-attack scenes were immortalized by the photographer Charles Moore, whose pictures were printed in a 1963 *Life* magazine issue. Those pictures would later be iconized by Andy Warhol in his own rendition of the tragic scenes in his 1974 "race riots" series.

By 2015, the "white dog" or the "Connor dog" became the "Ferguson dog." After the Ferguson race riots, the Department of Justice initiated an investigation of the police department in Ferguson, Missouri. The report from the investigation concluded that police dogs in the city had been made to discriminate against Black people. As the report stated, "in every canine bite incident for which racial information is available, the subject was African American" (US Department of Justice 2015, 31). There was no denying it: the Ferguson dog was officially anti-Black. In modern history, there is no shortage of stories about dogs trained to be racist by proxy. The so-called racist dog is an inextricable part of US history. It mutates to adapt to the successive eras with no signs of extinction. It is almost as if this dog is undying, its algorithm reinventing itself ad infinitum. Could it be that one day, through a process of genetic mutation and conditioning, dogs would no longer need to be trained to act on racist cues because they would be atavistically predisposed to be racist?

If in the US, the problem is the color line, as W. E. B. Du Bois stated at the turn of the twentieth century in *The Souls of Black Folk* (1903), the dog may have a role to play in maintaining that line. Thomas Jefferson, in his memoir *Notes on the State of Virginia* (1787), raised concerns about miscegenation if the US were to abolish slavery. For him, after slavery, it would be best if former slaves were to leave the US. As he wrote, "when freed, [the slave] is to be removed beyond the reach of mixture" ([1787] 1997, 103). Today, in a world where the color line becomes more and more imperceptible due to miscegenation, the racist dog, through centuries of experience tracking Afro-descendant people, could be the only one genetically predisposed to retrace Blackness. As I wrote in *Afro-Dog*, "through atavism and by way of conditioning, dogs could one day respond to race as a biological phenomenon even though humans, by then, will no longer be able to track the racial difference" (2018, 64). This is of course a hypothesis that is neither scientifically nor biologically sound, but it is science fiction ready.

Digidog

On Tuesday, February 23, 2021, a robot police dog walked out of a Bronx apartment with a man in handcuffs escorted by police officers. The robot police dog nonchalantly walked on the street in front of passersby. It was quite a sight for witnesses, who filmed the awkward scene and published it online. The video quickly became viral. The robot dog is called "digidog." The *New York Times* describes it as "a 70-pound robotic dog with a loping gait, cameras and lights affixed to its frame, and a two-way communication system that allows the officer maneuvering it remotely to see and hear what is happening" (Crammer and Hauser 2021). The purpose of this remotely controlled robot was allegedly to assess situations without putting police officers at risk. In this case, the police were confronted with a hostage situation in which two men had been held at gunpoint in a Bronx apartment for hours by two other men. The digidog was not a welcome sight in the neighborhood, in part because it evoked the militarization of police surveillance against civilians. In defense of the backlash caused by the viral video, the New York Police Department (NYPD) explained on Twitter, "The NYPD has been using robots since the 1970s to save lives in hostage situations & hazmat incidents. This model of robot is being tested to evaluate its capabilities against other models in use by our emergency service unit and bomb squad" (NYPD 2021). The digidog feels like a déjà vu, but in the future. The police tool of surveillance looks like a dog, just in time to replace the Ferguson dog, thereby giving the police the presumption of color-blindness with a robot dog. The white dog has reached the technological stage: it is now undying. The "white dog" is indeed science fiction ready.

In H. G. Wells's 1898 science fiction novel *The War of the Worlds*, the English author envisions a Martian attack on Earth threatening human existence. In the late nineteenth century, the British Empire was the most powerful colonial power in the world, and the author uses this story to make a point about colonialism. As he says in the opening chapter, no one should clutch their pearls at the idea of a ruthless extraterritorial imperialistic mission against humans, since this is already what humans are doing to each other on Earth. As he writes, "And before we judge of them too harshly we must remember what ruthless and utter destruction our own species has wrought, not only upon animal, such as the vanished bison and the dodo, but upon its inferior races. The Tasmanians, in spite of their human likeness, were entirely swept out of existence in a war of extermination waged by European immigrants, in the space of fifty years. Are we such apostles of mercy as to complain of the Martians warred in the same spirit?" (Wells [1898] 2007, 7). Wells's Martians are described as physically abject. What comes out of the cylinder-shaped alien ship that just landed on Earth is a blob with tentacles. The narrator refers to it as "The Thing." "Monstruous," "fungus-like," "nasty," "inhuman," and "crippled" are some of the words used to describe it. Horror is conveyed through the description of an alien entity that looks nothing like humans, though, to some extent, they do act like humans.

In a 2019 Anglo-French adaption of Wells's classic adapted to television in a miniseries also titled *The War of the Worlds*, the creator, Howard Overman, reimagines Wells's original extraterrestrial invasion. What comes out of the alien ship is not a fungus-like Thing but canine robots. The horror, this time, is conveyed through headless quadruped machines relentless in their mechanical pursuit of human survivors. Hybridity is what makes the robot dogs particularly uncanny. They are not all machine: the insides are organic with neuron density, which makes them not only mortal but also sentient. As viewers soon find out, they are not like robots: they want to live, and they are afraid to die. By the end of the first season and through the second season, viewers also find out that the robot dogs are not the brains of the attack on Earth. In season 2, the real extraterrestrial invaders are revealed to be humans from the future. Those human offspring have genetic flaws that will lead to their extinction if they do not start an intervention. They need to travel back in time and through space to proleptically change the course of their genetic fate. The plan is to attack their ancestors on Earth and steal their babies to get their healthy DNAs.

At first glance, Overman's adaption of Wells's classic seems to have kept nothing of the original tone of Wells's anticolonial message. But history has proven that, when humans want to control other races or species, they launch dogs after them. Overman's idea of having dogs, even mechanical ones, hunt humans brings a colonial dimension to the story. Science fiction is often an amplified and sublimated version of our history. As attack dogs become more and more technological, they escape humans' mortal fate and become the dominant power on Earth.

What makes Overman's cynodog horror inspiring is its "uncanny valley" effect on the audience. The phrase "uncanny valley" usually applies to a humanoid entity. Some humanoid robots look uncannily human. A part of us is drawn to their human-like side, until it becomes too close for comfort, and then it feels uncanny. The phrase "uncanny valley" (first coined by Masahiro Mori in Japanese in 1970) pinpoints the transitional moment from comfort to discomfort and from the familiar to the unfamiliar (Mori, MacDorman, and Kageki 2012), what Sigmund Freud (2003) calls, in his 1919 essay, the *Unheimlich*. But with mechanical dogs, the "uncanny valley" effect is reversed. The cynobot first feels unfamiliar, until something about it starts feeling very familiar. The Overman dogs are first science fiction, until they become real. They are our history.

Overman's 2019 cynobots are probably inspired by the dogs from a 2017 episode of *Black Mirror*, the Netflix original science fiction series. Written by the series creator Charlie Brooker and filmed in black and white, the episode titled "Metalhead" appears in the fourth season and tells the story of a postapocalyptic world in which headless dog-looking robots have exterminated most of the human population and are intent on finishing the mission. The dogs look like those in Overman's series. The few humans left are running for their lives, among them a woman named Bella and two men. The three have decided to risk it all to retrieve an unknown object stored in a warehouse. The targeted object is intended to give comfort to Bella's terminally ill nephew. But before the three even have time to retrieve the object, the robot dogs kill the two men and redirect their full attention on Bella. After being shot by one of the robots with GPS bullets, which are able to geolocalize the prey once inserted in the flesh, it becomes clear that the woman is destined to be tracked down to the end. The merciless robots are programmed to complete the mission without fail. The robots are, as Brooker says in the collection of essays *Inside Black Mirror*, "pragmatic killing machines" (Brooker, Jones, and Arnopp 2018, 286). The episode focuses on Bella's doomed pursuit and the chilling relentlessness of the machine.

In spite of a similar design, this is where Brooker's cynobots differ from Overman's. The dogs in "Metalhead" are meant to show no signs of sentience or will to live. They are pure machines. The *Black Mirror* episode is mainly about human compassion in the context of technological supremacy. The woman's programmed demise and the robot's monomaniac determination call attention to the intended contrast between the woman's humanity and the robot's lack thereof. The woman's fatal weakness is her ability to feel for the dying boy at the expense of her own life. Compassion for the dying is seen as not practical or programmable, as it outweighs the protagonists' survival instinct. The Achilles' heel of these three humans is indeed their feelings in the face of human death. As *Black Mirror* producer Annabel Jones points out in *Inside Black Mirror*, "The biggest distinction between Bella and the robot is humanity. She could hunt for survival, but the thing that undoes her is her intended quest to give some comfort to a dying nephew" (Brooker, Jones, and Arnopp 2018, 293). In this human-versus-machine story, programmability is inherent to both the machine and the human. The robot cannot be deprogrammed in its mission to exterminate humans, while humans cannot avoid the inevitability of their death. Humans are left with feelings as their only claim to agency. The three humans are willing to meet their fate sooner to get their hands on that mysterious object. The show would have you believe that the sought-after object is the black box of the human condition, and somehow, it is. Only at the end do the viewers find out what the mysterious object stored in the warehouse was. What the three wanted to grab for the dying nephew was a teddy bear, in a box filled with teddy bears.

The role of animals in the story is understated, maybe because there are no real animals left; all we see are simulacra in the guise of teddy bears and robot dogs. The teddy bear here is a symbol of compassion and comfort in the face of death. Charlie Brooker and Annabel Jones's interview in *Inside Black Mirror* does not address the meaning of the animal presence in the episode, but it seems that the animal ersatz stands as an allegory of both human and nonhuman extinction. Even though the emotional support animals (teddy bears) are synthetic and hunting dogs are metal, animal-shaped objects are still meant to fulfill their original function as if of flesh and blood. Brooker and Jones present a dystopian world where representability takes precedence over existence, where animals have lost their "aura" in the age of mechanical reproduction, to paraphrase Walter Benjamin (1969). We are led to understand this episode within the context of what Antoine Traisnel calls the "technological reproducibility" (2020, 9) of animal life. In industrial farming but also in conservationist efforts, living and breathing animals have lost significance in the pursuit of the bigger picture of representability and fungibility. Animals have become more of a species that a living entity. As John Berger says in "Why Look at Animals?," "an animal's blood flowed like human blood, but its species was undying and each lion was Lion, each ox was Ox" ([1980] 1991, 6–7). The animal is in capital letters when it stands for its species, to the detriment of its flesh-and-blood existence. In the era of mechanical reproduction, slaughter, and life, the animal is undying. As Traisnel writes, "Death for animals becomes legible predominantly in terms of extinction, of species death—which paradoxically sanctions both conservation efforts and mass slaughter" (2020, 22). "Metalhead" envisions a world where dogs and bears would keep their function as service animals but are devoid of all that makes them alive, feeling, and breathing. This is an extreme case of the programmability of life. As the episode predicts, after animals, humans are the next to be extinct. We can also assume that after their extinction, humans will also be represented in a nonliving form at the service of the dominant class, the machines. The teddy bear, as a token of a dying humanity, is the decoy that lures the remaining humans to their untimely death.

Brooker and Jones designed the robot as headless to prevent viewers from reading any kind of feelings on the canine robot's face. If robots are often inclined to be anthropomorphized or, in this case, cynomorphized and potentially deemed "sentient," it is because of a false sense of agency created by their programmability, which is exactly—as stated earlier—the common reaction from viewers that Brooker and Jones wanted to avoid. The robot exhibits a hunting dog's natural predisposition. The relentlessness and determination of the robot is very much in line with what you would expect from a hound, while the GPS bullets are equivalent to the scent that help the hunting dog to track its prey. It is not just the dog that has lost its sentient existence; Bella is also being technologized, as the GPS bullets replace her human smell, the very essence of her humanity. The momentum of the pursuit between robot dog and human prey creates an amalgam between human, animal, and machine. What is missing in this entanglement is the question of race, not far behind.

There is a reason why the dog machine in "Metalhead" looks like the digidog from the Bronx, which itself looks like the cynobot from Overman's *War of the Worlds*. Brooker reveals in *Inside Black Mirror* that the design for the dogs in the episode was inspired by robots made by a Boston-based robotics company called Boston Dynamics, which is where the digidog from the Bronx police was also produced. And since Overman seems to have been inspired by Brooker himself, we have here several versions of the same dog initially produced by Boston Dynamics. The viral video taken in the Bronx is a case of reality catching up with fiction. The use of robotized police dogs sends an ominous message, introducing another form of repressive state apparatus, more remote from its subject and completely devoid of sentience. With this quadrupedal drone of surveillance, there is a complete disconnect between police repression and the population and a general sense that digidog is meant to be the next step after the Ferguson dog. The digidog is a police dog robot with a new technology of surveillance that, again as Ruha Benjamin would say, "[is] promoted and perceived as more objective or progressive than the discriminatory systems of a previous era" (2019, 3).

With the digidog, we have reached the age of science fiction, a world where the alien is no longer perceived as monstrous, a world where the Thing lives among us. As Haraway says in "A Cyborg Manifesto," "the boundary between science fiction and social reality is an optical illusion" ([1985] 2016, 6). What "Metalhead" offers is a parable of what Achille Mbembe (2017) calls, in his book *Critique of Black Reason*, the becoming Black of the world. The corporatization, digitalization, and technologization of human existence has brought global humanity to the brink of nonhumanity, a condition, as Mbembe argues, that was formerly unique to the Black man. As the author says, in a neoliberal, digital, and capitalistic age, humans are "abandoned subjects, relegated to the role of a 'superfluous humanity'" (2017, 3). Human essence has become increasingly linked to market value, corporate logic, and digital technology, making the human a human-machine. If Boston Dynamics resorted to a canine body to design the perfect digital tool of surveillance, it is because in the American collective consciousness, the animal is never far from the racialized, even if it must be in a digital form. Bella is being technologized as she runs, the GPS bullets in her body being the symbol of her machine-transmutation in a *becoming Black of the world.*

The Science Fiction of Blackness

For Mbembe, the original human-machine is the Black man. As he writes, racial slavery created a first of its kind, "when a human being of bone, flesh, and spirit made its first appearance under the sign of the Black Man, as *human-merchandise*, *human-metal*, and *human-money*" (2017, 180). "Chattel" not only connotes the condition of human property as human cattle but also indexes a leaked distinction between human and technology. "Chattel," from the Latin *capitalis*, means "capital." The Black Man is both capital and the tool that builds capital. As Mbembe states, "The Black Man, despised and profoundly dishonored, is the only human in the modern order whose skin has been transformed into the form and spirit of merchandise—the living crypt of capital" (2017, 6). The original cyborg is, as it were, Black.

What we see today is a new version of human-machine. In the digital and neoliberal age of global markets, as Mbembe argues, human capital is no longer only the Black man: it now affects everyone. This is what Mbembe refers to as the "becoming Black of the world." Neoliberalism, capitalism, and animism together have blurred the boundaries between human and technology in a global context. The cyborg is the new universal Man. There is "little distinction remaining between psychic reflexes and technological reflexes, the human subject becomes fictionalized as 'an entrepreneur of the self,'" Mbembe writes (2017, 3). In the first phase of capitalism, the word "Black" referred to the enslaved people of African descent. In its second phase, as Mbembe posits, the word now also applies globally to the new human, the human-machine. "There are no longer any limits placed on the modification of his genetic, biological structure" (4), he writes. Artificial intelligence has stripped Man's golden ticket to human exceptionalism. The world becomes Black, in Mbembe's technological and digital sense of the word. Blackness now comes out as what it always was: the ultimate science fiction.

The word "Afrofuturism" was coined by Mark Dery in a 1994 essay, "Black to the Future." Dery defines it as a "speculative fiction that treats African-American themes and addresses African-American concerns in the context of twentieth-century technoculture" (1994, 181). As the Middle Passage attests, the extraterrestrial is an essential part of the Black experience. Think of it: Africans were captured by people who seemed to be coming from nowhere. The captives were then crammed into a slave ship taking them to an outer world. The slave ship might as well have been a hydraulic spaceship for all they knew. On the ship, before they even set foot on the other side of the Atlantic, African captives underwent a process of chattel mutation through dehumanization. The dystopian experience of the Middle Passage is what science fiction stories are made of.

The former slave Olaudah Equiano, who published *The Interesting Narrative of Olaudah Equiano* in 1789, a slave narrative credited for being the only full account of the Middle Passage from the captive's perspective, offers a unique account of on the extraterritorial nature of racial slavery. Unlike Frederick Douglass, Equiano was said to have been born free in Africa. He was in a unique position to recount the experience of an African captive. Through his lens, the white slave hunters come across as an odd species with little in common with the human form known in Africa. Equiano's abductors had, as the author writes, "complexions differing so much from ours, their long hair, and their language they spoke, which was very different from any I had ever heard" ([1789] 2021, 56). Equiano felt like they belonged to a world of "bad spirits" with extreme barbarianism and cruelty (56). The onboard technology used to steer the ship is described by Equiano as magical, in an awe- and fear-inspiring kind of way. Equiano is simply introduced to a different species with no earthly connection, a bit like the Homo sapiens in the original *War of the Worlds*. Dery rightfully calls African Americans "the descendants of alien abductees" (1994, 180).

Science fiction, however, is not just a narrative about Black suffering; it is also a tool of Black empowerment. Drexciya, a Detroit-based electronic music band, created a powerful Afrofuturist mythology around the alien-evoking Middle Passage. The artist duo envisioned an underwater fantasy world made of unborn babies from pregnant slaves who had been thrown overboard from the slave ship. In their mythology, those babies survived and learned to breathe underwater, eventually creating a submarine colony named Drexciya. Drexciya's mythology shows that the production of Blackness can be generative. Drexciya embodies Afrofuturist plasticity and evokes new modes of being, seeing, and creating beyond the world of Man.

Lisa Yaszek, in "An Afrofuturist Reading of Ralph Ellison's *Invisible Man*" (2005) touches on the creative porosity of Blackness and highlights the liberating effect of technology for the Black experience. As she sees it, technology, once complicit in the exploitation of Black bodies, can be also emancipatory. She quotes Ralph Ellison in "Some Questions and Some Answers" to prove her point: "It is precisely technology which promises [us] release from the brutalizing effects of over three hundred years of racism and European domination. Men cannot unmake history, thus it is not a question of reincarnating those cultural traditions which were destroyed, but a matter of using industrialization, modern medicine, modern science generally to work in the interest of these peoples rather than against them. Nor is the disruption of the past a totally negative phenomenon; sometimes it makes possible a modulation in a people's way of life that allows for a more creative use of its energies" (quoted in Yaszek 2005, 304).

Before Ellison, Frederick Douglass had expressed a similar view of technology with his obsession with photography, which was at the time a new technology. Douglass strongly believed in photography as a weapon to abolish slavery because he saw this technology as a human privilege, a privilege owed to Black men. Only humans can produce and appreciate photography, and for Douglass, getting his photograph taken was proof of his humanity. Douglass was photographed more than any other (white) men in the US. Photography was vouching for his humanity and for the humanity of the Black man. As Douglass writes in his 1861 essay "Lecture on Pictures," "It is worthy of remark to begin with that of all the animal world man alone has a passion for pictures. Neither dogs nor elephants ranging nearest to man in point of intelligence show any sensation of pleasure in the presence of the highest work of art. The dog fails to recognize his own features in a glass. The power to make and to appreciate pictures belongs to man exclusively" ([1861] 2015, 131). To fully appreciate this passage, one must go back to Douglass's experience with animals as described in his 1845 slave narrative. In it, Douglass offers a vivid image of combined racialization and animalization, as he describes an estate valuation following the death of his master. Douglass explains that the property of his deceased master was to be shared among two heirs. In the assessment of property, chattel slaves (including him) and animals were said to be treated on the same footing. "Men and women, old and young, married and single, were ranked with horses, sheep, and swine. There were horses and men, cattle and women, pigs and children, all holding the same rank in the scale of being" (Douglass 1845, 45). This passage underscores the role of race in the human-animal divide, showing how the racialized enslaved blurred the frontier between human and animal. The nonperson legal status of the slave as chattel property is like that of the animal, but not quite.

Years after Douglass's 1845 slave narrative, the author returned to the animal question but in a very different light. Douglass had discovered that photography for a Black man can speak louder than words. There is no doubt that Douglass's eloquence and literacy as an orator and author helped him to claim his status as a man in an abolitionist context, but photography offered something more. It transcended the logos, circumventing a Western idea of human exceptionalism. Douglass found a unique way to claim humanhood, through technology rather than reason. The ability to produce photography may be a human privilege, but the ability to be reproduced is a human enigma. The photographic portrait distances itself from the material body, making the image of humans reproducible, plastic, and fungible. The more Douglass duplicates his image, the more impenetrable the idea of Man becomes in the smoke-and-mirror duplicity of his face. The photograph *looks like* the real, but not quite. The photograph is the epitome of the crossover, as it presents the human as bendable, flexible, and reproducible just like any other forms of existence. The goal is no longer to prove one's humanity against the animal but to show the plasticity of humanity, to flaunt the porosity of its essence. Douglass revisited the meaning of Man through his ubiquitous representation in photography. The making of Man is a learned technology. Man is in fact a production. Douglass foresaw that the technologization of the Black man was a path to liberation.

Feeling It

At the dawn of the twenty-first century, Donna Haraway published "A Cyborg Manifesto," an ode to the transmutation of human cells in modern times. "We are cyborgs," she wrote. Prescient of an emerging high-tech culture steadfast in its pursuit to recode the human condition, Haraway looked at the meshing of human and machine as a sign of porosity in the world. In addition to what she named the "breached boundary between human and animal" ([1985] 2016, 11), her essay brought attention to "a second leaky distinction between animal-human (organism) and machine" (11). A new hominin taxonomy was emerging, and the cyborg was its latest installment.

Today, Haraway's words sound prophetic. In the 2020s, we have witnessed in some parts of the world an accelerated redefinition of the human as cyborg. The novel coronavirus brought humanity to its knees, ushering us toward an inevitable digital existence. As it were, the pandemic-induced digitalization of human existence has paved the way in the US for a racial reckoning of historic proportions. The fact that the COVID-19 pandemic led to a collective racial reckoning highlights a long-standing tradition of cross-fertilization between the technological and Blackness. From the pictures of the 1955 death of Emmett Till to the 1991 televised beating of Rodney King and the 2021 recorded murder of George Floyd, the impact of violence on the Black body has repeatedly been experienced through the camera lens of a witness, and most often a Black witness. The recorded image as a path toward racial justice is an act of resistance against the institutional voicelessness of the Black witness. As Frederick Douglass points out in *Narrative of the Life of Frederick Douglass*, masters and overseers used to murder slaves with impunity because slaves could not legally testify as a witness in court. Douglass mentions a particular instance in which an overseer executed a slave in front of other slaves for refusing to receive more lashes. As Douglass writes, "His horrid crime was not even submitted to judicial investigation. It was committed in the presence of slaves, and they of course could neither institute a suit, nor testify against him; and thus the guilty perpetrator of one of the bloodiest and most foul murders goes unwhipped of justice, and uncensored by the community on which he lives" (1845, 23–24). Black witnessing is today haunted by a lingering historical past in which slave's firsthand witnessing had no legal bearing. The number of Black whistleblowers equipped with a camera has grown exponentially over the years to circumvent remnants of a social system notorious for giving little credibility to the Black witness. Black witnessing needs to be digitally enhanced to carry some sort of admissibility. Technology, therefore, has been instrumental in speaking on behalf of Black victims. The proof is now in the lens.

Again, the idea of technology as an ally to Black witnessing started with Frederick Douglass, the first American to see the power of photographic representation for Black liberation. Douglass, as the most photographed American of the nineteenth century, ahead of Walt Whitman and Abraham Lincoln, embodies Black empowerment through the lens. John Stauffer, Zoe Trodd, and Celeste-Marie Bernier, authors of *Picturing Frederick Douglass* (2015), have identified 160 separate photographs of Douglass in distinct poses. As Stauffer and his coauthors write, "the only contemporaries who surpass Douglass are the British royal family and other British celebrities" (2015, x). Douglass also published four essays on photography during the Civil War. The former slave saw the objectivity of photographic representation as a countervoice to Black caricatures prevalent at the time. His ubiquitous portrait was a constant reminder of what a free, dignified Black man looks like. As John Stauffer et al. write, "Even more than truth-telling, the truthful image represented abolitionists' greatest weapon, for it gave the lie to slavery as a benevolent institution and exposed it as a dehumanizing horror" (2015, xi). Photography, which started precisely at the time of Douglass's freedom, was here to attest to the birth of Black liberation in the US. Technology was about to become the main weapon of racial justice.

On May 25, 2021, the Minneapolis policeman Derek Chauvin was caught on video choking George Floyd to death as the policeman kept his knee on the victim's neck for more than eight minutes. The phone recording of the incident by an African American teenager, Darnella Frazier, shook Americans to the core, taking them out of the slumber of their shelter-in-place and into the streets. The digital nudge brought life into human existence and made America feel for the Black man and feel for his death. We start feeling for the Black man, not in his presence but in the representation of his death. The video is like Douglass's photograph, a way to show the Black man's right to existence against his state of subjection. Floyd's recorded death *moved* people into action; it was the catalyst for a massive Black Lives Matter mobilization. As the viral video startled Americans out of their racial torpor, antiracism took center stage overnight. The Black Lives Matter mobilization was not only about racial reckoning but also about getting in tune with the country's capacity to feel. As the poet Claudia Rankine argues in her essay "The Condition of Black Life Is One of Mourning" (2015), "National mourning, as advocated by Black Lives Matter, is a mode of intervention and interruption that might itself be assimilated into the category of public annoyance. This is altogether possible; but also possible is the recognition that it's a lack of feeling for another that is our problem. Grief, then, for these deceased others might align some of us, for the first time, with the living." The world is now in search of that teddy bear, to learn how to feel, grieve, and live again.

In a footnote to *An Introduction to the Principles of Morals and Legislation*, published the same year (1789) as Equiano's narrative, the English philosopher Jeremy Bentham reorients the debate about the meaning of human and nonhuman existence. The philosopher debunks René Descartes's theory of the animal as no other than a complex machine, by shifting the focus from "I think therefore I am" to "I *feel* therefore I am." As the author argues, "What else is it that should trace the insuperable line? Is it the faculty of reason, or, perhaps, the faculty of discourse? . . . The question is not, Can they *reason*? nor, Can they *talk* but, Can they *suffer*?" (Bentham 1789, 311). Bentham shows how flawed the human-animal divide is, by arguing that human and nonhuman animals are all sentient beings entitled to rights. Bentham does away with the insuperable line of reason; for him, sentience is the new logos.

Bentham's footnote has drawn much attention for its analogy between the fight to abolish slavery and the animal rights movement. We are all sentient beings capable of suffering in the hands of Man. Bentham's axiom, however, is not so much about the sentience of the Black person and the animal as that of Man. Bentham's note is a plea for Man to start *feeling*. The burden of proof of sentience is not on the victim but on the assailant. Can Man *feel* the pain inflicted on the Other, human and nonhuman alike? The question is not, indeed, Can they (Man) reason? but Can they *feel*, feel the Other's pain? With technology in the mix, the real question is actually, Who is doing the "feeling," the video, the portrait, or the witness? How much can technology be a compassionate ally to the Black cause? The viral video of George Floyd's dying extracted us from our screen, as if to suggest that technological reproduction has the power to make us feel more than the real does. To what extent can Douglass's portrait or Floyd's recorded murder convey the pain more than Douglass or Floyd could ever do? Does technology have the ability to make us feel?

When Thomas Jefferson addressed the evils of slavery in his journal *Notes on the State of Virginia* (1787), his biggest concern was not the condition of the slave but that of a society based on slavery. Jefferson questioned the impact of the banality of evil on masters. He confided, "There must doubtless be an unhappy influence on the manners of our people produced *by* the existence of slavery among us. The whole commerce between master and slave is a perpetual exercise of the most boisterous passions, the most unremitting despotism on the one part, and degrading submissions on the other" ([1787] 1997, 96). The US plantation system was based on a lack of compassion passed down from one generation to the next, to the point of Rankine asserting hundreds of years later that it is a "lack of feeling for another that is our problem" (2015). Little has been said on the specular nature of Bentham's famous axiom. The question of sentience raised in his footnote ricochets back today, forcing Man to question his own capacity to feel.

As much as the recorded and photographed deaths of Black men seem to have jolted a moribund humanity into compassion, it is still to be determined whether Black death is grievable at all. The fact that Black suffering and Black death can only be conveyed by way of a technological proxy indicates that Blackness is not truly relatable. Saidiya Hartman, in *Scenes of Subjection*, addresses the complexity of empathy, particularly as it relates to Black suffering. Empathy comes with a form of identification. One feels for the other, and to feel the pain, one must identify with the victim. In the case of white abolitionism, as Hartman argues, empathetic identification is a slippery slope. Feeling for the Black person, projecting oneself into that space to feel the lashes, the rape, and the torture, is filled with good intentions, but it misses the mark. The identification ultimately obliterates the Black person by occupying their space. As Hartman writes, "empathy fails to expand the space of the other but merely places the self in its stead" ([1997] 2022, 26). Empathy is a common issue in an abolitionist context, as abolitionists have struggled to convey the horror of slavery to a white audience. In an abolitionist context, cross-racial and cross-species empathetic identifications have been common tropes. The tragic mulatto trope was based on an identification with a Black woman who looks white. The white reader was meant to feel for the white-looking woman who had a tragic fate due to her putative Blackness. The tragic mulatto trope is a perfect example of placing "the white self in its Black stead," to paraphrase Hartman. Here, the Black woman is only relatable because she comes across as white.

Cross-species empathy is a bit more complex. As Brigitte Nicole Fielder explains in "Animal Humanism" (2013), in abolitionist children's literature, the point of identification was often the domesticated animal. The young reader was meant to feel for the enslaved person via a comparison with animals that inspired fuzzy feelings. The comparison in this case, as Fielder explains, is not due to identification but proximity. The reader feels close to the animal and is invited to transfer those feelings to the enslaved person. Today, the new mode of empathetic identification is technology. Through a screen, a photograph, or a video, the viewer is meant to feel for the Black victim. But the technological medium cannot account for the flesh and the immediacy of the Black existence. Nothing can fully bridge the distance between the white witness and the Black subject.

The New Cyborg

Despite the limitations of technology, the recorded death of George Floyd in the summer of 2021 announced the science fiction of Blackness as a new reality with infinite possibilities for transmutation, leaking, and entanglement. Technology as an inherent part of Blackness has often been overlooked at the expense of the animal question, even though both together contribute to the porosity of Man. In *Becoming Human* (2020), Zakiyyah Jackson underscores the plasticity of Blackness as a form of power and strength. For her, the point is not to try to claim a human status delineated by colonization. On the contrary, Blackness should embrace its porosity, plasticity, animality, and any other nonhuman expression. There is no need for Blackness to claim a seat at the table of a so-called humanity informed by Man. And indeed, any claim to humanity will only relegitimize the flawed premise of the human-animal divide. As Jackson argues, the point of Blackness is to embody "modes of being/knowing/feeling that gesture toward the overturning of Man" (2020, 4). But even more importantly, as Jackson asserts too, "the animal is one but not the only form Blackness is thought to encompass" (3). It is time to think of Blackness as an all-encompassing porosity. Blackness must own up to its animality, technology, and whatever else comes its way in a nonhuman form. Blackness is science fiction.

NOTE

I would like to thank Christy Hoffman (Canisius College) for our correspondence about digidogs.

REFERENCES

Alexander, Michelle. 2012. *The New Jim Crow: Mass Incarceration in the Age of Colorblindness*. New York: New Press.

Benjamin, Ruha. 2019. *Race after Technology: Abolitionist Tools for the New Jim Code*. Oxford, UK: Polity.

Benjamin, Walter. 1969. "The Work of Art in the Age of Mechanical Reproduction." In *Illuminations*, translated by Harry Zohn, 219–53. New York: Schocken Books.

Bentham, Jeremy. 1789. *Introduction to the Principles of Morals and Legislation*. London: T. Payne.

Berger, John. (1980) 1991. "Why Look at Animals?" In *About Looking*, 3–28. New York: Vintage.

Boisseron, Bénédicte. 2018. *Afro-Dog: Blackness and the Animal Question*. New York: Columbia University Press.

Brooker, Charlie. 2017. *Black Mirror*. Season 5, episode 5, "Metalhead." Aired December 29, 2017, on Netflix.

Brooker, Charlie, Annabel Jones, and Jason Arnopp. 2018. "Metalhead." In *Inside Black Mirror*, 282–93. London: Ebury.

Chamoiseau, Patrick. 1997. *L'esclave vieil homme et le molosse*. Paris: Gallimard.

Crammer, Maria, and Christine Hauser. 2021. "Digidog, a Robotic Dog Used by the Police, Stirs Privacy Concerns." *New York Times*, February 27, 2021. www.nytimes.com.

Dery, Mark. 1994. "Black to the Future: Interviews with Samuel R. Delany, Greg Tate, and Tricia Rose." In *Flame Wars: The Discourse of Cyberculture*, edited by Merk Dery, 179–222. Durham, NC: Duke University Press.

Douglass, Frederick. 1845. *Narrative of the Life of Frederick Douglass, and American Self. Written by Himself.* Boston: Published at the Anti-Slavery Office. https://docsouth.unc.edu.

———. (1861) 2015. "Lecture on Pictures." In *Picturing Frederick Douglass*, edited by John, Stauffer, Zoe Trodd, and Celeste-Marie Bernier, 126–41. New York: Liveright.

Du Bois, W. E. B. 1903. *The Souls of Black Folk: Essays and Sketches*. Chicago: A. C. McClurg.

Equiano, Olaudah. (1789) 2021. *The Interesting Narrative of the Life of Olaudah Equiano, or Gustavus Vassa, the African*. New York: Signet Classics.

Fielder, Brigitte Nicole. 2013. "Animal Humanism: Race, Species, and Affective Kinship in Nineteenth-Century Abolitionism." *American Quarterly* 65 (3): 487–514.

Freud, Sigmund. 2003. "The Uncanny." Translated by David Mclintock. In *The Uncanny*, 123–62. London: Penguin Books.

Gary, Romain. 1972. *Chien blanc*. Paris: Gallimard.

Haraway, Donna. (1985) 2016. "A Cyborg Manifesto: Science, Technology, and Socialist Feminism in the 1980s." In *Manifestly Haraway*, 3–90. Minneapolis: University of Minnesota Press, 2016.

———. 2003. *The Companion Species Manifesto: Dogs, People, and Significant Otherness.* Chicago: Prickly Paradigm.

Hartman, Saidiya. (1997) 2022. *Scenes of Subjection*. New York: Norton.

Jackson, Zakiyyah Iman. 2020. *Becoming Human: Matter and Meaning in an Antiblack World*. New York: New York University Press.

Jefferson, Thomas. (1787) 1997. "The Difference Is Fixed in Nature." In *Race and the Enlightenment: A Reader*, edited by Emmanuel Chukwudi Eze, 95–103. Malden, MA: Blackwell.

Kendi, Ibrahim X. 2019. *How to Be an Antiracist*. London: One World.

Koul, Scaachi. 2021. "Crocs Are Ugly!" *BuzzFeed News*, May 11, 2021. www.buzzfeednews.com.

Las Casas, Bartolomé de. (1542) 1992. *A Short Account of the Destruction of the Indies.* Translated by Nigel Griffin. London: Penguin Books.

Mbembe, Achille. 2017. *Critique of Black Reason*. Translated by Laurent Dubois. Durham, NC: Duke University Press.

Mori, Masahiro, Karl F. MacDorman, and Norri Kageki. 2012. "The Uncanny Valley [From the Field]." *IEEE Robotics & Automation Magazine* 19 (2): 98–100.

NYPD (@NYPD News). 2021. "Emergency Service Unit and Bomb Squad." Twitter, February 23, 2021. https://twitter.com/NYPDnews/status/1365083501989609477.

Overman, Howard. 2019. *The War of the Worlds*. 2 seasons. EPIX.

Rankine, Claudia. 2015. "The Condition of Black Life Is One of Mourning." *New York Times*, June 22, 2015. www.nytimes.com.

Stauffer, John, Zoe Trodd, and Celeste-Marie Bernier. 2015. *Picturing Frederick Douglass*. New York: Liveright.

Traisnel. Antoine. 2020. *Capture: American Pursuits and the Making of a New Animal Condition*. Minneapolis: University of Minnesota Press.

US Department of Justice. 2015. *Investigation of the Ferguson Police Department, Civil Rights Division*. March 4, 2015. www.justice.gov.

Wells, H. G. (1898) 2007. *The War of the Worlds*. New York: Signet Classics.

Yaszek, Lisa. 2005. "An Afrofuturist Reading of Ralph Ellison's *Invisible Man*." *Rethinking History* 9 (2–3): 297–313.

5

The Governance of Avian Influenza in the United States

CARRIE DUCOTE

Humans and other animals have a long history of interactions. Nowhere is that history more evident or more deeply rooted than in our eating habits. Meat eating has been slowly increasing over the past century (Barclay 2012). On Super Bowl Sunday alone, Americans eat more than 1.4 *billion* chicken wings (Garcés 2019). But this increase in meat consumption has not come without consequences. In addition to ethical and environmental issues, the production of large quantities of meat raises major public health concerns for human and nonhuman animals. As Aysha Aktar writes, "The industrialization and mass production of animals for food is now among the biggest contributing factors to emerging infectious diseases over the past few decades" (2012, 87). Capitalism, with its hunger for land and meat and other animal assets, is feeding zoonotic outbreaks.

Since the start of the COVID-19 pandemic, people around the globe have learned more about infectious diseases and developed new vocabularies for talking about them. Media attention to the origins of the COVID-19 pandemic have highlighted the significance of a so-called wet market in Wuhan, China, where various types of animals, including chickens, ducks, badgers, crocodiles, snakes, pangolins, and bats, were present and may have come into contact with each other and with humans. However, the general human population in the United States and elsewhere still does not seem familiar with what pandemics look like for species other than humans or with the massive number of deaths that pandemics which affect nonhuman animals cause. As of this writing, roughly one million humans have died of COVID-19 in the United States. In the six-month period between December 2021 and May 2022, over thirty million chickens died because of the way the US government and farmers seek to contain highly pathogenic avian influenza (HPAI), also commonly referred to simply as "avian influenza," "bird flu," or "H5N1CD" (although there are bird flus that are not HPAI). Another outbreak in late 2022 and into 2023, which garnered some public attention because of its apparent impact on the price of eggs, will probably have an even higher death toll.

Of course, death and the animal agriculture industry are deeply entwined. The whole point of raising an animal for food is to kill them to be consumed. But what happens when food animals cannot be killed for food because of public health concerns? What happens if you find yourself, as Rembrandt Enterprises of Iowa did, with over five million egg-laying hens and an outbreak of avian influenza that is likely to lead to a painful death for all of the chickens and that poses a contagion threat to neighboring farms? Who decides on strategies for containment? What happens to the animals living on or near a farm with an outbreak of avian influenza? And who benefits from the response to avian influenza outbreaks?

In this chapter, I examine the governance of avian influenza through an analysis of the state policies and practices in response to disease outbreaks. I invoke governance to highlight the importance of state policies and practices in addressing avian influenza outbreaks once they occur and also the absence of state policies and practices to prevent such outbreaks. I illuminate the connection between the housing conditions of animals raised for human consumption and the contribution of these conditions to outbreaks of avian influenza in the United States, leading to the deaths of nearly seventy-three million birds—the vast majority of them farmed animals being raised for meat and/or eggs—between the two major US outbreaks of highly pathogenic avian influenza in the 2000s. There is no humane way to kill that many potentially contagious birds, leading farmers to employ ethically questionable methods as they struggle to kill their flocks quickly. As property that, under existing legal and social frameworks, "has no rights and can literally be killed without it constituting either homicide or sacrifice," farmed animals, including the chickens and turkeys at the center of this chapter, live a bare life and constitute the category of *bestia sacer* (Abrell 2021, 18). In discussing the deaths of these animals, not even for consumption but simply as a hidden cost of profit, my hope is to draw attention to the way the US Department of Agriculture (USDA) and the factory farming industry collaborate to create the conditions of disease outbreak.

Avian Influenza among American Birds

Avian influenza is a virus that infects several types of birds including chickens, turkeys, quail, geese, and some wild birds. The history of bird flu dates back to at least the 1870s, when scientists in Italy identified what they called "fowl plague" as a disease unique from avian cholera (Lupiani and Reddy 2009). More than fifty outbreaks occurred in the latter half of the twentieth century, with a notable uptick in the 2000s. In 1997, H5N1 jumped the species barrier and infected humans for the first time (or at least this was the first time that it was recognized and documented). After infecting eighteen people and killing six of them, the outbreak was contained through mass culling of poultry and a ban on imports from the region of China where it was suspected the outbreak started. Importantly, H5N1 usually cannot be transmitted between humans: that is, except in very rare circumstances, humans contract it only directly from infected birds.

Transmission among birds occurs quickly and easily, through both direct physical contact and aerosolized vapors. Avian influenza is frequently spread to commercial flocks being raised as part of food production via the droppings of migratory waterfowl, who are typically asymptomatic, flying over commercial poultry operations (Coston 2015). Ducks, in particular, are highly susceptible to H5N1 and, as migratory animals, have the capacity to carry the virus for hundreds or even thousands of miles. The virus can also travel in manure, egg flats, crates, and other farming materials and equipment, and people can pick up the virus on their clothing, shoes, or hands, carrying it between barns or farms. Because of this type of transmissibility, biosecurity is a major issue in the prevention and management of avian influenza outbreaks.

After an incubation period of three to fourteen days, avian influenza attacks an infected bird's nervous, respiratory, and gastrointestinal systems. Clinical signs of infection in birds include lack of energy and appetite; decreased egg production and/or soft-shelled or misshapen eggs; swelling of the head, eyelids, comb, wattles, and hocks; purple discoloration of the wattles, combs, and legs; runny nose; coughing; sneezing; stumbling or falling down; diarrhea; and sudden death without any clinical signs. Most avian influenza virus strands are classified as low pathogenic avian influenza (LPAI) and produce mild respiratory infections. All avian influenza strains start off as mild, LPAI viruses, but once they enter domestic bird populations, they can rapidly mutate into HPAI viruses that cause a much more severe infection, with a mortality rate of close to 100 percent among infected birds (Romich 2008). Death from HPAI is near certain and gruesome: a chicken's eyes and head will swell; they will bleed from their nostrils, lose the ability to walk, get diarrhea, struggle to breathe, and experience multiple organ failure (Rogers 2015). Most chickens die within two to three days of infection.

Understanding housing conditions in the commercial poultry industry is essential for comprehending the spread of avian influenza. The scale and conditions under which industrial agriculture houses chickens results in what Sunaura Taylor (2017) calls "captive disability," or the creation of disability through the routine operation of captivity. Factory farms cause disability through the conditions of confinement: farmed birds suffer from numerous ailments specifically as an outcome of the way farms force them to live. This debilitation is made largely invisible to the consumers of chicken and other animal products as the chicken industry plies consumers with claims about chicken being raised "responsibly" (Foster Farms 2023) and depicts "happy chickens," as in the advertising of one the largest chicken producers in the United States, Perdue Chicken, and legitimizes its practices through humane certification programs supported by the industry. Ultimately, "factory farms and other forms of animal institutionalisation simultaneously obscure the institutions' disabling of non-human bodies while killing those whose bodies [including those who are the wrong sex for the type of farm or who are identified as diseased and/or contagious] will not transform into profit" (Arathoon 2022, 10–11).

Numerous animal welfare organizations, as well as several scholarly works, have documented the problematic conditions in which farmed chickens and turkeys are typically forced to live in the US. Turkeys and chickens raised for meat are usually housed in large grower houses, which are devoid of sunlight and stimulation and in which strict confinement, overcrowding, and the use of growth hormones result in conditions like broken bones, being unable to stand, pterotillomania (or feather plucking), vision loss, and infections of various types, among other ailments. Battery chickens are crowded into tiny cages, debeaked, and inoculated with numerous antibiotics to maximize control of their reproductive output, eggs (Davis 1995). Differences in the sexed bodies of chickens also shapes their fates: male chicks in battery contexts are usually selected for death shortly after hatching because they do not produce eggs and thus are of limited economic value. Broiler chickens, or chickens raised for meat, are both male and female. Whatever the sex of the animal, they live in conditions in which they are typically unable to engage in behaviors that are typical for chickens, such as dust bathing, nesting, or flying (Gaard 2010).

The generally inhumane conditions in the housing of turkeys, chickens, and other birds farmed for meat serve the interests of profit. Breeding larger (i.e., meatier) birds and more of them for lower cost is key for corporations seeking to extract as much profit as possible from chickens. Selective breeding and use of medications result in chickens and turkeys who grow much larger and faster than would be considered typical for their breed outside of a factory farming context; broiler chickens today grow about six times faster than a century ago (King, Westbrook, and Kessel 2022). Chickens are unable to use their legs due to their staggering weight and are frequently immobile. Farmers typically amputate the beaks of egg-laying hens at a young age and house them in battery cages so small that they are unable to stretch their wings. The animal advocate Leah Garcés, speaking in a documentary film about chicken meat production in the United States, describes the buildings in which broiler chickens live in the United States as being so toxic and unhealthy that they are like "nuclear waste sites" (King, Westbrook, and Kessel 2022). Under strict control from the corporations that dominate the chicken industry in the United States, farmers have little, if any, leeway to improve conditions for chickens in their care. According to the National Chicken Council (2023), the primary trade association representing the interests of the broiler chicken industry, over twenty-five thousand farmers have production contracts with a mere thirty corporations producing chicken meat in the United States. Just three of these corporations are responsible for more than half of the chicken meat production in the United States (King, Westbrook, and Kessel 2022).

Beyond these issues, which animal rights advocates have long made central in their criticisms of industrial poultry farming, the sheer number of birds in factory farms contributes to the huge loss of life when pandemics do emerge. With such a large number of animals packed together, their waste piles up quickly, and they are continuously inhaling the recirculating aerosolized fecal matter, methane, and ammonia. Large numbers of highly stressed animals in close quarters with unclean conditions create ideal circumstances for pathogen strengthening and emergence. Stress is known to increase animals' vulnerability to disease, and the close quarters and circulation of waste create an environment where pathogens are frequently reproducing and gaining opportunities for mutation. Once a pathogen is present, the overcrowding enables the pathogen to race through farmed populations. It is possible that without commercial poultry farming, avian influenza would not have found an opportunity to mutate into the highly pathogenic virus it is today. And the more a virus mutates, the more opportunity it has to become highly infectious *and* zoonotic, opening the possibility of spread to other animals, including humans.

Death through Depopulation

The process of killing infected and exposed animals in factory farms in the US unfolds in a regulated, bureaucratic way that centers on containing disease and protecting farmers from financial losses while rendering invisible the suffering and deaths of animals who are diseased, or who, because of fear of exposure, the state determines must be killed. In this way, the physical and financial costs of virus management are borne primarily by the chickens themselves and by the state, rather than by the large corporations that control the chicken-farming industry.

When a farmer thinks they may have an infection of HPAI on their farm, they contact the USDA, which responds by visiting the farm and assigning a caseworker to help the farmer through the process. The farm is placed under quarantine, and the birds on the farm, as well as birds on nearby farms, are tested for HPAI. Testing is done by swabbing the throat of live or dead birds suspected to be infected. The swab is then sent to one of more than fifty USDA-approved laboratories that are part of the National Animal Health Laboratory Network. If one of these tests is positive for HPAI, the sample is then forwarded to the USDA's National Veterinary Services Laboratories in Ames, Iowa, for further testing and final confirmation. While the samples are being tested, the USDA and local agricultural agencies work with farmers to get an accurate inventory of their birds, including numbers, ages, and species, so that they can prepare to reimburse the farmer "100 percent of fair market value" for any birds who die without being able to be sold or who would still be viable egg-laying hens had they not been exposed to or infected with avian influenza (USDA 2015a).

Once the final positive HPAI result is confirmed, what farmers and USDA officials call "depopulation" begins immediately, with the goal of having the entire farm depopulated within twenty-four hours (USDA 2015b). The American Veterinary Medical Association (AVMA) "Guidelines for the Euthanasia of Animals" defines depopulation as "the killing of animals in large numbers in response to an animal health emergency (eg, catastrophic infectious disease, mass intoxication, natural disaster) where all due consideration is given to the terminal experience of the animal, but the circumstances surrounding the event are understood to be exigent and extenuating. Depopulation may not meet the requirements of euthanasia due to situational constraints" (2019). Here, the AVMA is clear that depopulation is a type of extraordinary measure and may not satisfy expectations for euthanasia because time, resources, access to means of killing, or other elements may not be in place. While slaughterhouses can efficiently kill thousands of chickens each day, farms themselves are not set up to do this, and yet, in the case of an HPAI outbreak, the USDA expects farmers to kill their own infected or possibly infected birds. These birds cannot be transported to slaughterhouses once exposed or infected as they could spread the disease further and will contaminate any other location through which they pass.

The USDA (2022) elaborates on the differences between depopulation and euthanasia: "Mass depopulation and euthanasia are not synonymous, and APHIS [the Animal and Plant Health Inspection Service of the USDA] recognizes a clear distinction. Euthanasia involves transitioning an animal to death as painlessly and stress-free as possible. Mass depopulation is a method by which large numbers of animals must be destroyed quickly and efficiently with as much consideration given to the welfare of animals as practicable, given extenuating circumstances.

Mass depopulation is employed in an HPAI response to prevent or mitigate the spread of HPAI through elimination of infected or potentially infected poultry." The USDA thus acknowledges that depopulation is a suboptimal response to HPAI outbreaks but sees it as an emergency measure that must be taken to "prevent or mitigate the spread of HPAI." The USDA further limits how much consideration farmers and USDA representatives must give to animals' welfare to what is "practicable." This functionally is a carte blanche for farmers to do whatever they see as necessary to kill birds quickly; the USDA expects them to complete depopulation within twenty-four hours of notice to do so.

Depopulation techniques include spraying a water-based foam into the houses to suffocate the chickens or placing them in a chamber with carbon dioxide gas (Rogers 2015). Neither of these methods is kind to the birds. When depopulating through foaming, a foam similar to what firefighters use in their struggles against wildfires is sprayed onto all of the birds in the barn, obstructing their airways so that they asphyxiate. Death takes at least six minutes for most birds, and some will survive for up to fifteen minutes in the foam. Critics of foaming as a depopulation method, including the animal advocacy group United Poultry Concerns, note that we have very little knowledge of what the chickens are experiencing as they die because the foam literally completely covers them up, making their reactions invisible. Many reports from farmworkers suggest that the birds actively struggle for at least four minutes. The foam also burns mucous membranes, causing the chickens to feel additional discomfort and pain while they are asphyxiated.

After the 2015 avian influenza outbreak, the USDA began recommending a third method of depopulation, ventilation shutdown, which is even more controversial than foaming. The APHIS fall 2016 "HPAI Preparedness and Response Plan" (USDA 2015c) says the following regarding approved depopulation methods for commercial poultry:

> Standard methods (foaming, CO2) are preferred, as they are the most humane and effective methods to depopulate large poultry flocks. However, if standard methods cannot achieve the 24-hour goal, the APHIS National Incident Commander will approve—on a case-by-case basis—the use of ventilation shutdown for depopulation. While not a preferred method, it could save the lives of thousands of birds by reducing the risk

> of disease spread. Ventilation shutdown requires no specialized equipment or personnel, and can be implemented immediately upon recommendation by Federal, State and industry participants at the affected flock to the National Incident Commander that all other options have been considered and that no other option will achieve the 24-hour depopulation goal.

Ventilation shutdown is the name of a process whereby all of the air systems providing ventilation to a poultry house or houses are shut off, resulting in death by hypoxia and hyperthermia. Once the ventilation systems are shut off, temperatures slowly rise, and the birds' internal organs start to fail, the small amount of oxygen in the house is quickly inhaled, and, without a way to replenish the supply, the birds suffocate. Ventilation shutdown does not require specialized equipment that can take time and resources to procure. It is easy and inexpensive for farmers to carry out and has a reliably high mortality rate. Especially on large farms—like the Rembrandt Enterprises farm, with over five million hens—locating and purchasing foam sufficient to kill the entire flock may be near impossible, especially within the twenty-four-hour time frame that the USDA demands.

In 2016, the US Poultry and Egg Association funded research at North Carolina State University (NCSU) to "examine the humane aspects and effectiveness of ventilation shut down for depopulating laying hens in cage systems" (Bolotnikova 2022). Videos of this research are available online and are difficult to watch. In the laboratory setting, a single chicken in a plexiglass cube took ninety-one minutes to die from ventilation shutdown alone; the time to die was slightly shorter when additional heat or carbon dioxide was used, known as "ventilation shutdown plus" (VSD+). These deaths are more likely due to the heat (hyperthermia) than from lack of oxygen (hypoxia) (Zhao, Xin, and Li 2019). However, ventilation shutdown takes longer to kill birds in commercial poultry conditions outside a laboratory setting: 3.75 hours with ventilation shutdown alone and somewhat less with VSD+ (Eberle-Krish et al. 2018). As the air supply depletes, the birds struggle to breathe and appear to panic. In the videos from the NCSU experiments, a chicken pants, his body heaving as he gasps for air. He alternates between lying down, his face pressed against the clear front of the death box into which experimenters have placed him, and flapping his wings and jumping in desperate attempts to escape. These experiments were conducted on chickens singly: it is even more painful to imagine what this experience of death must be like for thousands of chickens who are watching and feeling one another's suffering in addition to their own.

In the case of the ventilation shutdown video, the stress and panic of the birds being killed is unquestionable. Marina Bolotnikova (2022) shares the following interpretation from a veterinarian: "'These are birds in extreme distress,' said Sherstin Rosenberg, a veterinarian who has cared for thousands of chickens and other poultry birds at an animal sanctuary in California, after reviewing the NC State footage. 'They are literally fighting for their lives, they're gasping for air, they're struggling.' The videos don't have any audio, but Rosenberg added: 'These birds look like they're vocalizing to me. I think they were probably crying out.'" One of the researchers from NCSU seems to defend ventilation shutdown using the strategy common within the poultry industry, claiming that death from influenza is worse: "While the depopulation methods we investigated are not painless, neither are poultry diseases such as avian influenza that has recently infected many farms in NC. Chickens infected with respiratory diseases such as avian influenza also suffer shortness of breath and other painful symptoms and the suffering continues to happen for several days until death occurs. I wish there were less painful options" (Bolotnikova 2022). The AVMA "Guidelines for the Depopulation of Animals" recommends ventilation shutdown alone as a depopulation method for poultry only as a last resort and states that it must only be considered when all other options have been thoughtfully considered and ruled out. After COVID shut down many processing plants and farmers were using ventilation shutdown to depopulate animals they could not sell, AVMA issued a follow-up resolution on the use of VSD, reiterating that in poultry, VSD is not recommended unless no other reasonable option exists.

Yet, it is not clear that the poultry industry as a whole shares the hope for "less painful" options. Its slaughter practices, which include scalding chickens alive, have been subject to criticism by animal rights organizations for decades. Certainly, some chicken farmers, as documented by Leah Garcés (2019), have opened up to new, more humane practices and in some cases have joined forces with animal rights activists to make the public more aware of the animal, human, and environmental costs of chicken and turkey production. Still, chickens and turkeys enjoy almost no legal protections in the context of factory farms. In some states, like California, conditions for egg-laying hens in particular improved only through the passage of voter-initiated laws dictating increased space for the birds. Further, consumption in the US shows no signs of trending downward, and to keep chicken profitably on Americans' plates, farmers and the USDA continue to embrace inhumane practices that maximize efficiency and fail to account for the welfare of the chickens.

Alas, ventilation shutdown as a depopulation method is still on the rise in the US. Rembrandt Enterprises' use of ventilation shutdown to kill over five million chickens in March 2022 may be the single largest case of depopulation in the 2022 outbreak, but as avian influenza pandemics continue, it is highly likely that millions more birds will suffer the same fate. At the Rembrandt Enterprises farms, foaming the birds was considered an inappropriate method due to the number of trucks required to be on-site and the additional cleanup required (Cullen 2022). Human interests in limiting cost thus trumped any purported government or industry commitment to reducing the suffering of animals.

Governing Loss

The US government, primarily through the USDA's APHIS, supports the poultry industry by providing services to identify avian influenza outbreaks, regulating the response to such outbreaks, and compensating farmers for the value of the chickens they lose to depopulation. Once all of the confirmed infected birds are depopulated at a farm, the farm must continue to operate to control possible contagion. The APHIS sets up a ten-kilometer "control zone" around the perimeter of the known infection. Animals in that zone, which may include animals at nearby farms, are then monitored closely for signs of infection. To decrease the population density of susceptible poultry, "certain circumstances" may warrant accelerating the depopulation of birds *not* confirmed to be infected with HPAI in the control zone. That is to say, sometimes birds on farms that are not infected are nonetheless depopulated due to the risk that they could potentially become infected in the future.

After the birds have been depopulated, disposal, cleaning, and disinfecting begins. Disposal methods include composting, burial, incineration, rendering, or landfilling. The USDA recommends sanitizing the barn, equipment, and all affected areas of the farm and helps farms with the cleaning and disinfecting process. After cleanup and a two-day waiting period, the USDA returns to the farm to test for any traces of HPAI left in the environment. Once cleared, the farm may restock with a new flock of birds and begin production again. Depending on the size of the farm, fully restocking can take months or even a year. At Rembrandt Foods, over 250 workers lost their jobs in the wake of the HPAI-triggered depopulation of 5.1 million birds at the facility.

The poultry industry is a large contributor to the US economy. According to one study commissioned by the US Poultry and Egg Association and other poultry and egg trade associations, the chicken and egg industries provide 1.6 million jobs, $101.8 billion in wages, $450.7 billion in economic activity, and $27.3 billion in government revenue (US Egg and Poultry Association 2022). Therefore, a blow to the industry like HPAI infection could mean a blow to the entire US economy. To avoid repercussions, shortly after the initial positive HPAI test is confirmed, the USDA provides an indemnity payment for fair market value of depopulated birds, as well as costs of disposal, cleaning, and disinfecting to the farmer. Indemnity payments are meant to encourage the early, voluntary identification and destruction of diseased birds, in the hope that such identification can slow outbreaks. During the 2014–15 avian influenza outbreak, which overwhelmingly impacted egg-laying chickens, the USDA paid out $200 million in indemnity claims for the deaths of fifty million chickens, or roughly $4 per chicken, plus an additional $600 million for virus elimination and disinfection (Weinraub 2017). In total, the 2015 HPAI outbreak cost US taxpayers an estimated $950 million (USDA 2015d).

As of November 2022, the recent HPAI outbreak in the United States had resulted in the deaths of forty-nine million birds (Centers for Disease Control 2022), and it is expected that the total chicken deaths will exceed that of the 2014–15 outbreak (50.5 million birds). Further, birds were infected in forty-six US states in the more recent outbreak, compared to twenty-one states in the 2014–15 outbreak, suggesting that efforts at managing contagion are not effective. Worldwide, nearly nine hundred cases of humans contracting avian influenza have been confirmed to date, with 50 percent of human infections resulting in death (Centers for Disease Control 2023). Most human cases of H5N1 virus infection have occurred in people who had recent close contact with sick or dead poultry. Since most people do not have close contact with sick or dead poultry, it is unlikely that H5N1 will become a large threat to humans unless the virus gains the ability to be transmitted directly from one human to another.

A version of avian influenza, H1N1 or swine flu, became infectious in humans and spread quickly throughout the United States. Luckily, the symptoms were relatively mild, and the 2009 pandemic was not very deadly to humans. However, the 2009 H1N1 outbreak should serve as a reminder that pigs are highly susceptible to avian and human influenza A viruses and are commonly referred to as the "mixing vessels" in whom avian and human viruses commingle. New influenza strains frequently emerge from pigs since multiple virus strains can infect pigs and exchange genes during reproduction. Pigs raised for human consumption are kept in cramped gestation crates while pregnant and housed in small, indoor feeding houses after being separated from their mother. These housing conditions prevent the animals from exhibiting normal behavior and increase their stress. Just as for chickens, the cramped and unclean housing conditions of pigs on factory farms are also likely to provide an ideal environment for viruses to reproduce and mutate.

If H5N1 has a high mortality rate among infected humans but does not transmit from human to human easily and H1N1 transmits from human to human easily but does not have a high mortality rate, is there a chance the two could exchange genes within the mixing vessel (pig) and create a supervirus capable of both transmitting from human to human easily and killing many of those who become infected? Quite possibly. It is becoming increasingly popular in Asia and the United States to localize pig and chicken farms within the same region, increasing the likelihood of HPAI being transmitted from chicken to pig farms. Pigs may easily become infected with H5N1 by chickens during transport of either species or, as mentioned before, by migratory waterfowl. In fact, a study published in 2010 found that 7.4 percent of pigs tested on farms in Indonesia already carried H5N1 (Nidom et al. 2010). Worse yet, the pigs showed no clinical signs of infection, "indicating that influenza A (H_5N_1) viruses can replicate undetected for prolonged periods, facilitating avian virus adaptation to mammalian hosts" (Nidom et al. 2010, 1515).

One strategy for preventing future outbreaks in birds and for protecting human public health would be vaccination. According to the USDA, vaccination of uninfected birds living near a confirmed HPAI infection may be considered in place of depopulation (USDA 2020), but it is not clear how this decision is made or how often vaccination is used in lieu of depopulation.

The National Institute of Food and Agriculture is funding research to develop a HPAI vaccine, which is currently being tested on mice (Lawrence 2022). However, the USDA is worried that vaccinated birds would be ineligible for export to other countries because they could falsely test positive for HPAI, so it is currently investigating vaccines that would allow importers to distinguish between vaccinated and infected birds (Polansek 2022). Vaccines may be too expensive for farmers to purchase for each bird (Polansek 2022), at least not without cost consequences for consumers and attendant issues with competition from imports. Vaccines have also proved to be ineffective in preventing the spread of HPAI in the past (Amen et al. 2015). Researchers studied a large poultry farm in Egypt, where avian influenza is endemic and a vaccination policy is in place, but found that the vaccine offered little protection (Amen et al. 2015). A virus that is given free range to constantly mutate as it spreads from animal to animal and reproduces will constantly be changing, and vaccine science cannot keep up. Some public health officials predict that if a deadly and contagious influenza outbreak occurred that could spread readily among and to humans, we would see a large number of deaths before we were able to produce vaccines and treatments to treat sick people and protect us from the virus, as has been the case with COVID-19.

Unlike the recent race to find a vaccine that could be mass-produced for humans to slow the spread of COVID-19, there is relatively little incentive to try to find a useful vaccine for avian influenza. The current system of culling millions of birds and reimbursing farmers for the lost market value of those birds appears to be a status quo that the US government and farmers are willing to accept. Neither farmers nor consumers/taxpayers want to bear the costs of reorganizing how chickens are farmed so that farms are not sites of debilitation and contagion. While farmers see firsthand the devastation wrought by HPAI, chicken farms are almost always located in rural areas and are closed to the public, such that consumers/taxpayers are generally shielded from seeing the conditions in which farmed chickens live and the specific horrors of depopulation. Nor do we typically give poultry animals much consideration in the United States; in fact, the only federal legislation mandating the treatment of food animals, the Humane Methods of Slaughter Act, does not cover poultry.

In a 2015 interview with me, Michael Blackwell pointed to a key aspect of the 2014–15 avian influenza outbreak as it relates to conditions on factory farms: most of the infected farms were large-scale, egg-laying operations; not many cage-free or backyard flocks were affected (personal communication, December 14, 2015). What accounts for the difference in infection rates? Blackwell blames it on a few distinct differences in the way the birds live: cage-free birds have more space, experience more natural temperature variations, and have access to direct sunlight. Blackwell also said the following:

> The industrial operations are less natural for the animals. There are some where you've got tens of hundreds or thousands of individuals in fairly crowded conditions, artificial ventilation pretty much, artificial lighting. It's an unnatural set of conditions. Avian influenza virus, like most influenza viruses, does not survive very long in sunlight. It's considered to be maybe a two-hour life expectancy when in direct sunlight. When you go to a facility where the sunlight is not there but also the air is such that an individual sneezes or coughs, there are a lot of individuals within ten feet of that, then you have this whole line of individuals pretty much lined to pick up the viral particles from the coughing and sneezing, which wouldn't be the same if the birds were in less intensive conditions.

The USDA does not currently recommend, let alone require, that chicken farms be built in ways that provide sunlight. To do so would undermine profit: chickens are more active when they are exposed to sunlight and thus burn more calories and weigh less. Nor has it taken other steps to promote housing practices that could reduce rates of infection and the threat of infection, thereby reducing the need to depopulate.

The experts I spoke with all agreed that, although avian influenza outbreaks are clearly tied to conditions within the agriculture industry, those conditions are not likely to change anytime soon. Melissa Warren, senior specialist for influenza at the Association of Public Health Laboratories, did say that she sees the public health sector and the animal agriculture industry beginning to recognize that connection and are working together more frequently (personal communication, December 10, 2015).

The housing conditions of animals raised for human consumption contribute to the frequency and scale of avian influenza outbreaks in the United States, leading to the deaths of nearly one hundred million birds. This is death on a scale we can hardly wrap our heads around—it is the same number of individuals as the entire human population of Vietnam. Some proponents of meat consumption attempt to validate eating meat by saying that the animal's life was not a waste if their flesh was consumed. But what of these millions of birds who lived a short time, had painful and stressful deaths, and then went on to be compost or trash? Can we say that their lives and deaths had meaning and purpose, or are they just the collateral damage of a broken food system?

The Next Pandemic

Since the housing conditions that chickens and turkeys must endure on factory farms are ideal for a virus to reproduce and mutate, as the ease with which HPAI has spread demonstrates, some public health experts predict that HPAI will ultimately jump from a poultry farm to a nearby hog farm, where it could combine with swine flu, H1N1, or some other strand of influenza that easily effects humans. The result would be a virus to which humans have no immunity and that is both highly contagious and highly deadly. Awareness of such a possibility should be greater following the COVID-19 pandemic, with its roots in human-animal contact. Dr. Aysha Akhtar offered predictions regarding the scale of an HPAI outbreak, were it to mutate to a form where it could be transmitted from humans to humans easily:

> We have close to eight billion people on the planet. We have more than ten times that number of animals in farms now. So, the chances of pro-

> ducing another virus in pigs or in birds, and that includes chickens or turkeys, is extremely high, and the chances are that we will produce a virus that will be not only lethal in us but also very contagious among humans. It's also extremely high given the fact that there are more people now, so many more people that are traveling around the world. If and when such a pandemic occurs, it's going to be far worse than the influenza outbreak was in 1918. That's what I predict. (personal communication, 2015)

The 1918 influenza pandemic—the pandemic whose history reared its head as policy makers, pundits, and the public reflected during the COVID outbreak on what a pandemic that killed tens of millions people worldwide would be like today—was ultimately traced back to an avian influenza virus that had adapted itself to humans. So, concerns about bird flu again taking hold in humans are not science fiction or dystopian imagination—it has happened, and it could happen again. What will it take to prevent pandemics from emerging out of the animal agriculture industry in the future?

At present, the governance of avian influenza focuses on contagion control and remediation far more than on prevention. Yet, provided with better living conditions, these animals will be at lower risk for a disease that harms them, farmers, taxpayers, and consumers and that poses at least some risk of mutating into a virus that would be debilitating and/or deadly for members of other species, including humans. Ebola, Zika, COVID, and other diseases of animal origin that infect humans have already shown us that predicting the next outbreak of a highly lethal and contagious virus is nearly impossible. Yet, we *can* identify the conditions that set us—and members of other species—up for disaster.

Like COVID-19 and other pandemics, avian influenza is a global pandemic. While outbreaks may start locally, avian influenza spreads virtually everywhere free-flying birds fly, which means that preventative measures also need to be scaled up to engage with the problems inherent in poultry production globally. This creates challenges, as the cultural, institutional, and legal norms around meat and egg production vary considerably. Working toward global governance focused on prevention is thus essential.

The sheer volume of chicken farming in the US (and many other parts of the world) and both the industry's and the society's desire to maximize profit and minimize cost to the consumer make sanitary and spacious housing for poultry birds unpopular choices. But these changes need to happen. Consumers are paying more attention to the welfare of the animals they eat, by looking for grass-fed and pasture-raised meats, for example. If more chickens were raised outdoors, the threat of new viruses emerging would lessen, due to additional airflow and sunlight. It is less clear if consumers would be willing to pay more for their meat if they knew the long-term benefits of such a change both for the chickens and for the humans consuming them. One of the lessons of the COVID pandemic, at least in the United States, seems to be that people are more interested in immediate gratification and economic stability than in making sacrifices for the greater good. If consumers are unwilling to bear the costs of more expensive chicken or to reduce their chicken consumption altogether, the federal government could take the initiative to protect avian and human health by making better living conditions for battery and broiler chickens more affordable for farmers. Rather than using federal funds to pay for the costs associated with depopulation, the federal government could subsidize programs to help farmers transition to lower-confinement chicken production. Moving away from mass farms, like the Rembrandt facility where over five million chickens were killed through ventilation shutdown in an effort to contain avian influenza, would benefit the welfare of chickens, save farmers the emotional and economic stress of disease outbreaks, and reduce government expenditures for loss amelioration. For decades, the poultry industry (like others) has moved toward centralization and even monopolization. Moving back in the other direction by providing government subsidies for the construction and maintenance of low-confinement chicken housing offers one possible pathway for better lives for chickens and members of other species at risk from avian influenza.

While an in-depth analysis of the structure of the poultry and egg industries is beyond the scope of this chapter, it seems clear that those industries have no intention of moving toward changing practices without additional pressure to do so. Thus, good governance would be essential for effecting change. Simultaneously, consumers need to pay more attention to the consequences of their consumption. Continuing to eat chicken, eggs, turkey, duck, and other birds farmed in high-volume, low-welfare conditions places all of us—human and bird—in peril.

REFERENCES

Abrell, Ethan. 2021. *Saving Animals: Multispecies Ecologies of Rescue and Care*. Minneapolis: University of Minnesota Press.

Akhtar, Aysha. 2012. "Foul Farms: The State of Animal Agriculture." In *Animals and Public Health: Why Treating Animals Better Is Critical to Human Welfare*, 86–116. London: Saffron House.

Amen, Omar, S. V. Vemula, Jingming Zhao, Ragab Sayed Ibrahim, Asmaa Hussein, Indira K. Hewlett, S. Moussa, and Suresh K. Mittal. 2015. "Identification and Characterization of a Highly Pathogenic H5N1 Avian Influenza A Virus during an Outbreak in Vaccinated Chickens in Egypt." *Virus Research* 210:337–43.

Arathoon, Jamie. 2022. "Towards a Research Agenda for Animal and Disability Geographies: Ableism, Speciesism, Care, Space, and Place." *Social & Cultural Geography*, December 5, 2022, 1–19.

AVMA (American Veterinary Medical Association). 2019. "Guidelines for the Depopulation of Animals." www.avma.org.

Barclay, Eliza. 2012. "A Nation of Meat Eaters: See How It All Adds Up." *NPR*, June 27, 2012. www.npr.org.

Bolotnikova, Marina. 2022. "Amid Bird Flu Outbreak, Meat Producers Seek 'Ventilation Shutdown' for Mass Chicken Killing." *The Intercept*, May 1, 2022. https://theintercept.com.

Centers for Disease Control. 2022. "US Approaches Record Number of Avian Influenza Outbreaks in Wild Birds and Poultry." November 3, 2022. www.cdc.gov.

———. 2023. "Reported Human Infections with Avian Influenza A Viruses: Highly Pathogenic Avian Influenza A Virus Infections." April 17, 2023. www.cdc.gov.

Coston, Susie. 2015. "What You Need to Know about Avian Influenza and Factory Farming." *One Green Planet*, December 10, 2015. www.onegreenplanet.org.

Cullen, Tom. 2022. "Five Million Layers Snuffed as Avian Flu Hits." *Storm Lake Times*, May 1, 2022. www.stormlake.com.

Davis, Karen. 1995. "Thinking like a Chicken: Farm Animals and the Feminine Connection." In *Animals and Women: Feminist Theoretical Explorations*, edited by Carol J. Adams and Josephine Donovan, 192–212. Durham, NC: Duke University Press.

Eberle-Krish, Krista N., Michael P. Martin, Ramon D. Malheiros, Sanjay B. Shah, Kimberly A. Livingston, and Kenneth E. Anderson. 2018. "Evaluation of Ventilation Shutdown in a Multi-level Caged System." *Journal of Applied Poultry Research* 27 (4): 555–63.

Foster Farms. 2023. "Our Story." www.fosterfarms.com.

Gaard, Greta. 2010. "Reproductive Technology, or Reproductive Justice? An Ecofeminist, Environmental Justice Perspective on the Rhetoric of Choice." *Ethics and the Environment* 15 (2): 103–29.

Garcés, Leah. 2019. *Grilled: Turning Adversaries into Allies to Change the Chicken Industry*. New York: Bloomsbury Sigma.

King, Lucy, Adam Westbrook, and Jonah M. Kessel. 2022. "The Cost of Your Cheap Chicken." *New York Times*, February 22, 2022. www.nytimes.com.

Lawrence, Margaret. 2022. "Creating Better Vaccines." US Department of Agriculture, February 28, 2022. www.usda.gov.

Lupiani, Blanca, and Sanjay M. Reddy. 2009. "The History of Avian Influenza." *Comparative Immunology, Microbiology and Infectious Diseases* 32 (4): 311–23.

National Chicken Council. 2023. "Broiler Chicken Industry Key Facts 2021." www.nationalchickencouncil.org.

Nidom, Chairul A., Ryo Takano, Shinya Yamada, Yuko Sakai-Tagawa, Syafril Daulay, Didi Aswadi, Takashi Suzuki, Yasuo Suzuki, Kyoko Shinya, Kiyoko Iwatsuki-Horimoto, Yukiko Muramoto, and Yoshihiro Kawaoka. 2010. "Influenza A (H5N1) Viruses from Pigs, Indonesia." *Emerging Infectious Diseases* 16 (10): 1515–23.

Polansek, Tom. 2022. "U.S. Considers Vaccines to Protect Poultry from Deadly Bird Flu." *Reuters*, April 4, 2022. www.reuters.com.

Rogers, Kaleigh. 2015. "Ventilation Shutdown: The Gruesome Last Resort for Bird Flu-Infected Farms." *Vice*, September 22, 2015. http://motherboard.vice.com.

Romich, Janet. 2008. *Understanding Zoonotic Diseases*. Clifton Park, NY: Thomson / Delmar Learning.

Taylor, Sunaura. 2017. *Beasts of Burden: Animal and Disability Liberation*. New York: New Press.

USDA (US Department of Agriculture, Animal and Plant Health Inspection Service [APHIS]). 2015a. "Highly Pathogenic Avian Influenza: A Guide to Help You Understand the Response Process." www.aphis.usda.gov.

———. 2015b. "HPAI Outbreak 2014–2015 Stamping-Out & Depopulation Policy." www.aphis.usda.gov.

———. 2015c. "HPAI Preparedness and Response Plan." www.aphis.usda.gov

———. 2015d. "Final Report for the 2014–2015 Outbreak of Highly Pathogenic Avian Influenza (HPAI) in the United States."

———. 2020. "Prevention and Control of H5 and H7 Avian Influenza in the Live Bird Marketing System." Animal Disease Information. www.aphis.usda.gov.

———. 2022. "Confirmations of Highly Pathogenic Avian Influenza in Commercial and Backyard Flocks." May 1, 2022. www.aphis.usda.gov.

US Egg and Poultry Association. 2022. *2022 Poultry and Egg Economic Impact Study*. Tucker, GA: US Egg and Poultry Association.

Weinraub, Mark. 2017. "USDA Has $80 Million–$90 Million to Fight Bird Flu." *Reuters*, March 17, 2017. www.reuters.com.

Zhao, Yang, Hongwei Xin, and Lihua Li. 2019. "Modelling and Validating the Indoor Environment and Supplemental Heat Requirement during Ventilation Shutdown (VSD) for Rapid Depopulation of Hens and Turkeys." *Biosystems Engineering* 184:130–41.

6

Animals Don't Fully Understand Death, but Do Humans?

YAIR DOR-ZIDERMAN AND JULIAN PAUL KEENAN

As happens in science, the authors sit to draft an article of well-summarized findings only to be alerted to the latest publication. Just as we were finalizing this current chapter, *Frontiers in Ageing Neuroscience* published the first "recorded" death in neuroscience (Vicente et al. 2022). The death was seen as novel because according to all accounts, this was the first time a human had passed while having a full array of EEG (electroencephalogram) electrodes recording his brain. This allowed the researchers to observe the brain as it went from a state of living to a state of death. The eighty-seven-year-old was "wearing" a full suite of brain-recording equipment (for epilepsy monitoring) at the time his body ceased activity.

One of the main findings was that human death looks very similar to rodent death (with regard to brain activity). That is, similar patterns exist, such as that the brain remains active for seconds after cardiac arrest. The other major discovery is that there was an increase in gamma-band activity. What this could translate to is that humans, unlike rodents, may have a self-aware event at death (Li et al. 2015). The "seeing my life pass before my very eyes" may be quite a real phenomenon, but as scientists tend to do, the authors caution us that more data are needed.

Bigger than the results or the brain correlates of death is the questioning of understanding. Do humans and nonhuman animals understand death the same way? This initial question has led authors in many directions. Here we examine how this research has led us to understand humans to a greater extent, with results that may take us back to the actual experience of death.

We Don't Get It

Both life and death are difficult to define on a biological level. For example, the debate over the "living" status of viruses remains, and the actual definition of death in humans varies across religions, countries, scientists, and philosophers; the topic of death, because of its ambiguity, raises many questions in ethics and morals and one's outlook on life itself (Verheijde, Rady, and Potts 2018).

Of interest is the notion that humans have an understanding of death and animals do not. For an evolutionary biologist, the notion of "humans do, animals do not" has formed the basis for centuries of research. We have examined thumbs and tool use, vision and abstract thinking. We have looked at art and numbers, language and murder and slavery. At each step, we discover both differences and similarities.

"Do animals understand death?" is a simple-enough question. However, researchers are quickly confronted with the dilemma of how you know whether an organism understands death. That is, what test do we have and what evidence for that test being valid and reliable do we have as a gauge of death (Watson and Matsuzawa, 2018)? What we and others have thought is that humans have an understanding, and we should model our tests after our own cognition. That is, a test of understanding should be based on what humans know, as humans obviously comprehend death. However, before this thought gets past the zygotic stage, one realizes that perhaps humans do not fully understand death, and if any nonhuman animal reached our level, it means confusion at best. But that is not to say that humans cannot grasp most aspects of death. We can, as demonstrated by the fact that most of us understand that we will die. That is, most humans understand that we are mortal.

However, that is where things get quite fuzzy. According to recent Pew Research Center data, which is in line with other large-scale US studies, the majority of Americans believe in fantastical things (Nortey, Lipka, and Alvarado 2021). Most Americans believe that there is a heaven (73 percent) and a hell (62 percent). One-third of Americans believe in reincarnation. Furthermore, two-thirds of Americans believe that they will reunite with loved ones in the afterlife. Of note for this chapter, 48 percent of Americans believe that they will be reunited with a pet. These data were collected in late 2021, and over sixty-four hundred people were sampled.

We therefore are in a quandary: If *Homo sapiens* are the benchmark of understanding death, we would need to test for similar beliefs in nonhumans. If we discover that nonhumans do not believe in the afterlife, their understanding is incomplete. We reject this idea. But we ask, How is it possible to know that your physical life ends but your "soul" or "spirit" continues? A final question from the Pew survey indicates a possibility. Approximately 60 percent of the people surveyed believe that their physical bodies will be perfectly healthy in the afterlife. In other words, the afterlife provides an avenue for the self to continue, not just as it is but in an even better form.

Self-Awareness

Before moving on, researchers have examined the moment of death looking for scientific indications that the soul leaves the body upon death. A study on the Buddhist practice of Tukdam might be the most interesting. "Tukdam" is the term given to a postmortem state of meditation that is said to delay physical decomposition. The notion is that we can all reach this state, but only practiced meditators actually achieve it. Using a similar EEG setup to the one we saw previously, researchers attempted to measure the brain state of people entering Tukdam. Because the deaths were unpredictable, it took hours to days postmortem to commence recording, but this should be well within the window, according to tradition. As one might predict, no discernable brain activity was detected (Lott et al. 2021). It is not that science does not take accounts of the afterlife seriously; it is simply that all evidence points to a negative result.

Nonhumans and humans are varied in the ways they treat the dead (Reggente et al. 2018; Watson and Matsuzawa 2018). For example, there are accounts of crows attempting to engage in sexual behaviors with the corpses of other crows (Swift and Marzluff 2018), which may or may not indicate a similar mentality between species (i.e., both have similar behaviors but may or may not have similar motives/beliefs/cognitions). But like the varied behavior of humans toward a corpse, different behaviors toward a corpse by animals do not necessarily equal different understandings by those animals. We think a major cognitive difference lies in self-awareness. That is, the differences that exist between "selves," comparatively speaking, lead to very different understandings of death, such that those animals that possess self-awareness have a greater likelihood of understanding the finality of existence that death brings about.

The most reliable and valid method of testing for self-awareness across most animal species is the mirror-recognition test, which measures mirror-self recognition (MSR). This test has over fifty years of testing in science (Anderson and Gallup 2015), and while it is far from perfect (Guenther 2017), it is the best that science has developed. The basic notion is that animals that recognize themselves can only do so because they have a sense of self-awareness or "meta" understanding of the self. Self-face recognition correlates with other known variables of the self, which is one reason that people believe it to be somewhat valid. For example, infants who have self-face recognition also tend to possess self-conscious emotions (LaVarco et al. 2022). Narcissism can be gauged via self-face recognition, and autism, a disorder of self, is associated with disrupted self-face recognition (Kramer et al. 2020). Few animals possess MSR. They include humans, chimps, and orangutans, for sure; magpies, dolphins, and elephants as probable/possible (Anderson and Gallup 2011; Gallup and Anderson 2018). Even in those animals that do, such as the chimps, levels of not passing the test are at about 50 percent. Assuming that the test is measuring at least some aspect of self-awareness, we can assume the data indicate that nonhuman animals experience the self differently than humans do. That is, self-awareness across organisms is not equal, similar to memory, learning, depth perception, and so on.

Neuroscience has tried to take some of these concepts to the brain to truly determine the self. For example, Bill Hopkins examined the brains of sixty-seven chimpanzees, some with MSR and some without. He found significant brain difference in regions associated with higher-order thinking and attention. That is, chimps with MSR had different brain anatomy (Hopkins et al. 2019).

In humans, MSR has been examined in-depth. One of the first studies involved patients who had one-half of their brains anesthetized. That is, for about five minutes, the right hemisphere was completely asleep (and later the left hemisphere). This was done for medical reasons, but we used this time to show the self-face to these patients and found that the right hemisphere was needed for self-face recognition (Keenan et al. 2001). Along with others, we have discovered the frontal lobes (the medial prefrontal cortex, to be specific) and regions of the right hemisphere to be critical for both MSR and all aspects of self-awareness. That is, when humans see themselves, think about themselves, or remember themselves, the frontal lobes and the right hemisphere are critical (Feinberg and Keenan 2005; Uddin et al. 2007). These brain areas are underdeveloped or completely absent in nonhumans. In animals such as the chimpanzees or dolphins in which there are signs of self-awareness, we see these areas expanded. However, even in our closest relatives, there are tremendous neuroanatomical and functional differences, which probably lead to the differences we see behaviorally with regard to the self.

But why is the self so important to humans *not* understanding death?

The Self Loves Itself at All Costs

Neuroscience has revealed a few surprises about the self. In our early examinations of the self, we were looking into introspection. We had participants look at adjectives and decide whether a word described them. We thought this would get them thinking about themselves. As a control, we had them think whether the adjectives described their best friend. We did not think much about the control until a pattern emerged. Participants were significantly more favorable to themselves compared to their best friends (Luber et al. 2012). This finding was seen again and again, and the notion that people were self-enhancers and self-deceivers was emerging. Across a number of studies, we kept finding the same results (Amati et al. 2010; Barrios et al. 2008; Kwan et al. 2007; Luber et al. 2012; Taylor-Lillquist et al. 2020). First, participants self-deceive in a direction that makes the self look favorable. Second, people self-enhance across a number of tested methods including what they know and their own basic attributes.

Mainly, deceiving makes participants feel better (Duran et al. 2021). When people self-enhance, their affect goes up. In other words, self-deception has a clear benefit, one we think involves an antidepressant buffer.

What is critical about these studies is that we had the brain regions isolated. Mainly, the exact same areas that are involved in self-awareness are involved in self-deception. The frontal cortex seems to be at the center of both. When we used techniques to measure the frontal cortex, this part of the brain got excited during self-awareness and self-enhancement. When we temporarily disrupted this area, the participants deceived less and felt worse.

With regard to death itself, the frontal cortex plays a similar "feel better" or "antidepressant" role. Disrupting the frontal cortex reduces self-reported religious belief in the context of a recent, vivid reminder of death and bodily decomposition (Holbrook et al. 2020). In other words, the frontal cortex is necessary for religious beliefs surrounding death. When the frontal cortex is disrupted, religious beliefs are reduced when a person has "death on their mind." We interpret this as evidence that the frontal cortex aids in managing a threat to the self. That is, death is a threat to the self; the response is religious belief. As noted earlier, these beliefs preserve the self.

The Self Believes It Will Live Forever

Sigmund Freud, the "father of psychoanalysis," tended to ignore death as a phenomenon of importance in our psychic structure and dynamics. Nevertheless, in the midst of the devastation brought about by the First World War, he wrote, "Our own death is indeed unimaginable, and whenever we make the attempt to imagine it we can perceive that we really survive as spectators" (Freud 1915, 289). Thus, "at bottom no one believes in his own death, or to put the same thing in another way, in the unconscious every one of us is convinced of his own immortality" (289). On the other hand, Freud observed, "for strangers and for enemies, we do acknowledge death, and consign them to it quite as readily and unthinkingly" (297).

While knowledge about the brain was greatly limited in Freud's time, these statements foreshadow contemporary notions of the way the brain encodes certain aspects of its embodied selfhood, as well as the protective mechanism by which it denies its mortality. We will review evidence showing that on a prereflective and automatic level, the brain is incapable of combining self- and death-related information, categorizing death as an event that only befalls others.

But before moving to the discussion of the way the self protects itself from the existential threat of death, we first need to establish some basic ideas about the way contemporary cognitive neuroscience views the brain and the self. In particular, we refer to the predictive processing theory of brain function (Clark 2013; Friston and Kiebel 2009). The predictive processing theory is currently the most influential neurocomputational framework for understanding how the brain works on all levels—from perception and movement to attention, cognition, and emotion. The brain is understood to be primarily and foremost (some people, e.g., Friston 2009, would say exclusively) a prediction machine trying to make sense of the multitude of incoming sensory information by using predictions about the world. These predictions, or neuronally encoded statistical "beliefs" (Rao and Ballard 1999; Bastos et al. 2012), serve as sorts of heuristics, allowing the brain to limit itself to the processing of discrepancies between what it expects the world to be and what its senses say the world is. The argument is that a brain that would have to process, from the bottom up, all the information picked up by all the different senses and then combine and integrate them into higher-order representations would not endow the human animal with the processing speed necessary for survival.

In order to be one step ahead of the game, we constantly simulate the world, adjusting the simulations' predictions and models only when they conflict with reality. Importantly, the brain generates predictions not only of the external world but also of the internal one. Bodily sensory information such as information about the body's temperature, pH level, energy, balance, and so on are constantly processed and maintained within tight boundaries. Here again, a "self" as the null center of gravity (Dennett 1992) at the eye of this interoceptive and exteroceptive informational storm comes in useful. In this view, the self is nothing other than a higher-order prediction (Seth and Friston 2016; Limanowski and Blankenburg 2013), developed as an evolutionary necessity for making it possible for the human organism to navigate physical and social reality. Finally, and this is a crucial point to take into account, the beliefs encoded by our brain are constrained by their adaptive value—not their ontological validity (Seth and Tsakiris 2018). Thus, the brain will, at times, go out of its way to maintain beliefs that are clearly not true but that are important for the organism's functioning. One such belief is that the self is immortal.

But wait, did we not say before that humans are able to grasp their mortality? We all know we are going to die, right? The answer to this conundrum is that the self is both able and unable to grasp mortal truth. And that is because there is no *one* self.

The Self Is Not a Unitary Entity

One of the great realizations of modern cognitive neuroscience is that the self is unitary in name alone. The self is rather viewed as an umbrella term for a host of different processes operating at different levels of the cognitive hierarchy, manifesting different phenomenal signatures, and mediated by distinct neural substrata.

The most basic division of the self is into a narrative autobiographical sense of self and a minimal embodied sense of self. This basic division goes back to the works of William James (1890), who distinguished between the "Me" and the "I." Recent parallel formulations include Antonio Damasio's (2012) "extended/autobiographical" versus "core" self and the philosophers of mind Shaun Gallagher's (2000) and Dan Zahavi's (2006) "narrative" versus "minimal" self.

The narrative self is the autobiographical story we tell ourselves about ourselves. It is the organizing thread running through our past history and onward toward our future imagined possibilities. It includes our characteristics, or how we view ourselves, and also how we suppose others view us. The narrative self can thus be defined as the construction, that is, mental image, of one's own personal identity shaped by social and cultural factors (Gallagher 2000; Zahavi 2006). It is cognitively associated with high-level functions such as language and autobiographic memory (Christoff et al. 2011; Damasio 2012), and it is neuroscientifically associated with the default mode resting-state network (Northoff et al. 2006; Buckner, Andrews-Hanna, and Schacter 2008) and in particular with the medial prefrontal region (Whitfield-Gabrieli et al. 2011; Gusnard et al. 2001), mentioned previously as the region implicated in both self-enhancement and self-deception.

Thus, we are prone in our self-narratives, as we often see in daily life, to misrepresent ourselves with a particular emphasis on story lines that allow some form of self to persist beyond death. But even if we close the book of "me" and just pay attention to present-moment experience, we will discover a very different but no less real sense of self. We will notice that we are located inside a body that we "own" and can control. We will notice a clear sense of separation from the world, which we view through a first-person perspective and which we feel to be at the center of this experience. The embodied self thus refers to the basic experience of "being a self," a momentary awareness endowed with a sense of agency and ownership (the subjective experience of being in control of one's body and thought, as well as owning the body), first-person perspective (1PP, the sense of being localized in space, having a point of view) (Gallagher 2000), and self-other differentiation (what is me and what is not me; Christoff et al. 2011). Neurally, it has been shown to be rooted in bodily and multisensory processes (Seth 2013) and in particular a region known as the right temporal parietal junction (Ionta et al. 2011). Our own neurophenomenological (Berkovich-Ohana et al. 2020) work has contributed to this literature by showing that these two modes of self experience were different not only in brain topography but also in their underlying brain waves' frequency. Faster waves in the gamma band were associated with the narrative self, while slower beta-band brain waves were associated with the minimal embodied self (Dor-Ziderman et al. 2013, 2016).

Going back to Freud, let us try for a moment the thought experiment that he describes. Try to imagine your own death. What you will notice is that you indeed "survive as a spectator." Close introspection will reveal someone there observing the whole thing. The mere fact of trying to imagine or think of your own death necessarily gives rise to a minimal phenomenal self with a location in space and a first-person perspective who owns and directs the experience (Blanke and Metzinger 2009). It is indeed ironic that we create a self by imagining its demise.

Note that this problem does not arise when we imagine, or indeed see, someone else's death. Thus, the brain implements a neat trick. As death is a *fact of experience* (Heidegger 1962), it accepts death as a universal all-encompassing phenomenon on a narrative-conceptual level; as death can cause debilitating anxiety (Becker 1973), it categorizes death as pertaining to the "other" on an embodied-experiential level.

This may seem to be a ridiculous solution, but remember, brains did not evolve to accurately portray reality but rather to help the organism pass on its gene pool. The immortal self illusion, not unlike visual illusions, tends to persist even in the face of rational certainty. We know we will die but, at the same time, do not really believe it.

The Brain Shields Its "Self" from Existential Threat by Attributing Death to the "Other"

Detecting change is a basic function of what brains do. Gazelles peacefully grazing on the savanna plains must be finely tuned, at all times, to even the slightest changes in visual scenery that might indicate a lion getting ready to pounce. Babies' attention is automatically attracted to novelty. Brains automatically represent statistical regularities of the environment and register "surprising" events.

A well-established neuroscience paradigm for gauging this phenomenon is the mismatch negativity paradigm (MMN), originally discovered in the auditory domain (Näätänen, Gaillard, and Mäntysalo 1978), later extended to visual changes (Kremláček et al. 2016), and currently widely understood in predictive processing terms (Stefanics, Kremláček, and Czigler 2014; Friston 2005). The idea behind this paradigm is simple. Participants view a stimulus that is flashed several times (the standard stimulus), causing the brain to establish the prediction that the same stimulus will appear again. If this prediction is violated, that is, if a different stimulus (the deviant stimulus) appears instead, the brain registers a surprise signal roughly three hundred milliseconds after the deviant's onset.

Building on the work of others (Sel, Harding, and Tsakiris 2016), we devised a version of this paradigm (reported in Dor-Ziderman, Lutz, and Goldstein 2019) in which participants viewed their own faces as standard stimuli ("self" condition) and the faces of gender-matched strangers ("other" condition) as controls. Deviant facial stimuli were created by morphing the self and stranger faces with equal proportions. Participants lay in a magnetoencephalogram (MEG) brain scanner and viewed, in succession, between three and six faces either of their own or of the stranger, followed by the morphed deviant facial stimuli. What made the paradigm relevant to death processing were prime words that appeared before each sequence of faces commenced and remained present above the faces for each sequence's duration. These words were either death-related words (such as "burial" or "funeral") or merely negative words (serving as a control condition).

As expected, the deviant morphed face was marked by the characteristic "surprise" brain wave in all the control conditions (that is, when negative prime words appeared with either self or stranger faces and when death-related words appeared with stranger faces). However, when self faces followed death-related words, the MMN surprise signal was absent. Note that the only difference between the death-self and negative-self conditions was the preceding death-related or merely negative prime word, respectively; the standard and deviant facial stimuli were identical. While this may not impress the average reader, the notion that the mere presence of a word could suppress a basic automatic perceptual brain signal is quite shocking. It was as if the brain refused to link the self with death, causing the brain's predictive mechanism to malfunction.

A second finding of the study was a functional self-other relation in the processing of death stimuli. Following death-related words (but not negative words), a linear relation emerged between the "self" and "other" MMN signals. The weaker the effect was for the former, the larger it was for the latter. To us, this indicated that the brain dealt with self-related information under a deathly context by "pushing" death onto the "other." This effect was interpreted as a "shielding" of the self from existential threat by attributing death to the "other" at a prereflective perceptual level of processing. The brain categorizes death as something that befalls others but not oneself.

Can We Learn to Fully Understand Death?

The question that this chapter set out to explore was whether humans fully understand death. We argued that different selves may lead to different understandings of death. After outlining the self's fragmented, constructed, and deceptive nature, we can summarize that on a narrative conceptual level of the self, humans, perhaps uniquely, can understand their mortality but choose not to. Rather than recognizing that like all stories, our personal story too has an end, we go to great lengths to preserve the self through various afterlife beliefs and immortality schemes. On the other hand, on the minimal embodied experiential level of the self, a level of the self we at least partially share with some nonhuman animal species (Northoff and Panksepp 2008), humans may lack the ability to fully understand their mortality. We may be neurally wired to deny our own death. Thus, it may be the case that even within the same brain, different selves understand death differently.

Before trying to address the question of whether we can fully understand death, it is important to understand that there is a cost to *not* attempting to understand death, to leaving death-denial processes unchecked.

The denial of death is necessarily bounded by time and circumstance. Facing one's own imminent death after a lifetime of denial, one often feels surprised, afraid, and unprepared (Jenkinson 2015). This sense of unpreparedness and fear clearly marked the global societal responses to the COVID-19 pandemic (Menzies and Menzies 2020; Pyszczynski et al. 2020). As death anxiety has been argued to be a transdiagnostic construct underpinning a multitude of mental illnesses (Iverach, Menzies, and Menzies 2014), these prolonged elevated levels of death anxiety are likely to cause increases in psychopathology (Menzies and Menzies 2020).

The account of the way humans are affected by the prospects of their own death cannot be complete without mentioning terror management theory (TMT). TMT is the most comprehensive scientific research paradigm investigating the effects of death denial on the human psyche and society. TMT has received much attention for revealing the dark side of death-anxiety defenses, showing that they strip the human psyche of a degree of its freedom, where, unaware, it aligns itself with salient cultural values and adopts a prejudiced, intolerant, and even aggressive attitude toward those who fall outside its boundaries (Greenberg and Kosloff 2008; Pyszczynski, Solomon, and Greenberg 2015). Of special interest to this chapter are the TMT studies showing that death reminders impact how humans view and feel toward nonhuman animals. Jamie Goldenberg et al. (2001) have shown that death reminders increase disgust toward animals and strengthen views of human exceptionalism. Other studies have found that death reminders increase hostility toward animals (Beatson and Halloran 2007), including one's own pets (Loughnan, Halloran, and Beatson 2009), and even lead to a greater endorsement of killing them (Lifshin et al. 2017). Finally, and perhaps most importantly, it has been argued that mortality awareness drives climate (in)action at the individual and societal levels (Wolfe and Tubi 2019) and that making peace with our existential fears is an unavoidable crossing point on the road to reconnection with nature and degrowth (Koller 2021).

So this brings us to the all-important question of whether and how our brains can be retrained to face up to mortal truth. Again, the key lies in self-awareness. We made the case that different selves may give rise to different understandings of death. The philosopher Derek Parfit (1984) argues that coming to believe that there is no unitary enduring self should lead to changes in our attitude toward death. Perhaps the way to understand death is to better understand our selves. Seeing the self as a set of impersonal transient processes, rather than an ontological truth, may diffuse its self-preserving protective mechanisms. The underlying machinery and processes that give rise to the self are clearly not something we are aware of in everyday life, in the same way that we are not aware of our digestive processes (that is, until something goes wrong). They are transparent to us (Metzinger 2004). However, certain radical self-disruptive experiences can make these processes opaque, even if temporarily, and both meditation and psychedelics have been shown to induce such "selfless" experiences (Millière et al. 2018).

Altered self-processing is one of mindfulness's mechanisms of action (Hölzel et al. 2011; Tang, Hölzel, and Posner 2015), linked with decreased trait default mode network (DMN) activity and connectivity (Brewer et al. 2011; Berkovich-Ohana et al. 2016). Experienced practitioners have also been shown to produce nondual (Josipovic et al. 2012), "selfless" (Ataria, Dor-Ziderman, and Berkovich-Ohana 2015; Nave et al. 2021) states of consciousness, tied with decreases in the parietal DMN nodes (Dor-Ziderman et al. 2013, 2016; Josipovic 2014). In the context of death processing, there is preliminary evidence linking reduced death thoughts and defensiveness to dispositional mindfulness (Niemiec et al. 2010), as well as meditation practice in a Korean Buddhist sample and a sample of US students receiving a brief mindfulness training (Park and Pyszczynski 2019).

In a similar vein, there is evidence linking psychedelics to altered self and death processing. Psychedelics have been shown to reduce DMN activity, connectivity, and structure (Muthukumaraswamy et al. 2013; Carhart-Harris and Friston 2010). These DMN changes were also shown to be correlated with ego dissolution degree (Lebedev et al. 2015; Carhart-Harris et al. 2016) and to persist even after the psychedelic experience has subsided (Smigielski et al. 2019; Barrett et al. 2020). In the context of death processing, psychedelics (mainly LSD) were researched already in the 1960s for alleviating the fear of death in the terminally ill (Dyck 2019), results that were corroborated by more rigorous recent studies (Grob et al. 2011; Gasser, Kirchner, and Passie 2015; Griffiths et al. 2016). While underlying mechanisms have not been empirically demonstrated, one explanation of this effect is that experiencing psychedelic-induced "ego-death" is perceived as mirroring the experience of actual death (Pahnke 1969). Having gone through self-annihilation and come back radically changes how the self is experienced and leads to reduced death anxiety and denial. In (simplified) predictive processing terms, such experiences alter top-down priors regarding the self and the advent of its nonexistence.

Can We Learn to Fully Understand Death? Part 2

If we go back to the moment of death and a burst of brain activity, we really do not know what it means. Like blood flowing to a brain area, we know that there is activity in that area, but we do not know for sure what cognitive processes are occurring. In the end of *The Sopranos*, a now-fading, decades-old TV show, the climax was a cut to black after the main character presumably gets assassinated. People hated the ending. In fact, most people thought that their cable went out or that something happened with their internet. Few people thought that going to black was an accurate depiction of death. If "going to black" is in fact the ending facing all of us, we are certain that it is not a reality that many of us wish to know of.

We think that brain research will bring us closer to understanding why comprehending death is so difficult. We also think that it will bring us a long way to understanding ourselves and our own animal consciousness.

REFERENCES

Amati, Franco, Hanna Oh, Virginia S. Y. Kwan, Kelly Jordan, and Julian Paul Keenan. 2010. "Overclaiming and the Medial Prefrontal Cortex: A Transcranial Magnetic Stimulation Study." *Cognitive Neuroscience* 1 (4): 268–76.

Anderson, James R., and Gordon G. Gallup Jr. 2011. "Which Primates Recognize Themselves in Mirrors?" *PLoS Biology* 9 (3): e1001024.

———. 2015. "Mirror Self-Recognition: A Review and Critique of Attempts to Promote and Engineer Self-Recognition in Primates." *Primates* 56 (4): 317–26.

Ataria, Yochai, Yair Dor-Ziderman, and Aviva Berkovich-Ohana. 2015. "How Does It Feel to Lack a Sense of Boundaries? A Case Study of a Long-Term Mindfulness Meditator." *Consciousness and Cognition* 37 (December): 133–47.

Barrett, Frederick S., Manoj K. Doss, Nathan D. Sepeda, James J. Pekar, and Roland R. Griffiths. 2020. "Emotions and Brain Function Are Altered up to One Month after a Single High Dose of Psilocybin." *Scientific Reports* 10 (1): 1–14.

Barrios, Veronica, Virginia S. Y. Kwan, Giorgio Ganis, Jaime Gorman, Jennifer Romanowski, and Julian Paul Keenan. 2008. "Elucidating the Neural Correlates of Egoistic and Moralistic Self-Enhancement." *Conscious and Cognition* 17 (2): 451–56.

Bastos, Andre M., W. Martin Usrey, Rick A. Adams, George R. Mangun, Pascal Fries, and Karl J. Friston. 2012. "Canonical Microcircuits for Predictive Coding." *Neuron* 76 (4): 695–711.

Beatson, Ruth M., and Michael J. Halloran. 2007. "Humans Rule! The Effects of Creatureliness Reminders, Mortality Salience and Self-Esteem on Attitudes towards Animals." *British Journal of Social Psychology* 46 (3): 619–32.

Becker, Ernest. 1973. *The Denial of Death*. New York: Free Press.

Berkovich-Ohana, Aviva, Yair Dor-Ziderman, Fynn Mathis Trautwein, Yoav Schweitzer, Ohad Nave, Stephen Fulder, and Yochai Ataria. 2020. "The Hitchhiker's Guide to Neurophenomenology—The Case of Studying Self Boundaries with Meditators." *Frontiers in Psychology* 11 (July).

Berkovich-Ohana, Aviva, Michal Harel, Avital Hahamy, Amos Arieli, and Rafael Malach. 2016. "Alterations in Task-Induced Activity and Resting-State Fluctuations in Visual and DMN Areas Revealed in Long-Term Meditators." *NeuroImage* 135 (July): 125–34.

Blanke, Olaf, and Thomas Metzinger. 2009. "Full-Body Illusions and Minimal Phenomenal Selfhood." *Trends in Cognitive Sciences* 13 (1): 7–13.

Brewer, Judson A., Patrick D. Worhunsky, Jeremy R. Gray, Yi-Yuan Tang, Jochen Weber, and Hedy Kober. 2011. "Meditation Experience Is Associated with Differences in Default Mode Network Activity and Connectivity." *Proceedings of the National Academy of Sciences* 108 (50): 20254–59.

Buckner, Randy L., Jessica R. Andrews-Hanna, and Daniel L. Schacter. 2008. "The Brain's Default Network: Anatomy, Function, and Relevance to Disease." *Annals of the New York Academy of Sciences* 1124 (March): 1–38.

Carhart-Harris, Robin L., and Karl. J. Friston. 2010. "The Default-Mode, Ego-Functions and Free-Energy: A Neurobiological Account of Freudian Ideas." *Brain* 133 (4): 1265–83.

Carhart-Harris, Robin L., Suresh Muthukumaraswamy, Leor Roseman, Mendel Kaelen, Wouter Droog, Kevin Murphy, Enzo Tagliazucchi, et al. 2016. "Neural Correlates of the LSD Experience Revealed by Multimodal Neuroimaging." *Proceedings of the National Academy of Sciences* 113 (17): 4853–58.

Christoff, Kalina, Diego Cosmelli, Dorothée Legrand, and Evan Thompson. 2011. "Specifying the Self for Cognitive Neuroscience." *Trends in Cognitive Sciences* 15 (3): 104–12.

Clark, Andy. 2013. "Whatever next? Predictive Brains, Situated Agents, and the Future of Cognitive Science." *Behavioral and Brain Sciences* 36 (3): 181–204.

Damasio, Antonio. 2012. *Self Comes to Mind: Constructing the Conscious Brain.* New York: Pantheon Books.

Dennett, Daniel C. 1992. "The Self as a Center of Narrative Gravity." In *Self and Consciousness: Multiple Perspectives*, edited by Frank S. Kessel, Pamela M. Cole, and Dale L. Johnson, 4–237. Hillsdale, NJ: Erlbaum.

Dor-Ziderman, Yair, Yochai Ataria, Stephen Fulder, Abraham Goldstein, and Aviva Berkovich-Ohana. 2016. "Self-Specific Processing in the Meditating Brain: A MEG Neurophenomenology Study." *Neuroscience of Consciousness* 2016 (1): niw019.

Dor-Ziderman, Yair, Aviva Berkovich-Ohana, Joseph Glicksohn, and Abraham Goldstein. 2013. "Mindfulness-Induced Selflessness: A MEG Neurophenomenological Study." *Frontiers in Human Neuroscience* 7 (January): 582.

Dor-Ziderman, Yair, Antoine Lutz, and Abraham Goldstein. 2019. "Prediction-Based Neural Mechanisms for Shielding the Self from Existential Threat." *NeuroImage* 202 (November): 116080.

Duran, Kelly A., Hannah O'Halloran, Heather Soder, Saeed Yasin, Rachel Kramer, Sydney Rosen, Janet Brenya, Katherine Chavarria, Liliia Savitska, Julian Paul Keenan. 2021. "The Medial Prefrontal Cortex: A Potential Link between Self-Deception and Affect." *International Journal of Neuroscience* 131 (7): 701–7.

Dyck, Erika. 2019. "Psychedelics and Dying Care: A Historical Look at the Relationship between Psychedelics and Palliative Care." *Journal of Psychoactive Drugs* 51 (2): 102–7.

Feinberg, Todd E., and Julian Paul Keenan. 2005. "Where in the Brain Is the Self?" *Consciousness and Cognition* 14 (4): 661–78.

Freud, Sigmund. 1915. "Thoughts for the Times on War and Death." In *The Standard Edition of the Complete Psychological Works of Sigmund Freud*, vol. 14, 273–300. London: Hogarth.

Friston, Karl. 2005. "A Theory of Cortical Responses." *Philosophical Transactions of the Royal Society B: Biological Sciences* 360 (1456): 815–36.

———. 2009. "The Free-Energy Principle: A Rough Guide to the Brain?" *Trends in Cognitive Science* 13 (7): 293–301.

Friston, Karl, and Stefan Kiebel. 2009. "Predictive Coding under the Free-Energy Principle." *Philosophical Transactions of the Royal Society B: Biological Sciences* 364 (1521): 1211–21.

Gallagher, Shaun. 2000. "Philosophical Conceptions of the Self: Implications for Cognitive Science." *Trends in Cognitive Sciences* 4 (1): 14–21.

Gallup, Gordon G., Jr., and James R. Anderson. 2018. "The 'Olfactory Mirror' and Other Recent Attempts to Demonstrate Self-Recognition in Non-primate Species." *Behavioural Processes* 148:16–19.

Gasser, Peter, Katharina Kirchner, and Torsten Passie. 2015. "LSD-Assisted Psychotherapy for Anxiety Associated with a Life-Threatening Disease: A Qualitative Study of Acute and Sustained Subjective Effects." *Journal of Psychopharmacology* 29 (1): 57–68.

Goldenberg, Jamie L., Tom Pyszczynski, Jeff Greenberg, Sheldon Solomon, Benjamin Kluck, and Robin Cornwell. 2001. "I Am Not an Animal: Mortality Salience, Disgust, and the Denial of Human Creatureliness." *Journal of Experimental Psychology: General* 130 (3): 427–35.

Greenberg, Jeff, and Spee Kosloff. 2008. "Terror Management Theory: Implications for Understanding Prejudice, Stereotyping, Intergroup Conflict, and Political Attitudes." *Social and Personality Psychology Compass* 2:1881–94.

Griffiths, Roland R., Matthew W. Johnson, Michael A. Carducci, Annie Umbricht, William A. Richards, Brian D. Richards, Mary P. Cosimano, and Margaret A. Klinedinst. 2016. "Psilocybin Produces Substantial and Sustained Decreases in Depression and Anxiety in Patients with Life-Threatening Cancer: A Randomized Double-Blind Trial." *Journal of Psychopharmacology* 30 (12): 1181–97.

Grob, Charles S., Alicia L. Danforth, Gurpreet S. Chopra, Marycie Hagerty, Charles R. McKay, Adam L. Halberstad, and George R. Greer. 2011. "Pilot Study of Psilocybin Treatment for Anxiety in Patients with Advanced-Stage Cancer." *Archives of General Psychiatry* 68 (1): 71–78.

Guenther, Katja. 2017. "Monkeys, Mirrors, and Me: Gordon Gallup and the Study of Self-Recognition." *Journal of the History of the Behavioral Science* 53 (1): 5–27.

Gusnard, Debra A., Erbil Akbudak, Gordon L. Shulman, and Marcus E. Raichle. 2001. "Medial Prefrontal Cortex and Self-Referential Mental Activity: Relation to a Default Mode of Brain Function." *Proceedings of the National Academy of Sciences* 98 (7): 4259–64.

Heidegger, Martin. 1962. *Being and Time*. Oxford, UK: Blackwell.

Holbrook, Colin, Marco Iacoboni, Chelsea Gordon, Shannon Proksch, and Ramesh Balasubramaniam. 2020. "Posterior Medial Frontal Cortex and Threat-Enhanced Religious Belief: A Replication and Extension." *Social Cognitive and Affective Neuroscience* 15 (12): 1361–67.

Hölzel, Britta K., Sara W. Lazar, Tim Gard, Zev Schuman-Olivier, David R. Vago, and Ulrich Ott. 2011. "How Does Mindfulness Meditation Work? Proposing Mechanisms of Action from a Conceptual and Neural Perspective." *Perspectives on Psychological Science* 6 (6): 537–59.

Hopkins, William D., Robert D. Latzman, Linsday M. Mahovetz, Xiang Li, and Neil Roberts. 2019. "Investigating Individual Differences in Chimpanzee Mirror Self-Recognition and Cortical Thickness: A Vertex-Based and Region-of-Interest Analysis." *Cortex* 118:306–14.

Ionta, Silvio, Lukas Heydrich, Bigna Lenggenhager, Michael Mouthon, Eleonora Fornari, Dominique Chapuis, Roger Gassert, and Olaf Blanke. 2011. "Multisensory Mechanisms in Temporo-Parietal Cortex Support Self-Location and First-Person Perspective." *Neuron* 70 (2): 363–74.

Iverach, Lisa, Ross G. Menzies, and Rachel E. Menzies. 2014. "Death Anxiety and Its Role in Psychopathology: Reviewing the Status of a Transdiagnostic Construct." *Clinical Psychology Review* 34 (7): 580–93.

James, William. 1890. *The Principles of Psychology.* New York: Dover.

Jenkinson, Stephen. 2015. *Die Wise: A Manifesto for Sanity and Soul.* Berkeley, CA: North Atlantic Books.

Josipovic, Zoran. 2014. "Neural Correlates of Nondual Awareness in Meditation." *Annals of the New York Academy of Sciences* 1307 (1): 9–18.

Josipovic, Zoran, Ilan Dinstein, Jochen Weber, and David J. Heeger. 2012. "Influence of Meditation on Anti-correlated Networks in the Brain." *Frontiers in Human Neuroscience* 5 (January): 183.

Keenan, Julian Paul, Aaron Nelson, Margaret O'Connor, and Alvaro Pascual-Leone. 2001. "Self-Recognition and the Right Hemisphere." *Nature* 409 (6818): 305.

Koller, Sarah. 2021. "Towards Degrowth? Making Peace with Mortality to Reconnect with (One's) Nature: An Ecopsychological Proposition for a Paradigm Shift." *Environmental Values* 30 (3): 345–66.

Kramer, Rachel, Kelly Duran, Heather Soder, Lisa Applegate, Amel Youssef, Matthew Criscione, and Julian Paul Keenan. 2020. "The Special Brain: Subclinical Grandiose Narcissism and Self-Face Recognition in the Right Prefrontal Cortex." *American Journal of Psychology* 133 (4): 487–500.

Kremláček, Jan, Kairi Kreegipuu, Andrea Tales, Piia Astikainen, Nele Põldver, Risto Näätänen, and Gábor Stefanics. 2016. "Visual Mismatch Negativity (VMMN): A Review and Meta-Analysis of Studies in Psychiatric and Neurological Disorders." *Cortex* 80 (July): 76–112.

Kwan, Virginia S. Y., Veronica Barrios, Giorgio Ganis, Jamie Gorman, Claudia Lange, Monisha Kumar, Alejandro Shepard, and Julian Paul Keenan. 2007. "Assessing the Neural Correlates of Self-Enhancement Bias: A Transcranial Magnetic Stimulation Study." *Experimental Brain Research* 182 (3): 379–85.

LaVarco, Adriana, Nathira Ahmad, Qiana Archer, Matthew Pardillo, Ray Nunez Castaneda, Anthony Minervini, and Julian Paul Keenan. 2022. "Self-Conscious Emotions and the Right Fronto-Temporal and Right Temporal Parietal Junction." *Brain Sciences* 12 (2).

Lebedev, Alexander V., Martin Lövdén, Gidon Rosenthal, Amanda Feilding, David J. Nutt, and Robin L. Carhart-Harris. 2015. "Finding the Self by Losing the Self: Neural Correlates of Ego-Dissolution under Psilocybin." *Human Brain Mapping* 36 (8): 3137–53.

Li, Duan, Omar S. Mabrouk, Tiecheng Liu, Fangyun Tian, Gang Xu, Santiago Rengifo, Sarah J. Choi, et al. 2015. "Asphyxia-Activated Corticocardiac Signaling Accelerates Onset of Cardiac Arrest." *PNAS* 112 (16): E2073–2082.

Lifshin, Uri, Jeff Greenberg, Colin A. Zestcott, and Daniel Sullivan. 2017. "The Evil Animal: A Terror Management Theory Perspective on the Human Tendency to Kill Animals." *Personality and Social Psychology Bulletin* 43 (6): 743–57.

Limanowski, Jakub, and Felix Blankenburg. 2013. "Minimal Self-Models and the Free Energy Principle." *Frontiers in Human Neuroscience* 7 (September): 547.

Lott, Dylan T., Tenzin Yeshi, N. Norchung, Sonam Dolma, Nyima Tsering, Ngawang Jinpa, Tenzin Wozer, et al. 2021. "No Detectable Electroencephalographic Activity after Clinical Declaration of Death among Tibetan Buddhist Meditators in Apparent Tukdam, a Putative Postmortem Meditation State." *Frontiers in Psychology* 11.

Loughnan, Stephen, Michael Halloran, and Ruth Beatson. 2009. "Attitudes toward Animals: The Effect of Priming Thoughts of Human-Animal Similarities and Mortality Salience on the Evaluation of Companion Animals." *Society & Animals* 17 (1): 72.

Luber, Bruce, Hans C. Lou, Julian P. Keenan, and Sarah H. Lisanby. 2012. "Self-Enhancement Processing in the Default Network: A Single-Pulse TMS Study." *Experimental Brain Research* 223 (2): 177–87.

Menzies, Rachel E., and Ross G. Menzies. 2020. "Death Anxiety in the Time of COVID-19: Theoretical Explanations and Clinical Implications." *Cognitive Behaviour Therapist* 13 (June): e19.

Metzinger, Thomas. 2004. *Being No One: The Self-Model Theory of Subjectivity.* Cambridge, MA: MIT Press.

Millière, Raphaël, Robin L. Carhart-Harris, Leor Roseman, Fynn Mathis Trautwein, and Aviva Berkovich-Ohana. 2018. "Psychedelics, Meditation, and Self-Consciousness." *Frontiers in Psychology* 9 (September): 1475.

Muthukumaraswamy, Suresh D., Robin L. Carhart-Harris, Rosalyn J. Moran, Matthew J. Brookes, Tim M. Williams, David Errtizoe, Ben Sessa, et al. 2013. "Broadband Cortical Desynchronization Underlies the Human Psychedelic State." *Journal of Neuroscience* 33 (38): 15171–83.

Näätänen, Risto, Anthony W. K. Gaillard, and Sirkka Mäntysalo. 1978. "Early Selective-Attention Effect on Evoked Potential Reinterpreted." *Acta Psychologica* 42 (4): 313–29.

Nave, Ohad, Fynn Mathis Trautwein, Yochai Ataria, Yair Dor-Ziderman, Yoav Schweitzer, Stephen Fulder, and Aviva Berkovich-Ohana. 2021. "Self-Boundary Dissolution in Meditation: A Phenomenological Investigation." *Brain Sciences* 11 (6): 819.

Niemiec, Christopher P., Kirk Warren Brown, Todd B. Kashdan, Philip J. Cozzolino, William E. Breen, Chantal Levesque-Bristol, and Richard M. Ryan. 2010. "Being Present in the Face of Existential Threat: The Role of Trait Mindfulness in Reducing Defensive Responses to Mortality Salience." *Journal of Personality and Social Psychology* 99 (2): 344–65.

Nortey, Justin, Michael Lipka, and Joshua Alvarado. 2021. "Few Americans Blame God or Say Faith Has Been Shaken amid Pandemic, Other Tragedies." Pew Research Center, November 23, 2021. www.pewforum.org.

Northoff, Georg, Alexander Heinzel, Moritz de Greck, Felix Bermpohl, Henrik Dobrowolny, and Jaak Panksepp. 2006. "Self-Referential Processing in Our Brain: A Meta-Analysis of Imaging Studies on the Self." *NeuroImage* 31 (1): 440–57.

Northoff, Georg, and Jaak Panksepp. 2008. "The Trans-species Concept of Self and the Subcortical-Cortical Midline System." *Trends in Cognitive Sciences* 12 (7): 259–64.

Pahnke, Walter N. 1969. "The Psychedelic Mystical Experience in the Human Encounter with Death." *Harvard Theological Review* 62 (1): 1–21.

Parfit, Derek. 1984. *Reasons and Persons*. Oxford: Oxford University Press.

Park, Young Chin, and Tom Pyszczynski. 2019. "Reducing Defensive Responses to Thoughts of Death: Meditation, Mindfulness, and Buddhism." *Journal of Personality and Social Psychology* 116 (1): 101–18.

Pyszczynski, Tom, Mckenzie Lockett, Jeff Greenberg, and Sheldon Solomon. 2020. "Terror Management Theory and the COVID-19 Pandemic." *Journal of Humanistic Psychology* 61 (2): 002216782095948.

Pyszczynski, Tom, Sheldon Solomon, and Jeff Greenberg. 2015. "Thirty Years of Terror Management Theory." In *Advances in Experimental Social Psychology*, vol. 52, edited by James M. Olson and Mark P. Zanna, 1–70. Amsterdam: Elsevier.

Rao, Rajesh P. N., and Dana H. Ballard. 1999. "Predictive Coding in the Visual Cortex: A Functional Interpretation of Some Extra-Classical Receptive-Field Effects." *Nature Neuroscience* 2 (1): 79–87.

Reggente, Melissa A. L. V., Elena Papale, Niall McGinty, Lavinia Eddy, Giuseppe Andrea de Lucia, and Chiara Giulia Bertulli. 2018. "Social Relationships and Death-Related Behaviour in Aquatic Mammals: A Systematic Review." *Philosophical Transactions of the Royal Society B: Biological Sciences* 373 (1754).

Sel, Alejandra, Rachel Harding, and Manos Tsakiris. 2016. "Electrophysiological Correlates of Self-Specific Prediction Errors in the Human Brain." *NeuroImage* 125 (January): 13–24.

Seth, Anil K. 2013. "Interoceptive Inference, Emotion, and the Embodied Self." *Trends in Cognitive Sciences* 17 (11): 565–73. https://doi.org/10.1016/j.tics.2013.09.007.

Seth, Anil K., and Karl J. Friston. 2016. "Active Interoceptive Inference and the Emotional Brain." *Philosophical Transactions of the Royal Society B: Biological Sciences* 371 (1708): 20160007.

Seth, Anil K., and Manos Tsakiris. 2018. "Being a Beast Machine: The Somatic Basis of Selfhood." *Trends in Cognitive Sciences* 22 (11): 969–81.

Smigielski, Lukasz, Milan Scheidegger, Michael Kometer, and Franz X. Vollenweider. 2019. "Psilocybin-Assisted Mindfulness Training Modulates Self-Consciousness and Brain Default Mode Network Connectivity with Lasting Effects." *NeuroImage* 196 (August): 207–15.

Stefanics, Gábor, Jan Kremláček, and István Czigler. 2014. "Visual Mismatch Negativity: A Predictive Coding View." *Frontiers in Human Neuroscience* 8 (September).

Swift, Kaeli, and John M. Marzluff. 2018. "Occurrence and Variability of Tactile Interactions between Wild American Crows and Dead Conspecifics." *Philosophical Transactions of the Royal Society B: Biological Sciences* 373 (1754).

Tang, Yi-Yuan, Britta K. Hölzel, and Michael I. Posner. 2015. "The Neuroscience of Mindfulness Meditation." *Nature Reviews Neuroscience* 16 (4): 213–25.

Taylor-Lillquist, Birgitta, Vivek Kanpa, Maya Crawford, Mehdi El Filali, Julia Oakes, Alex Jonasz, Amanda Disney, and Julian Paul Keenan. 2020. "Preliminary Evidence of the Role of Medial Prefrontal Cortex in Self-Enhancement: A Transcranial Magnetic Stimulation Study." *Brain Sciences* 10 (8).

Uddin, Lucina Q., Marco Iacoboni, Claudia Lange, and Julian Paul Keenan. 2007. "The Self and Social Cognition: The Role of Cortical Midline Structures and Mirror Neurons." *Trends in Cognitive Sciences* 11(4), 153–57.

Verheijde, Joseph L., Mohamed Y. Rady, and Michael Potts. 2018. "Neuroscience and Brain Death Controversies: The Elephant in the Room." *Journal of Religion and Health* 57 (5): 1745–63.

Vicente, Raul, Michael Rizzuto, Can Sarica, Kazuaki Yamamoto, Mohammed Sadr, Tarun Khajuria, Mostafa Fatehi, et al. 2022. "Enhanced Interplay of Neuronal Coherence and Coupling in the Dying Human Brain." *Frontiers in Aging Neuroscience* 14.

Watson, Claire F. I., and Tetsuro Matsuzawa. 2018. "Behaviour of Nonhuman Primate Mothers toward Their Dead Infants: Uncovering Mechanisms." *Philosophical Transactions of the Royal Society B: Biological Sciences* 373 (1754).

Whitfield-Gabrieli, Susan, Joseph M. Moran, Alfonso Nieto-Castañón, Christina Triantafyllou, Rebecca Saxe, and John D. E. Gabrieli. 2011. "Associations and

Dissociations between Default and Self-Reference Networks in the Human Brain." *NeuroImage* 55 (1): 225–32.
Wolfe, Sarah E., and Amit Tubi. 2019. "Terror Management Theory and Mortality Awareness: A Missing Link in Climate Response Studies?" *WIREs Climate Change* 10 (2).
Zahavi, Dan. 2006. *Subjectivity and Selfhood Investigating the First-Person Perspective.* Cambridge, MA: MIT Press.

7

Understanding the Taking of Animals for Food through an Indigenous Lens, Utilizing the Concepts of Food Sovereignty and ʔiisaak (Being Respectful)

CHARLOTTE COTÉ

I was born and raised in my community of Tseshaht, which is one of the Indigenous Nations that constitute the larger Nuu-chah-nulth Nation on Vancouver Island in British Columbia, Canada. We are marine-based cultures, and our communities have thrived in a reciprocal and respectful relationship with the lands, waters, plants, and animals within our environment.

I grew up on the Somass River, which flows a few hundred yards behind my family home. We refer to this river as c̓uumaʕas, meaning "cleansing" or "washing," but it became known as the Somass River, a name used by the mamałn̓i (white settlers), who began moving into our territory in the mid 1800s.[1] The c̓uumaʕas streams through our territory like a life vein, bringing the precious salmon that nourish and feed our community. Salmon is at the heart of our stories and shared experiences; it is the foundation of our culture and has remained an important nutritional food in our diets. As Tseshaht member Darryl Ross Sr. told me, we Tseshaht have a saying, "A happy Tseshaht has a drum in one hand and a sockeye in the other," which demonstrates how salmon and culture are intertwined (personal communication, August 11, 2015; Coté 2022).

I learned how to clean and process salmon from my mother when I was a young girl, and it is an activity I enjoy and have continued into my adulthood. Processing haʔum, or cultural food, such as salmon brought—and continues to bring—families and community members together. I enjoyed cleaning and processing salmon with my mum, who loved to share stories with me while we were cleaning the fish, especially cultural stories centered in teachings of ʔiisaak, being respectful, which helped lay the foundation of my cultural knowledge. As we cleaned the salmon, and mummy shared her stories, I listened attentively, taking in this cultural knowledge through our storytelling tradition. Sometimes she would hum one of her favorite tunes as she watched over me, making sure I was cleaning the salmon correctly. I became proficient in fish cleaning, and by the age of ten, I was adept in both cleaning and processing fish through the canning process. As an adult, after my mum passed, I learned how to smoke fish, a tradition taught to me by my aunty Marilyn, whom I get together with every summer to process fish.

Tseshaht community members come together every Sunday for a community fishing day in the summer months, when the miʕaat, sockeye salmon, are in season and making their way up the c̓uumaʕas to their spawning areas. The fish are caught using a large seine net that is set out in boats and then pulled to shore by our community members. As the net is being pulled onto the bank, the fish that are caught are removed and placed in bins that are later distributed to our members after the fishing has concluded.

As a young girl, I would watch the adults pulling in the net, carefully removing the fish, and placing them in large bins that were set up on the beach. Sometimes, community members would clean the salmon right there on the shore rather than wait until they got home. It was common for my mum to do this, and I share this story of one of those times when I was nine years old. After my mum received her fish allotment, we took our tub of fish to a spot on the bank to begin cleaning them. Mummy handed me a knife, and I sat and watched her clean a couple of fish before cleaning one on my own. Feeling comfortable enough to begin the cleaning process, I grabbed one of the salmon out of the tub filled with water. The fish was still alive and flicking its tail back and forth, making it difficult to hold onto its slippery skin. I managed to turn it over on its back, and I carefully cut into its belly. I quickly ran my sharp knife from under the gills to the beginning of its tail. I opened the belly and began removing the internal organs.

I must admit, the first time I cleaned salmon I was a little grossed out by the guts and blood. But sometimes I would find a pouch of eggs, which I loved to eat, and I would put these aside. Usually, after we finished cleaning the fish at home, mum would make a big pot of fish head soup, and if we had any eggs, she would throw them in too. I love fish head soup, which is basically fish heads, potatoes, carrots, and onions in a rich salmon broth. The addition of the eggs made it even tastier. But there were no eggs in this salmon, only guts. As I began pulling out the gut sack, to my surprise, the salmon's little heart was still beating. I gently took out the heart and held it in my hand, fascinated by how tiny it was and how soft it felt as it pulsed in my palm. With the tiny heart in my hands, I ran to my mother, who was on her knees cleaning a fish. I dropped down on my knees and showed her the "treasure" I held in my hand. I said excitedly, "Mummy, look. The heart is still beating." My mother looked at the little heart in my hand and then looked up at my little delighted face and said softly, "It gave its life to you." It was many years later that I realized the significance of this experience.

Cultures Based on Respect and Reciprocity

Salmon has always been a primary food source for Northwest Coast Indigenous people, and the spirit of the fish was celebrated through the First Salmon Ceremony that honored its return each year and maintained this important relationship. In the coastal Indigenous belief system, everything has a spirit (Kidwell 2005). The salmon's spirit is intimately tied to our societies, and salmon are shown the greatest respect and honor. During the first salmon run, tribal members gather along the waterways to catch the first salmon. These salmon are ceremonially cut up and divided among the guests to eat. While we are eating, prayers and ceremonies are conducted to show respect to the salmon's spirit and to thank them for bringing their physical bodies to us as food.

Once all the ceremonies are conducted and all the fish are eaten, the remaining bones and skin are collected and returned to the water. The spirits of the salmon return to their homes in the deep ocean waters, where they share with their relatives the great respect that was shown to them. This ensures that our salmon relatives continue to visit us and provide their physical forms to us as food (see Brown 2005; Drucker 1951; Geffen and Crawford 2005; Turner 2005).

During fieldwork with the Nuu-chah-nulth in the 1930s, the anthropologist Philip Drucker (1951) noted the importance of strict observances to these rituals, such as making sure all the bones of the salmon were returned to the river. He recounts a prayer conducted by a ḥaw̓iłʔ

(chief) to the spirits of the salmon that clearly demonstrates how the salmon were treated with the utmost respect and honor for bringing this nutritious food to our Nuu-chah-nulth communities each year: "The [chief] sprinkled them with [eagle] down and 'talked' to them saying, 'We are glad you have come to visit us; we have been saving these (feathers) for you for a long time. We have been waiting a long time for you, and hope you will visit us soon'" (Drucker 1951, 75).

Indigenous peoples have a belief that all life that gives itself to us—whether animals or plants—has a spirit, and taking that life is sacred and therefore should be respected, what we Tseshaht and Nuu-chah-nulth peoples call ʔiisaak, or being respectful. Our principle of ʔiisaak applies not just to life-forms but to the land and water as well. At its most basic understanding, the concept teaches that all life is held in equal esteem. Our relationships to the plants and animals that give themselves to us as food derive from this concept of ʔiisaak and are embedded within our overarching philosophy of hišukʔiš c̓awaak, meaning "everything is interconnected."[2] My mother wisely understood that taking the life of salmon was a sacred act because it provided sustenance for us. Her wisdom instilled in me this gratitude to our salmon relatives as well. Indigenous traditions such as the First Salmon Ceremony are what the plant ecologist and scientist Robin Kimmerer (Potawatomi) so aptly articulates as "feasts of love and gratitude" and are not just "internal emotional expressions but actually aided the upstream passage of the fish by releasing them from predation for a critical time. Laying salmon bones back in the stream returned nutrients to the system. These are ceremonies of practical reverence" (2013, 248–49).

Kimmerer explains in her book *Braiding Sweetgrass* how "cultures of gratitude" must also be "cultures of reciprocity." She explains, "Each person, human or no, is bound to every other in a reciprocal relationship. Just as all beings have a duty to me, I have a duty to them. If an animal gives its life to feed me, I am in turn bound to support its life. If I receive a stream's gift of pure water, then I am responsible for returning a gift in kind" (2013, 115). Placing this idea within the context of the First Salmon Ceremony, Kimmerer says that these ceremonies "were not conducted for the people. They were for the Salmon themselves, and for all the glittering realms of Creation, for the renewal of the world. People understood that when lives are given on their behalf, they have received something precious. Ceremonies are a way to give something precious in return" (253).

For some non-Indigenous people, who see the death of animals through a Western cultural lens, this concept may be difficult to understand. Significant to the obligations we have to our nonhuman relatives, we have strict protocols and rituals around killing animals for food. The justification for these rituals stems from our Indigenous belief system that animals have spirits, just like human beings, "and so the taking of an animal's life is intertwined with spiritual beliefs and obligations" (Deer and Murphy 2017, 713). In our belief system, when the ceremonies and protocols are conducted within the framework of respect, the animal thus chooses to be taken and offers up its physical body as food. This idea, Deer and Murphy argue, "presents an interesting distinction from JudeoChristian principles, which would see humans as deliberately choosing their prey" (2017, 715).

Mi'kmaq scholar Margaret Robinson, in her article "Animal Personhood in Mi'kmaq Perspective," examines the question, "How does a culture that recognizes other animals as persons and relations reconcile this worldview with a diet that is so heavily animal derived?" (2014, 674). The answer, Robinson maintains, is in understanding the Mi'kmaq worldview, which is centered in a belief system that animals willingly sacrifice themselves to become food. In the Mi'kmaq stories that Robinson shares in her article, Mi'kmaq members emphasize the importance of having a respectful relationship with nonhuman animals, which is essential to maintaining their willingness to sacrifice themselves as food. If proper respect and protocols are not observed, this could fracture the sacred relationships between humans and their nonhuman kinfolk, and animals would not allow themselves to be caught. This also pertains to taking only as many animals as are needed for subsistence, as articulated in one of the Mi'kmaq stories shared by Robinson: "Wolverine invites a large number of birds into his wigwam, asks them to close their eyes, and then begins to kill them silently, one after another. His younger brother is distraught at this bloodlust because Wolverine has already killed more birds than they can eat. The younger brother whispers for the smallest bird to open his eyes, at which point the young bird cries the alarm and the remaining birds escape with the help of Wolverine's younger brother" (676). This story demonstrates the importance of maintaining these cultures of reciprocity and respect. In the Mi'kmaq worldview, animals are perceived as giving themselves to provide food and clothing, shelter, and tools, but they must never be exploited or overhunted, which, Robinson asserts, could result "in a type of karmic retribution in which greed and arrogance bring their own punishment in the form of hunger and famine" (676).

Indigenous Food Sovereignty

Tseshaht, like other Indigenous peoples worldwide, are enacting food sovereignty, which is defined as "the right of peoples to healthy and culturally appropriate food produced through ecologically sound and sustainable methods" (Declaration of Nyéléni 2007). In the early 1990s, we saw the birth of the food sovereignty movement, and scholars throughout the world began framing their theories and ideas around global food security and insecurity. For Indigenous people, food sovereignty requires peeling away the layers of colonialism that have been the Indigenous lived experience and recentering our lives within our own philosophical and ancestral teachings and wisdom.

Enacting food sovereignty is positioned within our struggles for decolonization and self-determination and is central to restoring health and wellness in our Indigenous communities by revitalizing our sacred connections to our haʔum. "Indigenizing" food sovereignty places emphasis on Indigenous responsibility, mutuality, kinship, and relationships with the natural world, a world that, as the Indigenous scholar Robin Kimmerer contends, is built on reciprocity between humans and nonhumans, creating duties and responsibilities for both. As Kimmerer writes, "An integral part of a human's education is to know those duties and how to perform them" (2013, 15).

Embedded within the Indigenous eco-philosophy and worldview is the cultural knowledge and understanding that people, animals, land, water, and air are interconnected in a web of life that emphasizes good relationships based on gratitude and respect. Indigenous food sovereignty, therefore, embodies a deep spiritual appreciation for food as a sacred gift. As the Indigenous scholar/activist Dawn Morrison explains, to understand cultural foods as sacred gifts keeps "foods alive spiritually" (2006, 8) and is recognized in rituals, offerings, and ceremonies.

Nuu-chah-nulth hereditary chief Tom Mexsis Happynook maintains that embedded within human and nonhuman relations is the understanding of responsibilities that Indigenous peoples strive to uphold in our social, cultural, and economic practices, responsibilities that have evolved into unwritten laws over millennia: "These responsibilities and laws are directly tied to nature and [are] a product of the slow integration of cultures within their environment and the ecosystems" (2001, 2). Thus, Happynook says, "the environment is not a place of divisions but rather a place of relations, a place where cultural diversity and biodiversity are not separate but in fact need each other" (2). This is cultural biodiversity, which has developed and been nurtured over millennia and is the basis of the Nuu-chah-nulth philosophy hišukʔiš c̓awaak, that everything in our natural and spiritual worlds is interconnected (Happynook 2001).

As Indigenous peoples, we live in a world of reciprocal relationships with the plants and animals that provide us with food, clothing, shelter, and cultural and spiritual sustenance. In return, we treat plants, animals, water, land, and air as "gifts" from the Creator, and we are bound by a "covenant of reciprocity," as Kimmerer asserts (2013, 11). Within this symbiotic relationship is the understanding that death is ultimately integrated into life. In the next section of this chapter, I discuss how killing animals for food is embedded within our Nuu-chah-nulth principle of ʔiisaak, being respectful. I center my discussion on the Nuu-chah-nulth and Makah whaling tradition, and I focus on the Makah tribe's 1999 whale hunt and the antiwhaling coalition that arose in opposition to it. I assert that this opposition clearly demonstrates and highlights the problems that Indigenous peoples face in enacting food sovereignty when our food traditions are viewed through an ethnocentric Western cultural lens.

The Makah Whale Hunt

In 1999, the Makah tribe on the western tip of Washington State harvested a sixʷa·wix̌, the Makah word for a gray whale, and with one throw of their harpoon enacted food sovereignty by revitalizing and reinforcing a cultural tradition that is central to their identity.[3] For the qʷidičč̓aʔa·tx̌, or Makah, and my people, the Nuu-chah-nulth, whaling was the foundation of our political, social, spiritual, and economic structures.[4] However, colonization, federal policies, and the depletion of whales as a result of an unregulated West Coast whaling industry forced us to put away our harpoons in the early 1900s (Coté 2010).

Before the arrival of mamałn̓i, white settlers, the Indigenous people in the Northwest Coast lived in natural environments that were rich in material goods and a variety of haʔum, cultural foods. Our marine-based economies provided us with a wealth of haʔum that not only sustained our communities but were also naturally nutritious, rich in vitamins and minerals. Our societies maintained optimum health by consuming large quantities of meat, fat, and oil from whales and other sea mammals, which provided us with health-promoting nourishment and an overall sense of well-being. For example, studies conducted among the Indigenous people in northern Canada and Alaska affirm the health benefits of eating whale, finding that a diet rich in sea mammal oil dramatically decreases the risk of death from heart disease, reduces symptoms of diabetes, and helps alleviate symptoms of arthritis and other chronic diseases (De Caterina et al. 2007).

Three significant factors were key in the Makah tribe's decision to revive their whale hunts. First, the gray whale, the main whale that the Makah hunted, rebounded from near extinction to the point where it could be sustainably hunted again, and in 1994, the species was removed from the endangered species list. Second, in the 1970s, a major storm uncovered thousands of whaling artifacts in the abandoned Makah village of Ozette, sparking a cultural renaissance among tribal members and a renewed interest in their whaling tradition. Third, in the 1974 case *U.S. v. Washington* (also known as the Boldt decision), federal judge George Boldt reaffirmed the Washington State tribe's treaty rights, with one of them being the exclusive right to hunt whales. These factors created an opportunity for the Makah tribe to restore their whale hunts, placing them within a larger context of cultural revitalization and self-determination movements that Indigenous peoples have been experiencing since the 1960s (Coté 2010). The Nuu-chah-nulth, following the lead of our Makah relatives, announced the decision to revitalize our whale hunts as well, understanding this as a necessary part of decolonizing, a way to enrich and strengthen our cultures, to reestablish our identity as a whaling people, and to restore our sacred relationship to this important cultural food (Coté 2010).

While the Makah tribe's whale hunt was received with overwhelming support around the world, there were also those who opposed it and began organizing an antiwhaling campaign immediately after the tribe's announcement in 1994. An antiwhaling coalition consisting of a wide range of interests, from environmental groups to right-wing politicians, waged a campaign in the court of public opinion that relied on false stereotypes and misconceived ideas in an attempt to discredit the Makah and Nuu-chah-nulth whaling cultures. For example, in response to a Canadian radio program on the Makah tribe reviving their tradition of hunting whales, a reader wrote, "Personally, I think it is a stupid, senseless, and needless slaughter by a bunch of jerks. They didn't go out in their canoes as their forefathers had done, with spears, etc., no they went out with a motor driven craft, armed with high caliber rifles and took unfair advantage of a creature that was not bothering them. . . . Who do they think they are? . . . They still appear to be ruthless savages" (Ellingson 2001, 357). In a letter to the *Seattle Times*, a reader responded to the notion of revitalizing tradition, writing, "I am anxious to know where I may apply for a license to kill Indians. My forefathers helped settle the west and it was their tradition to kill every Redskin they saw. 'The only good Indian is a dead Indian,' they believed. I also want to keep faith with my ancestors" (Two Horses 2001, 121). When the Makah tribe began preparing for their hunt, members of the antiwhaling coalition condemned it, arguing that the hunt was not "traditional" because the Makah were using motorized boats, high-powered weapons, and cellular phones. By fixating on modern amenities, these opponents were ultimately denying us the very right that all societies strive toward: the right to cultural change and technological advancement (Coté 2015). Makah tribal member Janine Bowechop, director of the Makah Cultural and Research Center, responded to this argument:

> For some reason some people like to freeze us in the past. If you're not doing something the way it was done prior to contact, then you're not doing it right—you're not doing it in the Native way. But we allow other cultures to make changes. One of my friends said, "I'm a White American

> but I don't make my butter in a butter churn anymore, and I'm not criticized for that." . . . Folks don't ride around in covered wagons anymore, but we don't turn around and say, "Gee, you're not a real American. . . . But, unfortunately, we're continually criticized if we do anything different than we did 500 years ago. (quoted in Coté 2010, 154)

One of the main arguments made against the Makah tribe was centered in a foods-based discourse, claiming that the Makah and Nuu-chah-nulth peoples did not need to hunt whales for food because they had access to all the food they needed (Coté 2010). Historically, we know that Indigenous peoples around the world, to put it mildly, have struggled to control access to and production of their traditional food sources in the face of colonization and its centuries-long hegemonic control over food production and consumption (Coté 2010). As the whale hunt controversy reminded us, through these assertions of cultural and culinary imperialism, people from other cultures continue to impose their own symbolic and aesthetic food values on Indigenous societies, making it difficult for Indigenous peoples to stay connected to their traditional foods. These days, wealthy Western states and NGOs, through their political power, continue to influence what is acceptable as food and which animals should or should not be eaten. The antiwhaling discourse that arose over killing and eating whales was robed in moral and legal terms, but as the ecologist Russell Barsh maintains, the real issue at stake was power—the power to determine what we eat: "Privileged societies have acquired the power to determine what the world eats and to impose their own symbolic and aesthetic food taboos on others. Placed in proper historical context, contemporary efforts to abolish whaling and sealing are exposed as the flip side of Western European domination of world food supplies. . . . Moral indignation, rather than conservation, has driven the anti-harvesting campaigns for the last twenty-five years" (2001, 148).

The Makah people and my people have a whaling culture that goes back over two thousand years. We have lived alongside whales and have had a relationship with them for thousands of years, one that is sacred and respectful. Deep inside our cultures, we also have a belief and understanding that killing animals for sustenance is acceptable and necessary to our survival. Nevertheless, some non-Indigenous people, especially those involved in the animal rights movement, see our whale hunts as barbaric or cruel and see hunting animals as a violent and "primitive" practice. The antiwhaling groups saw the death of the whale through a Western cultural lens and, thus, ignored the spiritual and sacred elements attached to our whaling tradition. Antiwhalers argued that whales should not be eaten because they are intelligent and are conscious beings. But the fact that whales are conscious beings is exactly why we revere them and why we show the utmost respect for all lives that give themselves to us. Happynook says that according to our traditions, whales, and all other elements of nature, are our equals. He asks, "Is this not the ultimate expression of what has been called 'animal rights'? To address them as equals and respect them for their contribution to our health, cultures and economies?" (2001, 2).

Jessica Thornton (2018) argues that "Western society has found it necessary to create specific 'animal rights' as a response to its treatment of animals, while most indigenous peoples have always been aware of the fact that animals, like humans, are sentient beings which should be respected." Indigenous peoples' relationship with animals is one based on respect, gratitude, and a sense of sacredness attached to the spirit of the animal for giving itself to us for sustenance. For proof, one need look no further than the First Species Ceremonies of the Northwest Coast Indigenous peoples. Similar to the First Salmon Ceremony that I discussed earlier, the First Species Ceremony is a sacred event that affirms the "personhood" of these animals and honors them for giving themselves to feed us. And, as I have already explained, integration of death into life is part of this symbiotic relationship that we have to everything that gives itself to us as food, a sacred aspect of our cultures that some people in Western society have difficulty understanding.

I have previously written about the Makah and Nuu-chah-nulth whaling tradition and how special rituals, prayers, taboos, and ceremonies were central to a successful whale hunt, attributed to the ḥaw̓ił, chief, and his ḥakum, wife, which developed a respectful and sacred relationship with the animal. If the chief, his wife, and the whaling crew adhered to the proper protocols and ritual preparations, they then earned respect from the whale's spirit, and the whale allowed itself to be taken as food for them and their community (Coté 2005). Being physically, emotionally, and spiritually ready to whale was a prerequisite for the whaling crew members during the 1999 hunt. Moreover, the Makah Whaling Commission established a certification process for all the members who participated in the hunt to ensure that each member received sufficient training to perform their assigned role (Makah Tribal Council 1998). Theron Parker, who was designated as the harpooner for the 1999 whale hunt, said that the whaling crew followed the spiritual guidelines that were established by their ancestors, and they all underwent months of rigorous training, spiritual cleaning, sacred rituals, purification ceremonies, and prayer. In other words, the whale hunt was not taken lightly. The spiritual preparation was personally very important to the crew and to Theron Parker, who spent months conducting the proper rituals and purification ceremonies because, he said, "to take such a creature you must be clean in your heart, mind, body, and soul" (personal communication, June 17, 2000).

This cultural principle of ʔiisaak, being respectful to the whale's spirit, is exemplified in the Nuu-chah-nuth story of the great Ahousaht whaler Keesta, as told by Umeek Richard Atleo in his book, *Tsawalk: A Nuu-chah-nulth Worldview* (2004). Keesta, Umeek's great-grandfather, was born in 1866 and was raised to be a whaling ḥaw̓ił. Throughout his lifetime, he would ʔuusimč, which is a rigorous spiritual cleansing that involved prayer, fasting, and observances of taboos. Keesta understood that a successful hunt meant creating this sacred relationship and "that the great personage of the whale demanded the honor of extended ceremony. . . . Every protocol had been observed between the whaling chief and the spirit of the whale. Keesta . . . had thrown the harpoon, and the whale had accepted it, had grabbed and held onto the harpoon according to the agreement they had made through prayers and petitions. Harmony prevailed, whale and whaler were one" (Atleo 2004, 34–35).

The sacred rituals that are practiced around the taking of animals for food create what the Indigenous scholar Clara Sue Kidwell describes as a "sense of communion" (2005, 301). Animals and plants are considered our relatives, a concept that many non-Indigenous peoples have difficulty in understanding because they do not have—or have lost—their own spiritual relationship to the foods they eat. The physical act of eating plants and animals, Kidwell says, reinforces the social and sacred bonds we have to their spirits that give themselves as food: "Consuming food is the most basic form of establishing relationships among humans, plants, animals, and the forces in the environment that are the ultimate sources of life. It is an integral element of both physical and spiritual being. Gifts of food solidify human relationships; offerings of plant and animal life establish and maintain relationships between humans and the spiritual world" (2005, 306). Viewed from this standpoint of animals and plants as gifts, a culture of gratitude is embedded within the relationship between humans and nonhumans, where reciprocity is the foundation. Animals and plants that are treated with respect will, in turn, provide their physical forms as food and are regarded as "gifts from the earth," says Kimmerer (2013, 25), which establishes a particular relationship, an obligation of sorts to give, to receive, and to reciprocate.

In contrast, the global industrial food system treats animals as commodities and reduces them to machines, where meat, eggs, and milk are pumped out in mass quantities. Industrialized food production is supported by chemical-intensive agriculture and the mass production of animals as food, using steroids to make them grow quicker and bigger and pumping them with antibiotics to keep them from getting sick from the unnatural foods they are being forced to eat (Kenner 2008).[5]

The rise of cheap corn in the 1950s and '60s made it more profitable for farmers to fatten their animals with corn in feedlots instead of on grass or wheat in an open range and to raise chickens in large, closed-in factories rather than in open farmyards (Pollen 2006). Gone are the farms where cattle and pigs grazed openly on grass, where chickens moved about in large pens, eating natural food like earthworms and insects, and hens could take a break from their laying nests and walk freely outside their coops. Corporate factory farming reduced animals to nothing more than a commodity that led to inhumane conditions for the animals, locked in cramped pens and small cages where they can barely move.[6]

Indigenous food traditions are not just about preserving daily diets; they are central to food sovereignty and security, and they reinforce familial and social bonds of generosity and reciprocity in harvesting, sharing, and eating. For the Makah, the capture, sharing, and eating of the six^{w}a·wix̌ they harvested in 1999 strengthened their community; revived prayers, songs, ceremonies, and stories integral to their whaling tradition; and strengthened their cultural identity as whalers. Enacting food sovereignty through the revival of their whaling practices reaffirmed the spiritual, emotional, and physical relationships the Makah have to their waterways and to the whale. And it was not just during the hunt. Afterward, they followed the tradition passed down from their whaling ancestors: after all the sacred rituals were conducted to show respect to the whale's spirit and to the whale for giving itself to the Makah people, tribal members held a huge Potlatch, or gift-giving feast, in honor of the historic event, to thank the people who supported the revival of their hunts. On May 22, 1999, more than three thousand people came to the small Makah village of Neah Bay to share in the celebration and show their support for the revitalization of the Makah tribe's whaling tradition. There were people from the local Native and non-Native communities, people from tribes across the US and First Nations communities in Canada, and even people from around the world, as far away as Africa.

The Makah people sang songs and performed dances for their guests and to honor the return of the whale to their community. Living up to their Makah name, meaning "generous with food," the tribal members provided their guests with a traditional feast, serving them heaping plates filled with salmon, halibut, steamed clams, and oysters. And for the first time in over eighty years, whale was the main food on the menu. The Makah were excited about offering such an important food to their guests, and they experimented with various ways to prepare it so that even those with more finicky palates would enjoy it. The whale meat was baked, roasted, and broiled. The blubber was served both cooked and raw. Many people from my Nuu-chah-nulth communities attended the celebration and partook in the tasting of our shared traditional food for the very first time. Nuu-chah-nulth member Denise Ambrose (1999) said that sharing in this feast of whale meat made her feel proud of her own Nuu-chah-nulth identity: "This was the first time that I would taste whale meat, a food that I, as a Nuu-chah-nulth person, should have been brought up on. The meat looked somewhat like dark chicken meat. To me, it smelled and tasted like corned beef. It is hard to describe my feelings after tasting the roasted meat. I was proud to be Nuu-chah-nulth-aht. . . . So many other [Nuu-chah-nulth] people have passed on without having the opportunity to share in what was the most integral part of our culture: the whale. I felt honoured."

Two years after the Makah whale hunt, the Makah Cultural and Research Center administered a survey of Makah households to clarify and quantify the reactions of tribal members to the revival of their whaling practices. The results were overwhelmingly positive, with over 95 percent of the respondents indicating full support for restoring the whale hunts. The survey also indicated an eagerness of all Makah members to incorporate more traditions and cultural practices into their daily lives (Coté 2010). A second Makah Household Whaling Survey was conducted in 2006 to see if the community still supported continuing their whale hunts. The responses were still overwhelmingly positive. Over 88 percent of those surveyed believed that revitalizing their whaling tradition was a positive move, especially for its cultural value and political importance, and continued their support of whale hunts (Coté 2010, 203).

Food sovereignty is the right to healthy and culturally appropriate food, defined through one's own cultural food practices, but in December 2002, a Ninth Circuit Court of Appeals decision legally stopped the Makah tribe from exercising this right by banning their whale hunts. In the 2002 case *Anderson v. Evans* (314 F.3d 1006), the court ruled that Makah whaling must cease until the tribe prepares an environmental impact statement (EIS) under the National Environmental Policy Act (NEPA), which is more stringent than the Environmental Assessment (EA) that was conducted for the 1999 hunt. The court also determined that the Marine Mammal Protection Act (MMPA) also applied to the Makah tribe and that their 1855 treaty, which affirmed and protected their whaling right, did not exempt them from the scrutiny of this act.[7] The Makah were now required to obtain an MMPA waiver from the federal government through the National Oceanic and Atmospheric Administration (NOAA), which could authorize a whaling quota.[8]

In examining the Makah tribe's efforts to revitalize their whaling tradition, we see the complexities and challenges that Indigenous people face when attempting to enact food sovereignty. The Indigenous scholar Kyle Pows Whyte places these challenges squarely within colonialism—as a derivative of settler-colonial domination and food injustice. Food injustice, Whyte maintains, is a violation of Indigenous peoples' collective self-determination over their food systems: "Food injustice can manifest as violations of food sovereignty that some Indigenous people associate with the destruction of particular foods or food systems. Violations of food sovereignty are one strategy of colonial societies, such as U.S. settler colonialism, to undermine Indigenous collective continuance in Indigenous peoples' own homelands" (2017, 3). It has been more than twenty years since the Makah threw the harpoon that reaffirmed their cultural identity as whaling people, and since then, their cultural and treaty right to whaling has been tied up in political and legal challenges fueled by racial and food injustice that are at the core of settler colonialism. The destruction of Indigenous foodways was one of the many colonial erasures utilized by settler society in their attempts to dismantle Indigenous lifeways, and its weakening of our political, economic, social, and spiritual systems continues to this day.

The late Indigenous activist Billy Frank Jr. (2012), a leader in the fight for Northwest Coast treaty fishing rights, positioned food sovereignty at the core of Indigenous struggles for political and cultural sovereignty: "Our treaties recognize that food is at the center of our cultures. Indian tribes are sovereign nations, and part of that sovereignty includes access to the traditional foods needed to keep ourselves and our communities healthy and strong." As of 2022, the legal battle continues, as the Makah tribe continues to seek a federal waiver to exercise its treaty and cultural right to whale once again.

NOTES

1 Through elder accounts, we know that the name c̓uumaʕas comes from the word ts'oma:as, which was originally used to refer to a small creek running through one of the Tseshaht village sites along the river. The meaning "cleansing" or "washing down" refers to the autumn rains swelling the creek that would wash away fish guts that were left there after the fish were cleaned. See Arima et al. 1991. c̓uumaʕas is also the Nuu-chah-nulth name for the city of Port Alberni.

2 In the Tseshaht dialect, we refer to this as ḥačatakma c̓awaak.

3 The phonetic spelling of gray whale is si/khwah/wikh. The Nuu-chah-nulth word for gray whale is maaʔak (mah/uk).

4 The Makah people's name for themselves is phonetically pronounced kwih-dich-chuh-aht. The name Makah came from their neighbors, the Klallam peoples, a name meaning "generous with food."

5 Corn gives cattle acidosis, causing their neutral stomachs to become acidic. It also causes them to bloat, which inflates their rumen and presses against their ribs. As a way to keep the cows healthy, they are given antibiotics (Pollen 2006).

6 *Food Inc.* (Kenner 2008) is an American documentary film that examines the industrial food industry. It explores how corporate factory farming produces food that is unhealthy, environmentally destructive, and abusive to animals and the people working in these industries.

7 The Marine Mammal Protection Act (MMPA) bans all hunting and killing of whales, "except as expressly provided for by an international treaty, convention, or agreement to which the United States is a party and which was entered into before the effective date of this subchapter or by any statute implementing any such treaty, convention or agreement." MMPA, 16 U.S.C. 1372(a)(2).

8 Alaska Natives have an MMPA exemption that allows them to hunt whales and marine mammals for subsistence. The US government did not issue an MMPA exemption to the Makah because of the recognized fundamental legal principle that Indian treaty rights were exempt from its provisions. The federal treaty with the Makah specifically protects the Makah's right to hunt whales (Coté 2010, 176–82). According to the court, NOAA's issuance of a gray whale quota to the Makah tribe without compliance with the MMPA violated federal law. *Anderson v. Evans*, 314 F.3d 1006 (2002).

REFERENCES

Ambrose, Denise. 1999. "Thousands Enjoy Makah Traditional Feast." *Ha-shilth-sa*, June 3, 1999.

Arima, E. Y., Denis St. Claire, Louise Clamhouse, Joshua Edgar, Charles Jones, and John Thomas. 1991. *Between Ports Alberni and Renfrew: Notes on West Coast Peoples*. Hull: Canadian Museum of Civilization.

Atleo, E. Richard. 2004. *Tsawalk. A Nuu-chah-nulth Worldview*. Vancouver: University of British Columbia Press.

Barsh, Russell Lawrence. 2001. "Food Security, Food Hegemony, and Charismatic Animals." In *Toward a Sustainable Whaling Regime*, edited by Robert L. Friedman, 147–79. Seattle: University of Washington Press.

Brown, Jovanna. 2005. "Fishing Rights and the First Salmon Ceremony." In *American Indian Religious Traditions*, edited by Suzanne J. Crawford and Dennis F. Kelly, 320–24. Santa Barbara, CA: ABC/CLIO.

Coté, Charlotte. 2005. "Whaling, Religious and Cultural Implications." In *American Indian Religious Traditions*, edited by Suzanne J. Crawford and Dennis F. Kelly, 1141–53. Santa Barbara, CA: ABC-CLIO, 2005.

———. 2010. *Spirits of Our Whaling Ancestors: Revitalizing Makah and Nuu-chah-nulth Traditions*. Seattle: University of Washington Press.

———. 2015. "Food Sovereignty, Food Hegemony, and the Revitalization of Indigenous Whaling Practices." In *The World of the Indigenous Americas*, edited by Robert Allen Warrior, 239–62. New York: Routledge.

———. 2022. *A Drum in One Hand, a Sockeye in the Other: Stories of Indigenous Food Sovereignty from the Northwest Coast*. Seattle: University of Washington Press.

De Caterina, Raffaele, Alessandra Bertolotto, Rosalinda Madonna, and Erik Berg Schmidt. 2007. "n-3 Fatty Acids in the Treatment of Diabetic Patients." *Diabetes Care* 30 (4): 1012–26.

Declaration of Nyéléni. 2007. Declaration of the Forum for Food Sovereignty, Sélingué, Mali, February 27, 2007. http://nyeleni.org.

Deer, Sarah, and Liz Murphy. 2017. "'Animals May Take Pity on Us': Using Traditional Tribal Beliefs to Address Animal Abuse and Family Violence Within Tribal Nations." *Mitchell Hamline Law Review* 43 (4): 703–42.

Drucker, Philip. 1951. *The Northern and Central Nootkan Tribes: Bureau of American Ethnology Bulletin*. Washington, DC: Smithsonian Institution Press.

Ellingson, Ter. 2001. *The Myth of the Noble Savage*. Berkeley: University of California Press.

Frank, Billy, Jr. 2012 "Traditional Foods Are Treaty Foods." Northwest Treaty Tribes, March 5, 2012. https://nwtreatytribes.org.

Geffen, Joel, and Suzanne Crawford. 2005. "First Salmon Rites." In *American Indian Religious Traditions*, edited by edited by Suzanne J. Crawford and Dennis F. Kelly, 311–19. Santa Barbara, CA: ABC/CLIO, 2005.

Kenner, Robert, dir. 2008. *Food Inc.* Film.

Kidwell, Clara Sue. 2005. "First Foods Ceremonies and Food Symbolism." In *American Indian Religious Traditions*, edited by Suzanne J. Crawford and Dennis F. Kelly, 301–7. Santa Barbara, CA: ABC-CLIO.

Kimmerer, Robin Wall. 2013. *Braiding Sweetgrass. Indigenous Wisdom, Scientific Knowledge, and the Teachings of Plants*. Minneapolis: Milkweed Editions.

Makah Tribal Council. 1998. "Management Plan for Makah Treaty Gray Whale Hunting for the Years 1998–2002." www.ncseonline.org.

Morrison, Dawn. 2006. *1st Annual Interior of B.C. Indigenous Food Sovereignty Conference: Final Report*. Vancouver: Interior of B.C. Indigenous Food Conference Planning Committee.

Pollen, Michael. 2006. *The Omnivore's Dilemma. A Natural History of Four Meals*. New York: Penguin Books.

Robinson, Margaret. 2014. "Animal Personhood in Mi'kmaq Perspective." *Societies* 4:672–88.

Thornton, Jessica. 2018. "Animal Rights, Imperialism and Indigenous Hunting." *Indian Country Today*, April 13, 2013, updated September 17, 2018. https://indiancountrytoday.com.

Turner, Nancy J. 2005. *The Earth's Blanket: Traditional Teachings for Sustainable Living*. Seattle: University of Washington Press.

Two Horses, Michael. 2001. "'We Know Who the Real Indians Are': Animal-Rights Groups, Racial Stereotyping, and Racism in Rhetoric and Action in the Makah Whaling Controversy." Master's thesis, University of Arizona, 2001.

Whyte, Kyle Pows. 2017. "Food Sovereignty, Justice and Indigenous Peoples: An Essay on Settler Colonialism and Collective Continuance." In *Oxford Handbook on Food Ethics*, edited by Anne Barnhill, Mark Budolfson, and Tyler Doggett, 345–66. Oxford: Oxford University Press.

PART III

After

8

Understanding Death Using Animal Models in Forensic Taphonomy

PAOLA A. PRADA-TIEDEMANN

The cessation of life is always marked by a profound sense of emptiness and, when unexpected, comes with a series of questions to bring the death incident to justice. Forensic practitioners across the globe are tasked with the duty to implement an evidence-based approach for crime-scene processing to understand the who, what, when, where, and how of what happened. A major source of evidence (if available) is the human cadaver. The study of human decomposition or forensic taphonomy helps to determine circumstances and time of death. Decomposition evidence plays a significant role in murder cases; thereby, the need to uphold its significance in a court of law is vital to successful prosecution. Of crucial importance in this effort is the need to understand the process of decomposition and to utilize appropriate methods to standardize and validate obtained results in experimental designs, thereby allowing the investigator to extrapolate these implications in routine casework death investigations. It is important for researchers not only to utilize state-of-the-art instrumentation when processing samples for analysis but also to understand the fate and decay process of experimental cadavers to properly understand and estimate what occurs at the crime scene (Miles, Finaughty, and Gibbon 2020). The underlying push in forensic taphonomy to clear some common debates and obtain empirical data has produced a renaissance of research using animal analogues to understand death. Animal models have served as proxies to measure and monitor various decomposition parameters in a range of environments across the globe. Forensic taphonomic studies utilize these animal analogues to estimate processes that a human cadaver would undergo in a specific environmental condition.

From a forensic context, the death of an animal can become a pivotal tool in gaining an understanding of the biological and chemical processes that occur upon death. This chapter explores animal death from a forensic taphonomy perspective. It provides a brief introduction to the role of taphonomy in forensic science with respect to human decomposition and postmortem changes. It then presents the use of animal models in this framework, discussing historical and underlying foundations as to why certain types of animal models are used. Finally, it focuses on the value of implementing animal analogues in taphonomic research and provides perspectives on validation parameters in decomposition dynamics to generalize between animal results and practical forensic casework knowledge.

What Is Forensic Taphonomy?

During the past forty years, the field of forensic taphonomy has seen a steady increase. The meaning of "taphonomy" can vary among different disciplines; however, for the purposes of this chapter, the definition of forensic taphonomy is the study of the organism between its time of death and the recovery of its remains. It evaluates factors such as the deposition environment and postmortem processes (trauma, degradation, chemistry/biology) to reconstruct events and differentiate intentional human action from the natural decay process (Schotsmans, Marquez-Grant, and Forbes 2017, 2). It is a wide-ranging discipline incorporating the physical and biological changes of decomposition to improve estimates of time since death in various scenarios, to differentiate peri- and postmortem trauma, and to identify effects of clothing, burning, wrapping, confinement, and submersion on a decomposing individual, to name a few of its goals (Simmons and Cross 2013, 12).

The term "taphonomy" is said to refer to the laws of burial, a term introduced in 1940 by J. A. Efremov (1940) as he studied the transition of animal remains from the biosphere to the lithosphere. In the late 1990s, William Haglund and Marcella Sorg (1997) summarized the goal of traditional taphonomy as the observation, preservation, and discovery of dead organisms; the reconstruction of their related biology/ecology; and the reconstruction of events surrounding their death. Techniques and methods in taphonomic research are rooted in pathology, anthropology, and archeological search and recovery methods, as well as laboratory analysis of remains (soft tissue, adipocere, putrefied biological remnants) and a general knowledge of tissue degradation and bone modification and distribution. Literature and research in this dynamic area are concerned with monitoring and documenting body changes postmortem, from early putrefaction to skeletonized remains, in conjunction with the fate of human remains during natural weathering, transport, and so on (Simmons and Cross 2013, 12).

Taphonomy can be further separated into two subdisciplines: biotaphonomy and geotaphonomy. Biotaphonomy is linked with abiotic components such as climate (temperature, humidity, rainfall, soil, sunlight, wind) and biotic components such as animal activity, as well as individual characteristics of cadaver (body fat, weight, height). As the decomposition process progresses, geotaphonomy takes place, referring to the interaction between the cadaver and its immediate environment. This cadaver–deposition environment interaction yields changes in the chemistry and ecology of the surrounding terrain unique to a particular scenario (Rattenbury 2018, 38).

Upon a person's death, the lack of circulatory functions leads the body to enter a state of decay as a result cellular collapse. While the process of decomposition follows a predictable sequence of stages, the dynamics of the process are highly dependent on environmental factors on a case-by-case basis, with temperature being the main driver of the putrefactive process. Decomposition encompasses autolysis and putrefaction. In autolysis, intracellular enzymes aid in the postmortem self-digestion and degradation of body cells and organs. These endogenous enzymes aid in the breakdown of all macromolecules in the body, including carbohydrates, proteins, nucleic acid, and lipids (DiMaio and DiMaio 2001). Due to the higher number of enzymes in areas such as the stomach, liver, and pancreas, these body regions undergo a much faster deterioration compared to the rest of the body. A drastic pH change is observed due to the drop of oxygen levels in the body, which causes the loss of integrity in all cellular membranes. This process can take from hours to days before the putrefaction is notably visible because of environmental factors. The putrefactive process typically follows autolysis; however, both autolysis and putrefaction can occur at the same time on different body parts. Putrefaction is driven by microbial processes, mainly bacteria, that guide the degradation and liquefaction of soft tissue. This period is marked by bloating, green/purple discoloration of skin, and intense foul odor (Gill-King 1997).

Typically, decomposition can be divided into five stages: fresh, bloat, active decay, advanced decay, and skeletal/dry remains. Both fresh and bloat can be further classified as the early decomposition phase, which encompasses the immediate hours following death and marks the onset of autolysis and common pathological stages such as algor mortis (drop of body temperature), rigor mortis (stiffening of the body), and livor mortis (blood pooling). This early postmortem period also marks the onset of putrefaction, in which there is an increased accumulation of gas due to microbial and chemical breakdown. The late decomposition phase begins with active decay, in which there is a higher rate of soft tissue removal, followed by advanced decay, in which loss of tissue mass results in moisture reduction. The skeletal/dry stage is the final fate of the remains, in which only hair, cartilage, and bone remain due to complete degradation (Verheggen et al. 2017, 601).

Why Animal Models?

The need to understand the fate of human remains is central to forensic science research. Thus, the study of human cadavers provides a direct comparison and application to what can be encountered in practical death investigation scenarios. A great breakthrough in this area was the emergence of taphonomic research facilities. In the early 1980s, William Bass founded the Anthropological Research Facility at the University of Tennessee, and for many years, it remained the only research facility of its kind worldwide. Currently, there are a total of seven facilities in the United States, one in Australia, and one in Europe, with more in the planning (Wescott 2018). These so-called body farms allow researchers to observe decaying bodies in a natural environment re-creating burial and deposition contexts. The establishment of such facilities has enabled decomposition research to be performed from distinctive viewpoints, including insect succession and identification, evaluation of external factors such as body wrappings/coverings, varying climates/seasons, and the effect of scavenging activity, to name a few (Shirley, Wilson, and Jantz 2011).

Although human cadavers are the ideal population on which to conduct these types of studies, due to the scarcity of available donors and the complexities of both ethical and cultural constraints that restrict their implementation, taphonomic studies have relied heavily on different animal analogues to circumvent this challenge (Matuszewski et al. 2020). The variation of the decomposition process across different geographic locations and the need to consistently measure dynamic parameters over time have made the use of animal models a steady and critical necessity. The use of animal models in various scientific fields for research purposes is not new, dating back to ancient Greek times, when studies of anatomy and physiology were conducted with dogs and chicks (Ericsson, Crim, and Franklin 2013). During the Renaissance era, the use of animals to help understand scientific investigation continued, with scientists such as the anatomist Vesalius conducting parallel studies between humans and animals, thereby establishing the foundations of comparative anatomical principles (Franco 2013).

While animal experimentation has played a central role in biomedical research throughout history, ethical considerations cannot be neglected and continue to represent an area of debate and concern. Researchers must abide by standard animal care guidelines in order to justify the experiment (Mole and Heyns 2019). For postmortem research purposes, animals are required to be deceased for experimentation. Hence, a crucial area to consider is euthanasia methods. Euthanasia is geared toward inducing death without pain. The humane death of an animal, therefore, lies in an optimal protocol in which the animal is rendered unconscious (so that it can be insensitive to pain) as fast as possible, to reduce anxiety and stress. Euthanasia methods are typically chosen based on animal species, size, and general protocol requirements for the specific study, dictating needs for tissue collection and required analysis. This method selection process is also dependent on personnel skill, availability of resources, and the number of animals to be killed. Common methods employed include asphyxiation with carbon dioxide, overdose with barbiturates, cervical dislocation, and decapitation (National Research Council 1992). Although gunshot is another method used primarily in field/rural settings, this euthanasia method is not widely applicable in taphonomic research, as inflicting wounds on the carcass results in alteration of decomposition factors (i.e., entomological activity is increased in wounded areas due to easier access), thus skewing results.

A further concern in animal modeling for research purposes is the applicability of these studies to humans and society in general; in other words, is it justified to conduct the experiment proposed? From an animal use viewpoint, justifiability is a much more subjective idea. The applicability of this type of research does rest on following proper experimental guidelines and research design to acquire reliable and useful results. In forensic science, animal modeling can be utilized to understand mechanisms and processes associated with the fate of human remains. However, one can argue that understanding the decay process of a carcass will not bring the human victim back to life or enhance human health or welfare.

This issue raises the question, Is the death of an animal even justified to perform observations that will not directly help anyone in the immediate future (Mole and Heyns 2019)? To put this question in perspective, one must direct the viewpoint to the roots of forensic science, the use of scientific principles in matters of the law. Overall, violent crime is a global problem. In the United States, the FBI's Uniform Crime Reporting (UCR) Program estimated that the number of murders in the nation in 2019 was 16,425. This number was approximately an 11.6 percent increase from data reports from 2010 (Federal Bureau of Investigation 2019). Hence, it can be argued that the need for efficient forensic science techniques to bring these alarming murders to justice calls for optimal procedures and protocols to process death investigations. Understanding parameters such as time of death estimations and analyzing carcasses for variables such as entomological data, microbial activity, or even odor analysis not only open the door for enhanced knowledge in taphonomic principles from a scientific perspective but also allow for technological or detection development avenues. Thus, animal modeling can be a platform for translational research into operational settings. Examples include understanding the odor of death for enhanced canine cadaver detection training (Iqbal et al. 2017, 112) or understanding burial decomposition processes for testing remote sensing and search techniques for the localization of clandestine single and mass graves in both forensic and humanitarian investigations (Blau et al. 2018, 304). Each of these examples highlights the benefit of understanding the dynamics of decomposition for an immediate real-life application. In the case of canines as human remains detectors, the definition of the odor of death with respect to different decomposition stages is a topic of great interest, as a canine needs to be able to detect a victim at any stage in which they may be recovered. Hence, knowledge on the chemical characterization of volatile odor signatures at different phases of the postmortem interval, from matrices such as tissues, soil, bacteria, or whole bodies, can generate useful information for the creation of synthetic chemical training aids that can mimic decomposing tissue for canine training purposes, when true putrefactive bodily materials are not readily available. In the case of clandestine grave sites, it is essential to understand times between burial and search activities to evaluate and augment detection capabilities. The impact of localizing mass gravesites is a top priority from an international forensic perspective; however, information with respect to the interaction of the grave and buried remains within the surrounding environment continues to be a largely unexplored area. In this case, animal proxies can serve as a good tool to obtain baseline data for technological advancement (Schultz, Collins, and Falsetti 2006, 2008).

In a recent review of the literature focusing on the number of animal models used specifically for forensic science research, porcine analogues were almost exclusively utilized for postmortem interval estimation/taphonomy/odor research, while studies in the forensic toxicological or trauma themes typically utilized rats and mice. Figure 8.1 shows a distribution of animal models utilized out of a total of 1,512 total specimens (only corresponding to the PMI/taphonomy and volatile odor analysis research themes; Mole and Heyns 2019, 1100). Pigs (*Sus scrofa domesticus*) represent 43 percent of the total distribution when compared to other mammalian models. The applicability of animal proxies in this research framework relies significantly on the availability of animal carcasses killed in laboratories or obtained from industrial agriculture.

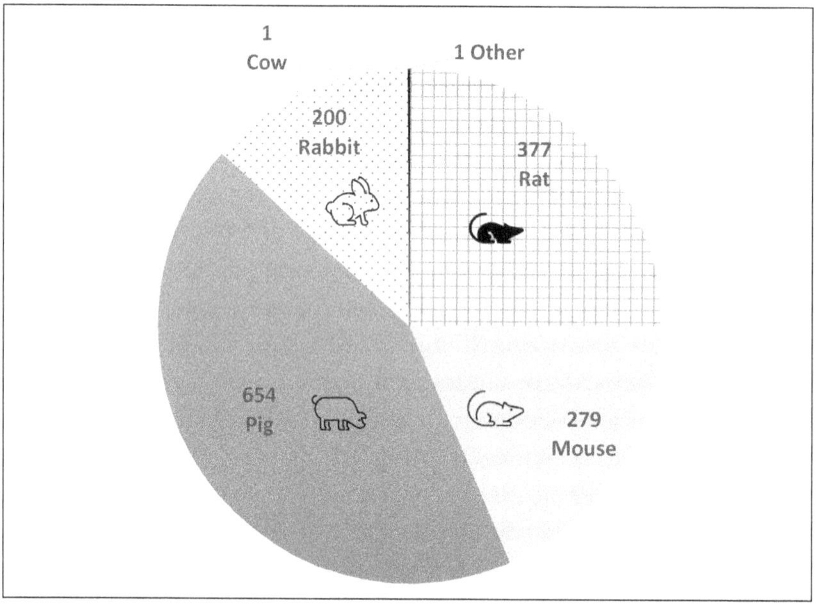

Figure 8.1. Distribution of animal models in forensic taphonomy research (Mole and Heyns 2019)

Pigs are the preferred animal model in taphonomic studies due to their availability in agricultural settings, which are typically geared for meat production and hence provide an ease of procurement services from local abattoirs. In addition to the relatively easier pathway for acquisition and wider availability, there are several other advantages of using the porcine model. Pigs have an all-season breeding capability, with large litter sizes (ten to twelve piglets per litter), as well as fully developed standardization of breeding conditions. Pigs have numerous anatomical similarities to humans that make them the go-to choice in taphonomic research. It is also known that there is a high genome and protein sequence similarity with human counterparts (Meurens et al. 2012, 51). With regard to the digestive system, both humans and pigs have distinct small and large intestines, which interact with a varied diet, thereby highlighting both plant and meat food groups in their system. With respect to dermal similarities, the two species share comparable amounts of hair distribution, in contrast to other, much-hairier mammalian analogues (Miles, Finaughty, and Gibbon 2020). This close resemblance in skin characteristics has led to genetic engineering of pig skin to provide skin grafts for burn patients (Yamamoto et al. 2018). Studies have also shown that pigs and humans have similar immunological systems, thereby sharing an infectious disease response, given comparable immune cell populations in the two organisms (Rothkötter 2009; Meurens et al. 2012). Fat-to-muscle ratio is also comparable between the two: the average body fat is around 20 percent (Dunshea and D'Souza 2003, 127).

Although the two species share similarities, it is important to note distinctions as well. When taking a closer look at the molecular level of fatty acid composition, relative proportions within the adipose tissues are different. Pigs have higher saturation of fatty acids such as stearic acid. In contrast, humans have a predominance of unsaturated fatty acids that include oleic, linoleic, and laurel acids (Notter et al. 2009). Another distinction in the two organisms is the intestinal length, as a human's average intestinal length is seven and a half meters, while pigs have twenty-three meters of intestine (Miles, Finaughty, and Gibbon 2020). Given these similarities and divergences between humans and pigs, the big question that forensic researchers are confronted with is, What do the results of animal proxies really mean in practical forensic casework? Can we trust and extrapolate the results to compare with a human death investigation? To provide some insight into this deliberation, it is important to understand the historical use of animals in decomposition-related research and to assess validation studies that have embarked on the human-animal model comparison paradigm.

History of Animal Modeling in Decomposition Research

The implementation of animals as human proxies for forensic taphonomic studies is rooted in ecological succession principles, tracing back to understanding entomological activity on animal carcasses. In the late 1800s, the French entomologist Pierre Megnin moved forward the notion that there is a predictable pattern of carrion-arthropod succession from his observations on exhumed and exposed human cadavers and that this pattern has utility in forensic applications. This groundbreaking discovery led to the origin of two important fields: carrion ecology and forensic entomology. Forensic entomology uses thermal changes (heat emission) and successional timelines of insects on the cadaver to provide estimates on time of death in criminal investigations (Michaud, Schoenly, and Moreau 2015). A seminal paper by Jerry Payne (1965) utilized species such as dogs, cats, squirrels, rabbits, chickens, birds, and pigs to evaluate carrion ecology. Payne selected domesticated pigs as the optimal species, given that he knew their time of death, could acquire them in higher numbers, could obtain them within a similar age range, and could obtain insect samples much easier from their hairless skin distribution (Payne 1965). These foundational experiments highlighted the importance of using larger-sized animals, the complexity of collecting entomological samples from mammals with other types of coatings such as birds' feathers, and the need for observations over long periods of time. In the early 1980s, William C. Rodriguez and William M. Bass compared insect succession patterns from a canine cadaver study (Reed 1958) and found significant overlap with human cadavers (Rodriguez and Bass 1983).

Other early foundational studies used a variety of species including cows, seabirds, and even sea mammals (Shafer 1978). These pioneering studies set forth an area of research that utilized animal samples as a pathway to understand the dynamic decomposition process. Given the multidisciplinary aspect of forensic science, this quest for understanding death comes from different angles to different topic areas. While all scientists seek to understand the postmortem interval, the underlying physical phenomena from which it is observed are not the same. To the entomologist, insect development, succession, and identification are key to understand what guides patterns of oviposition or visual/olfactory cues that govern insect patterns. To anthropologists, it is important to understand the gross changes of the decomposition process, how fast they develop, and what happens to tissue at each stage under distinctive environmental conditions. To chemists, the importance of the study of decomposition comes from exploring types and abundance of volatile emission at different stages, microbial activity in both the cadaver and surrounding areas, and soil changes and nutrient fluxes due to the new ecosystem provided by the carrion. Therefore, the study of animal analogues within a decomposition setting can be applicable and useful to several different scientific disciplines.

A Question of Transferability: Are Animal Proxies a Source of Forensic Knowledge?

While it is not the intent of this chapter to provide a comprehensive review of all the studies that have implemented animal models in the various themes of decomposition research, it is important to cite some representative studies and examine experimental variables affecting animal model comparisons. A recent review by Szymon Matuszewski et al. (2020) provides a detailed perspective on the use of animal analogues in forensic taphonomy, discussing methodological contexts of the pros and cons of animal proxies as a model for human cadavers. Major research areas depicted in this work include insect succession, seasonal and annual variability, surface/burial/water decomposition, trauma (wounds/hangings/dismemberment), refrigeration, burned remains, volatile odor analysis, wrappings, scavenging, microbial activity, concealment, thermal imaging, and soil biogeochemistry (Matuszewski et al. 2020). When evaluating these animal modeling experiments, vertebrate decomposition processes are sometimes different with respect to the decomposition rates and patterns observed when cross-linked with human cadaver results. There are fundamental intrinsic variables such as physiological differences of the carcass (body mass, fat, muscle tissue) as well as external experimental design variables (carcass distances and numbers, seasonal variability, scavenging activity, to name a few) that ultimately guide the results, and it is the responsibility of researchers to properly interpret the results and establish conclusions. Table 8.1 displays some of these important variables when comparing animal models to human cadavers in forensic taphonomic research applications. Given that there is an array of variables to take into consideration, it is essential that sample-selection processes in animal modeling studies are carefully designed within and between species to enhance the validity of the comparison context.

TABLE 8.1. Experimental Design Variables in Forensic Taphonomic Animal Modeling Research

Intrinsic (physiological) variables	External variables
Sex	Carcass distance during sampling
Age	Number of carcasses placed
Body mass (weight)	Season / temperature / longitudinal effects
Fat content	Scavenging activity
Tissue density	Use of cages/enclosures around carcass
	Wrappings/clothing
	Refrigeration (freeze/thaw) before carcass placement

An important variable when implementing animal models is carcass size and its influence on the rate or pattern of decomposition. Body mass is one parameter that will ideally be consistent across animals and humans in order to produce results that can be applied from animals to humans (Miles, Finaughty, and Gibbon 2020; Matuszewski et al. 2020). With respect to the rate of decay, it is logical to assume that a carcass of a greater body mass will take longer to decompose due to more available biomass and surface area, which gives decomposers more tissue for consumption, a pattern that can be expected irrespective of environment. Hence, even if multiple carcasses of varying weights were placed at the same time under identical field conditions, decomposition stages would be reached at unique points in time given that putrefactive processes and natural feeders and scavengers would take an extended time consuming the available tissue before skeletonization is observed. The first study to clearly depict and experimentally support this trend was that of Kenneth Kneidel in the early 1980s. Kneidel's study was conducted from an entomological perspective, assessing patterns of insect communities. He emphasized that carcasses of varying weights decompose at distinctive rates and therefore exhibit a different decomposition timeline as well as attract different carrion insect communities (Kneidel 1984).

In the 1990s, a study by Robert Mann et al. (1990) depicted discrepancies in decomposition rates between animal (dog carcasses ranging between 20 and 40 kilograms) and human cadavers (50–65 kilograms), showing a faster rate for the dog carcass decomposition. The only shared results across species were the faster decomposition of the head region in both matrices, which would have been expected due to existence of orifices in that body area, which provides easier body access, attracting greater entomological activity (Mann, Bass, and Meadows 1990). Later work conducted by Kamani Hewadikaram and M. Lee Goff (1991) comparing same-species sampling demonstrated that a carcass size variation of 6.7 kilograms (they used two pig carcasses, one weighing 8.4 kilograms and the other 15.1 kilograms) did not influence the composition or succession rates of detected arthropod fauna, while the rate of decay was more rapid for the heavier carcass than the lighter one, contrasting previous results. The lack of uniform carcass size was further exemplified in a Canadian study in which fourteen pig carcasses ranging in size from small (19–26 kilograms) to medium (36–80 kilograms) to large (156–62 kilograms) were allowed to decompose in shaded and sun-exposed field conditions. Study results highlighted that the smaller carcasses in both environments decomposed faster than the medium and larger carcasses did, reaching dry skeletal remains in as little as thirteen days. Again, using a same-species comparison experimental design with a wider weight range for observation clearly demonstrated differences in decay rates because of animal biomass (Komar and Beattie 1998).

Consecutive studies have reinforced the importance of carcass biomass as a critical factor in the decay rate, depicting that in the early postmortem stages, a rapid decomposition occurs regardless of size; however, as this putrefactive process progresses, higher body masses experience extended bloating periods, coupled to higher nutrient release into grave soil deposition sites, thereby exhibiting clear distinctions from their smaller-size counterparts (Spicka et al. 2011; Sutherland et al. 2013; Matuszewski et al. 2014). Ironically, a study by Tal Simmons et al. provided a degree of irrelevancy to previously cited research. In this study, carcass size appeared to have no influence on decay rates when insect activity was excluded from the postmortem process, as happens in environmental situations such as submerged, indoor, or buried scenarios (Simmons, Adlam, and Moffatt 2010). Again, the contradictions encountered only showcase the complex dynamics of the postmortem process, which interplay among each other to yield the results.

More recent studies have attempted to validate animal modeling with a direct comparison with human cadavers; however, standardization of variables such as carcass size has not always been followed. A study conducted by Melissa Connor et al. (2018) tested the use of pigs as human proxies; however, a major drawback of the study is the lack of information on the human cadavers, to be able to draw comparative results. The pig body sizes had a wide weight range, between 25 and 64 kilograms, rendering the animal carcass weight to be even highly variable within the species. Conclusions from this study need to be taken with caution as the lack of homogeneous weights affects the pattern of decomposition and thus makes decomposition scoring models challenging given animal subject variation that is not fully understood when extrapolating to statistical results (Connor, Baigent, and Hansen 2018). Another study reported in that same year conducted an animal modeling comparison to human cadavers utilizing pigs and rabbits as the animal species. Specifically comparing the pig carcass to human cadavers across three field trials, the cadavers had an average 21 kilograms weight difference between species. This discrepancy in the cadavers' weight skews the results, as previous literature has consistently reinforced the fact that body mass is a crucial factor in decay rates (Matuszewski et al. 2020). A closer body mass range between pig analogues and human cadavers was observed in a recent study by Zaccariah Knobel et al. (2019), who utilized carcasses from both species ranging between 60 and 80 kilograms for pigs and between 60 and 90 kilograms for human cadavers. The study was performed across two seasons, highlighting faster decomposition for both species at warmer temperatures, with rates being more comparable for both at cooler temperatures. However, a striking difference was the fact that pig carcasses underwent all decomposition stages, while their human counterparts underwent differential decomposition (meaning differing stages across different body regions), which resulted in dissimilar overall decay processes (Knobel et al. 2019).

Stemming from the physiological perspective, other studies have also investigated the validation of animal proxies from the viewpoint of fat and muscle tissue discrepancies. Adipose tissue, for example, has been compared between pigs and humans, showing that this fat had a higher rate of deterioration in the pig and showing a difference in nutrient fluxes. After thirty days, human fat had a mineral content of mainly potassium and sodium, while decomposed pig fat had more potassium and magnesium (Notter et al. 2009). The implications of these mineral composition variations across species are also relevant to cadaveric soil biogeochemistry, which can play an important role in decomposition ecology as well as cadaver dog detection training paradigms.

Muscle tissue is another tissue commonly investigated for taphonomic purposes in human decomposition. A comprehensive species study performed by Kathryn Stokes et al. (2013) used skeletal muscle tissue (SMT) from human, pork, beef, and lamb samples, which were buried in jars at a depth of one centimeter in standard laboratory conditions. Various physiochemical soil characteristics were measured and compared across all tissue types. There was not a single skeletal muscle tissue that represented an ideal predictor of the human SMT behavior in soil as it decomposed. Microbial activity was higher in soil exposed to pork and beef compared to human tissue. Lamb tissue was the most similar to human measured parameters. Although none of the animal tissue types were comparable for human tissue–soil interactions, all tissue types did offer some level of approximation in decomposition dynamics and offered useful baseline variables to measure and build on in future studies (Stokes, Forbes, Tibbett 2013).

Another important factor to consider when performing decomposition animal studies is the overall placement and distance between cadavers. The importance of understanding distance effect lies in the fact that insect colonizers can "compete," hence cross-contaminating the carcasses. The carcass that is more "attractive" to the insect can inadvertently mask the other cadaver, resulting in lower entomological activity in that carcass and hence in a slower decomposition timeline on the "less attractive" cadaver. Furthermore, larvae may disperse, thus becoming yet another mechanism that affects larval competition if the carcasses are placed too close together. This larval dispersal can yield to species composition differences and thus lead to a lack of "independence" across each replicate, further hindering statistical analysis assumptions. While distance plays a crucial role, sometimes this variable is inherently limited by the area in which researchers have access to conduct experiments. Some outdoor facilities are restricted in size, thus being a limiting factor with respect to resource availability and lacking in validated between-cadaver distance parameters (Matuszewski et al. 2020).

A closely related factor with respect to external experimental design considerations is the refrigeration of the animal carcass. From my own experience, it is sometimes difficult to begin an experiment concurrently with the time of death of the animal carcass. This can be due to the animal being donated at a time when the field site is not available or other experimental resources (cages, personnel, or instrumentation) are not ready to be deployed. Thus, in these instances, many researchers decide to store the carcass under refrigerated conditions prior to field placement. These carcasses are frozen at unmonitored temperatures for variable time intervals and ultimately thawed before experimentation begins. A seminal study conducted by Marc Micozzi (1986) evaluated the freezing-thawing process on animal carcasses in field conditions. Previously frozen-thawed animals showed predominantly decay, while freshly killed animals showed predominantly putrefaction (Micozzi 1986). Refrigeration affects microbial action, thus affecting decomposition rates and insect attraction and therefore leading to misleading results.

Besides initial considerations at or during carcass placement, another crucial variable to note in animal modeling in decomposition studies is scavenging effects. Scavenging can vary in the form of species availability and frequency. Studies try to eliminate this factor by using metal frames or cages to cover and protect the carcass from scavengers accessing the tissue, while simultaneously allowing access to weather conditions (rain, wind, sun, shade) as well as insect activity. From a validation perspective, it is important to clearly state this limitation in research results, as the rates obtained when scavenging is restricted may represent skewed results in the postmortem process observed. Scavenging restriction can also be directly refuted as it pertains to real forensic scenarios, with the argument that victims are not protected from scavenging in homicide events; hence, the results in experimental approaches cannot be directly linked to a forensic perspective (Miles, Finaughty, and Gibbon 2020).

Another substantial external experimental variable revolving around animal modeling with respect to the decomposition timeline is the effect of clothing and wrappings. As has been previously discussed, entomological activity plays a role in the putrefactive process, and thus the presence of clothing on the cadaver directly affects insects and retention of moisture within the tissues. Clothing is a common accessory in any victim, irrespective of age, sex, or manner of death. Whether the decomposition is indoor or outdoor, in land or in water, clothing and wrappings to conceal the body are a common artifact. Studies in this area have depicted a slower decomposition process, with clothed carcasses taking longer periods to reach full skeletonization. Clothing or wrapping constrictions can also affect the tightening of areas such as the abdomen, thus affecting the bloating stage and causing tissue rupture in these areas. Discoloration patterns are also critical when considering clothing as an experimental factor. It has been shown that clothing has a direct effect on the discoloration of the epidermis; thus, if a discoloration pattern does not match the location of clothing, it could indicate that taphonomic events moved the placement of clothing postdeath. Wrappings are yet another confounding variable. These can include plastic tarps or bags and textiles in the form of bedding materials (i.e., sheets, comforters, blankets). These materials not only have an insulation effect on the body but in some instances cause temperatures to increase in the interior of the material (Rojas-Guevara et al. 2020). While most experiments with animal analogues are conducted under unclothed situations, it is important to place this parameter in perspective, as experimentation might depict a faster decomposition timeline, when in operational scenarios, a victim's decomposition might be delayed due to the presence of clothing material.

The presented works suggest that a definitive model for cadaver experimental work is not clearly defined, with intrinsic and external variables affecting the comparative effort. It is thus up to researchers to be aware of parameters that might skew the results and clearly communicate the limitations of the observed results so that they can be taken with the level of accuracy and validity guided by the experimental design.

Conclusions

The perspective of animal death as an interface in forensic taphonomy experiments has been presented in this chapter. While it was not the intent to provide a comprehensive review of forensic decomposition research, this chapter presents an overview of the reason why animal models help advance taphonomic understanding. In this chapter, an overview of forensic taphonomy and gross decomposition changes was presented to understand the myriad of variables of interest to the forensic practitioner. Debate as to the use of animal models was presented, highlighting the need for the extended implementation of exploiting animal carcasses to observe the process of decay. A selected number of studies was presented to highlight important experimental parameters to consider when performing the animal-human comparison of the corpse entity.

Science has explored to a large degree what happens to the body after life ceases to exist. The human corpse undergoes both physical and chemical changes guided by biological breakdown processes that result in the decay or postmortem process. This dynamic decomposition phenomenon comprises distinctive stages in all living organisms. However, although reproducible with respect to stages observed, the timeline and degree of completion for each is highly variable. Numerous variables affect this process, including abiotic factors that can include temperature, humidity, wounds, and environment that interconnect with biotic factors such as scavenging activity and microbial communities.

The use of animal models by humans has come a long way since their use in pioneering anatomical and physiological studies in medical applications. The debate and controversy on their use continues; however, there is a divergence of opinion as to the best approach for obtaining fruitful scientific knowledge from animal experimentation. With respect to forensic applications, animal models have provided a good paradigm to obtain baseline and foundational data to monitor decomposition trends. Ideally, the use of human cadavers would prevent animal modeling from being a comparative resource, but realistically, not every researcher has access to a full body or body parts to undertake the needed research work. Taphonomic research facilities (body farms) do not exist in enough geographic locations to perform the amount of research being explored by the many disciplines of interest. Another factor that must be understood is that the limited awareness of forensic taphonomy and its applications to criminal justice limits the understanding of its advantages. Routine pathological and criminal investigations have access to deceased victims; however, due to legal and ethical restrictions, family considerations, and chain of custody implications, the use of human parts/tissues after the practice of medico-legal autopsy processes is not readily feasible. Hence, animal modeling is a necessity within forensic science research.

The overarching question central to this chapter is whether animal models are perfect for extrapolation to real forensic cases. As has been depicted in the literature reviewed, the answer is not a clear yes. However, with regard to systematic baseline data and the easier acquisition of animal analogues to explore research topics, the answer is yes, animal proxies are helpful. Pig carcasses have been highlighted as the animal species of choice due to various physiological and practical factors that allow their ease of implementation. Foundational studies with pig proxies have tackled entomological, taphonomy, chemical, and ecological questions. It is important to reinforce, however, that while research has demonstrated differences between animal and human cadavers, researchers have a responsibility to move this field forward by providing standardization and best practices. The need to clearly delineate cadaver weights, distance placements, field site characteristics, and environmental conditions and to acknowledge intrinsic limitations of the study will help to extrapolate collected data and establish trends with statistical validation. It is difficult to rely on results from a single replicate or geographic region, hence the need to extend scientific inquiry to many locations and conditions to evaluate the interconnection of factors. As human cadavers are difficult to obtain for experimental design, animal analogues provide an adequate avenue to investigate and test hypotheses of forensic interest. Thus, it is safe to assume that animal analogues will remain an integral tool in the forensic science toolbox to understand the decomposition timeline, which would otherwise be impossible without access to human bodies. Ironically, even though death in any organism is a difficult occurrence, animal death can help shed light on the understanding of death through a forensic lens, using death to understand death itself.

REFERENCES

Blau, Soren, Jon Sterenberg, Patrick Weeden, Fernando Urzedo, Richard Wright, and Chris Watson. 2018. "Exploring Non-invasive Approaches to Assist in the Detection of Clandestine Human Burials: Developing a Way Forward." *Forensic Sciences Research* 3 (4): 304–26.

Connor, Melissa, Christiane Baigent, and Eriek Hansen. 2018. "Testing the Use of Pigs as Human Proxies in Decomposition Studies." *Journal of Forensic Sciences* 63 (5): 1350–55.

DiMaio, Vincent J., and Dominick DiMaio. 2001. *Forensic Pathology*. 2nd ed. Boca Raton, FL: CRC Press.

Dunshea, Frank Rowland, and D. N. D'Souza. 2003. "A Review—Fat Deposition and Metabolism in the Pig." In *Manipulating Pig Production IX Proceedings of the Conference of the Australian Pig Science Association, Werribee, Australia, 23–26 November 2003*, 127–50.

Efremov, J. A. 1940. "Taphonomy: New Branch of Paleontology." *Pan-American Geologist* 74 (2): 81–93.

Ericsson, Aaron C., Marcus J. Crim, and Craig L. Franklin. 2013. "A Brief History of Animal Modeling." *Missouri Medicine* 110 (3): 201–5.

Federal Bureau of Investigation (FBI). n.d. "FBI URC 2019 Crime in the United States." Accessed January 29, 2022. https://ucr.fbi.gov.

Franco, Nuno H. 2013. "Animal Experiments in Biomedical Research: A Historical Perspective." *Animals* 3:238–73.

Gill-King, Harrell. 1997. "Chemical and Ultrastructural Aspects of Decomposition." In *Forensic Taphonomy: The Postmortem Fate of Human Remains*, edited by William D. Haglund and Marcella H. Sorg, 93–108. Boca Raton, FL: CRC Press.

Haglund, William D., and Marcella H. Sorg. 1997. "Method and Theory of Forensic Taphonomic Research." In *Forensic Taphonomy: The Postmortem Fate of Human Remains*, edited by William D. Haglund and Marcella H. Sorg, 13–22. Boca Raton, FL: CRC Press.

Hewadikaram, K. A., and M. L. Goff. 1991. "Effect of Carcass Size on Rate of Decomposition and Arthropod Succession Patterns." *American Journal of Forensic Medicine and Pathology* 12 (3): 235–40.

Iqbal, Mohammad A., Katie D. Nizio, M. Ueland, and Shari L. Forbes. 2017. "Forensic Decomposition Odour Profiling: A Review of Experimental Designs and Analytical Techniques." *Trends in Analytical Chemistry* 91:112–24.

Kneidel, Kenneth A. 1984. "Influence of Carcass Taxon and Size on Species Composition of Carrion-breeding Diptera." *American Midland Naturalist* 111 (1): 57–63.

Knobel, Zaccariah, Maiken Ueland, Katie D. Nizio, Darshil Patel, and Shari L. Forbes. 2018. "A Comparison of Human and Pig Decomposition Rates and Odour Profiles in an Australian Environment." *Australian Journal of Forensic Sciences* 51 (5): 557–72.

Komar, Damian, and Owen Beattie. 1998. "Effects of Carcass Size on Decay Rates of Shade and Sun Exposed Carrion." *Canadian Society of Forensic Science Journal* 31 (1): 35–43.

Mann, Robert W., William M. Bass, and Lee Meadows. 1990. "Time since Death and Decomposition of the Human Body: Variables and Observations in Case and Experimental Field Studies." *Journal of Forensic Sciences* 35:103–11.

Matuszewski, Szymon, Martin J. R. Hall, Gaetan Moreau, Kenneth G. Schoenly, Aaron M. Tarone, and Martin H. Villet. 2020. "Pigs vs People: The Use of Pigs as Analogues for Humans in Forensic Entomology and Taphonomy Research." *International Journal of Legal Medicine* 134:793–810.

Matuszewski, Szymon, Szymon Konwerski, Katarzyna Fratczak, and Michał Szafalowicz. 2014. "Effect of Body Mass and Clothing on Decomposition of Pig Carcasses." *International Journal of Legal Medicine* 128:1039–48.
Meurens, Francois, Artur Summerfield, Hans Nauwynck, Linda Saif, and Volker Gerdts. 2012. "The Pig: A Model for Human Infectious Diseases." *Trends in Microbiology* 20 (1): 50–57.
Michaud, Jean-Philippe, Kenneth G. Schoenly, and Gaetan Moreau. 2015. "Rewriting Ecological Succession History: Did Carrion Ecologists Get There First?" *Quarterly Review in Biology* 90 (1): 45–66.
Micozzi, Marc. 1986. "Experimental Study of Postmortem Change under Field Conditions: Effects of Freezing, Thawing and Mechanical Injury." *Journal of Forensic Sciences* 31 (3): 953–61.
Miles, Kelly L., Devin A. Finaughty, and Victoria E. Gibbon. 2020. "A Review of Experimental Design in Forensic Taphonomy: Moving towards Forensic Realism." *Forensic Sciences Research* 5 (4): 249–59.
Mole, Calvin Gerald, and Marise Heyns. 2019. "Animal Models in Forensic Science Research: Justified Use or Ethical Exploitation?" *Science and Engineering Ethics* 25 (4): 1095–1110.
National Research Council. 1992. *Recognition and Alleviation of Pain and Distress in Laboratory Animals*. Washington, DC: National Academies Press.
Notter, Stephanie J., Barbara H. Stuart, Rebecca Rowe, and Neil Langlois. 2009. "The Initial Changes of Fat Deposits during the Decomposition of Human and Pig Remains." *Journal of Forensic Sciences* 54 (1): 195–201.
Payne, Jerry A. 1965. "A Summer Carrion Study of the Baby Pig Sus Scrofa Linnaeus." *Ecology* 46 (5): 592–602.
Rattenbury, Amy E. 2018. "Forensic Taphonomy." In *Forensic Ecogenomics*, edited by T. Komang Ralebitso-Senior, 37–60. London: Academic Press.
Reed, H. B. 1958. "A Study of Dog Carcass Communities in Tennessee with Special Reference to Insects." *American Midland Naturalist* 59 (1): 213–45.
Rodriguez, W. C., and W. M. Bass. 1983. "Insect Activity and Its Relationship to Decay Rates of Human Cadavers in East Tennessee." *Journal of Forensic Sciences* 28 (2): 423–32.
Rojas-Guevara, Jorge Ulises, Paola Alexandra Prada-Tiedemann, Katherine C. Titus, Juan David Córdoba-Parra, and Gabriel Antonio Bohórquez. 2020. *Forensic Studies with Human Analogues: Evaluation of Decomposition and the Use of Residual Odor Detection Dogs*. Bogotá: National Police of Colombia.
Rothkötter, Hermann-Josef. 2009. "Anatomical Particularities of the Porcine Immune System—A Physician's View." *Developmental and Comparative Immunology* 33:267–72.
Schotsmans, Eline M. J., Nicholas Marquez-Grant, and Shari L. Forbes. 2017. Introduction to *Taphonomy of Human Remains Forensic Analysis of the Dead and the Deposition Environment*, edited by Eline M. J. Schotsmans, Nicholas Marquez-Grant, and Shari L. Forbes, 2–7. Hoboken, NJ: Wiley.

Schultz, John J., Mary E. Collins, and Anthony B. Falsetti. 2006. "Sequential Monitoring of Burials Containing Large Pig Cadavers Using Ground-Penetrating Radar." *Journal of Forensic Sciences* 51:607–16.

———. 2008. "Sequential Monitoring of Burials Containing Small Pig Cadavers Using Ground-Penetrating Radar." *Journal of Forensic Sciences* 53:279–87.

Shafer, Wilhelm. 1978. *The Ecology and Paleoecology of Marine Environments*. Chicago: University of Chicago Press.

Shirley, Natalie R., Rebecca J. Wilson, and Lee Meadows Jantz. 2011. "Cadaver Use at the University of Tennessee's Anthropological Research Facility." *Clinical Anatomy* 24:372–80.

Simmons, Tal, Rachel E. Adlam, and Colin Moffatt. 2010. "Debugging Decomposition Data—Comparative Taphonomic Studies and the Influence of Insects and Carcass Size on Decomposition Rate." *Journal of Forensic Sciences* 55 (1): 8–13.

Simmons, Tal, and P. A. Cross. 2013. "Forensic Taphonomy." In *Encyclopedia of Forensic Sciences*, 2nd ed., Jay A. Siegel, Pekka J. Saukko, and Max M. Houck, 12–17. London: Academic Press.

Spika, Ashley, Reyna Johnson, Jennifer Bushing, Leon G. Higley, and David O. Carter. 2011. "Carcass Mass Can Influence Rate of Decomposition and Release of Ninhydrin-Reactive Nitrogen into Gravesoil." *Forensic Science International* 209:80–85.

Stokes, Kathryn L., Shari L. Forbes, and Mark Tibbett. 2013. "Human versus Animal: Contrasting Decomposition Dynamics of Mammalian Analogues in Experimental Taphonomy." *Journal of Forensic Sciences* 58 (3): 583–91.

Sutherland, A., J. Myburgh, M. Steyn, and P. J. Becker. 2013. "The Effect of Body Size on the Rate of Decomposition in a Temperate Region of South Africa." *Forensic Science International* 231:257–62.

Verheggen, Francois., Katelynn A. Perrault, Rudy Caparros Megido, Lena M. Dubois, Frederic Francis, Eric Haubruge, Shari L. Forbes, Jean-Francois Focant, and Pierre-Hughes Stefanuto. 2017. "The Odor of Death: An Overview of Current Knowledge on Characterization and Applications." *Bioscience* 67 (7): 600–613.

Wescott, Daniel J. 2018. "Recent Advances in Forensic Anthropology: Decomposition Research." *Forensic Sciences Research* 3 (4): 278–93.

Yamamoto, Takayuki, Hayato Iwase, Timothy W. King, Hidetaka Hara, and David K. C. Cooper. 2018. "Skin Xenotransplantation: Historical Review and Clinical Potential." *Burns* 44 (7): 1738–49.

9

The Slow Death of Spider Goats

LISA JEAN MOORE

The Invention of Spider Goats

When I first met the herd of transgenic goats at an enclosed facility in Logan, Utah, they appeared like any other well-cared-for farm goat—all fluffy white and black fur and alert countenances. They ran to the fences of their pens to greet humans with enthusiasm and nibbled on my fingers. It was the summer of 2017, and I had only become aware of their existence a few months earlier. Intrigued by the idea of goats that could lactate spider silk, I had reached out to the current head of the project, Randy Lewis, and been granted permission to come to visit.

The goats had traveled to the western United States with Randy, a molecular biologist, after Nexia Biotechnologies, Inc., the Canadian biotech company responsible for engineering the herd, funded by the US Department of Defense, had become defunct. Engineered in the 1990s, the goats were part of a project to produce new fabrics both strong and flexible through the introduction of golden orb weaver spider deoxyribonucleic acid (DNA) into the goats' genome. Randy continued to do research with the spider goats supported by a variety of military and other federal agencies, and when he changed universities, the herd moved with him from Wyoming to Utah. Twenty-five years after their origin, I traveled to meet the spider goats, visiting the lab in the summers of 2017 and 2019. I conducted fieldwork at the farm and lab, interviewed several scientists and lab technicians, and observed the goats' everyday lives.

I am a medical sociologist who uses feminist qualitative methods to explore the entanglements of humans and nonhuman animals in a variety of ecological settings. Through sociological experiences of conducting ethnographies of honey bees, horseshoe crabs, and spider goats, I have witnessed animal death primarily through extractive, anthropocentric industries (Moore and Kosut 2013; Moore 2017). From my perspective, extracting honey or blood or milk from animals for human benefit has diminished and threatened the lives of nonhuman animals. This threat is despite the performative hand-wringing about the Anthropocene. I am interested in our repetition of behaviors toward nonhuman animals. Our species has the arrogance to exploit other species for their bodily fluids, endangering them, and then simultaneously we have the vanity to believe humans have some solution (at least in the case of honey bees or horseshoe crabs) to save the species. I have leveraged my feminism to foster my entangled empathy when considering animal death (Gruen 2015).

As a feminist researcher, even what I choose to study is based on my oft-acknowledged positionality and emotional investments in the world. This feminist stance comes from my reading of the philosopher Sandra Harding. Harding created standpoint theory as a way of epistemologically unsettling scientific knowledge production. Harding roots her analysis in the primacy of the visible and embodied subjects of knowledge as "the lives from which thought has started are always present and visible in the results of that thought" (Harding 1991, 63). For Harding, all knowledge production is inherently embodied. However, through the decontextualizing and erasure of the means of its production, certain forms and lineages of knowledge are privileged, resulting in knowledge that appears without origin. Harding asserts that objectivity in scientific research is contingent on strategic erasures: of the researcher's body and process and the historical context in which research is done. Because of these erasures, positivism is unable to critique its own form and context, no matter how rigorous its content may be. I work to enable enlivening critique of my own methodological interventions and epistemological creations by engaging in continuous reflexive analysis.

I am also influenced by the feminist science studies scholar Donna Haraway through her notion of situated knowledges, a reaction to the essentialism of Harding's knowledge "from below." While Harding calls for the primacy of the vision of the oppressed and the ability to see from another's embodied eyes, Haraway warns of the "serious danger of romanticizing and/or appropriating the vision of the less powerful while claiming to see from their positions" (1988, 579) and argues for a "view from a body, always a complex, contradictory, structuring, and structured body, versus the view from above, from nowhere, from simplicity" (589). Wary of essentializing and fetishizing the Other as a site of knowledge production, Haraway calls for situated knowledges, a contextualization of knowledge as a network emerging from the bodies of the object, the subject, and (more than) human agents involved in the production of knowledge. Embodied knowledge is thus messy and incomplete, less the product of any one embodied subject than a multiplicity of bodies, human and nonhuman.

While persuaded by this argument, I do wonder what is the standpoint when a human is trying to understand the experience of the animal within a fieldwork site. I suppose it is true that I am asking different types of questions with respect to transgenic goats who lactate spider silk protein because of my standpoint as a lactating mammal than, say, another scholar who does not have this standpoint experience. I believe my standpoint as a mammal who has lactated is an asset to my knowledge production, while at the same time, I fear the essentialism it flirts with. My feminist research is one of a situated knowledge that consistently interrogates my embodied relationships with the spider goats, the scientists, and myself.

The Disappearance of Spider Goats

My purpose in this chapter is to analyze the very recent "disappearance" of the spider goats, leading inexorably to their end. I caution you that this is a partial story about their ending and their slow death transpiring over their three decades of existence. The dying out of the spider goats is still happening. But before I explain this more fully, I describe the assignation of value of spider goats through scientific innovation. I also introduce the term "slow death," as offered by the cultural theorist Lauren Berlant (2007), and apply this idea through my interpretation of the life course of the spider goats. I end with considerations for what it means to make a species possible and then slowly let them wither away.

Through my experiences with all beings associated with the transgenic goats, I formed attachments to humans, spiders, and transgenic goats. It is hard to find the correct adjective to describe my time in Utah; I am still processing what I learned there and how I feel about it. I have worked over the past seven years to make sense of the spider goats and the social networks they have made possible. I go over and over my interviews, memories, photographs, and experiences in an attempt to understand the spider goats from their beginning to their end.

Randy, the director of the Spidersilk Lab, describes the beginning of the project, capturing some of its complexity:

> The full story goes as follows. The CEO of Nexia Biotechnologies in Canada had connections to the Animal Science Department at the University of Wyoming and was visiting them. Our department was in the same building, and the head of the AS Department suggested we meet, and we did. After a substantial conversation, we continued to explore the use of their goat system to produce proteins. They had already successfully done one protein and were looking to expand their products. So it was relatively easy for us to send them the cloned DNA we had for each of the spider dragline silk proteins to use in their transgenic goat system. In a little less than two years, they had produced the first "spider" goats. Before that they had made transgenic mouse mammary cells and demonstrated that they produced the spider silk proteins and secreted them, which is what would be needed for the goats to work correctly. Goats were used by Nexia as their gestation and time to first ovulation after birth were much shorter than other milking animals, thus cutting the time to production by over half. In addition, for reasons still not clear, cloning goats (which is essentially the same as creating and implanting the transgenic embryos) is highly successful compared to cattle. Goats also produce about the same amount of milk per pound of feed as dairy cattle and are much easier to handle. And, finally, we laughingly tell everyone that baby goats are much cuter than baby cattle.

The speed of goats' reproductive capacities, their dispositions for ease of human handling, a touch of mystery over the success rate of cloning, and their "cuteness" to humans all contributed to goats being selected as the appropriate animal to modify and turn into spider silk producers. Goats became a living factory, a bioengineered system, for the lead production of spider silk protein (Fish 2013). From the original engineered spider goats, the transgenic goats reproduced more or less naturally, creating over fifteen generational herds of spider goats.

To describe the process briefly, transgenic does are inseminated by a nontransgenic billy goat. Once pregnant, the does gestate and birth kids who are raised apart from their mothers and tested to see if they are transgenic. After birthing their kids, the lactating transgenic does are milked to retrieve the spider silk protein. This retrieval process is called "purification."

Purifying transgenic goat milk is a multistaged process that began in 2003 at the University of Wyoming. Over the years, a lot of tinkering has taken place in pursuit of "upping the recoveries," as the biologist Justin Jones, the current principal investigator of the spider silk lab at Utah State University (USU), puts it, or maximizing the amount of spider silk protein purified from the goat milk.[1] Once collected, the transgenic goat milk is immediately frozen, then thawed in a warm water bath in a lab sink. Goat milk from Saanen goats is typically between 2.9 and 4 percent milk fat (Kljajevic et al. 2018). Since this fat clogs the purification machine, thawed goat milk must first be defatted. I asked Justin to explain the program's goals, and he told me, "The process is a purification as we are isolating our target protein away from all of the contaminating milk proteins. The process of purification does begin with filtering the milk at the molecular level. We use the size of the fat micelles and normal milk proteins as a means by which to affect the first purification. We then selectively precipitate our spider silk protein away from the other milk proteins as a final step to purify the protein to greater than 80 percent purity." In this definition, then, the goat's milk has become a contaminant that must be drawn away from the spider silk protein or the target. The goat milk runs through the filter columns thousands of times over the course of a purification procedure. The result is a white, powdery substance—the spider silk protein—which can now be used to engineer objects with specific affordances.

The spider goats were made in a laboratory to extract as much silk protein from their milk as possible. And as long as they were able to produce the raw material, they were valuable. For the next roughly thirty years, the spider goats had been instrumental in producing spider silk protein to invent prototypes and applications using spider silk for military, medical, apparel, and cosmetic markets. These are some of the items that have been suggested as applications of spider silk protein inclusive of fibers:

- Bullet-proof clothing
- Parachute cords, parachutes
- Arresting gear ropes to catch a plane tailhook on aircraft carriers
- Active apparel, running shoes, jackets
- Seat belts
- Mesh covering of insertable devices in human bodies, such as catheter coverings, vaginal mesh, hernia repair mesh, mechanical insulin pump coverings
- Dental implants
- Biodegradable bottles
- Adhesives
- Sutures, bandages, surgical thread
- Artificial tendons or ligaments
- Applications in robotics
- Skin-care products

I chronicle the interspecies relationships of goats, spiders, and humans in the development and standardization of spider silk production in my book *Our Transgenic Future* (Moore 2022). That book concludes by contemplating the possible end of the spider goats, as their ability to make spider silk protein was starting to fail at the same time that the expense of maintaining the herd was rising. There were grumblings in the lab that the spider goats were no longer the best system to synthesize silk protein and that other systems (in this case, bacteria, alfalfa, or transgenic silkworms) were preferable. As my book was inching closer to being released, I thought it would be wise to check in with Justin about the status of the herd. I spoke with Justin and Randy in two separate interviews in May 2022. I spoke with Justin first, and after some COVID-19 chitchat and general catching up, I asked how the lab was doing. A week later, I interviewed Randy. In what follows, I share and unpack both those conversations. But first I review my application of the concept of slow death.

Slow Death and the Cull List

When Lauren Berlant (2007) coined the term "slow death," it was intended to be applied to humans. Described as a process of being worn out and worn down, depleted over time by the demands of capitalism, slow death is a concept that describes the mundane, repetitive, enduring everyday exhaustion of a population. As Berlant explains, slow death is an event of ordinariness and not immediate, blunt-force trauma: "the physical wearing out of a population in a way that points to its deterioration as a defining condition of its experience and historical existence" (754). In Berlant's work, she is expanding on the notion of human agency, and through nuance, she shares how human will can be inhabited differently than has previously been articulated. For my purposes, I am applying slow death to the spider goats to explore the gradual, yet seemingly foretold, decline of the population of spider goats. With the benefit of hindsight, I can see how over time each generation inches closer to obsolescence and extinction. This transgenic species experienced slow death as distinct from other (nontransgenic) types of goats.

The spider goats were made as part of an extractive economy, and their lives have always been highly regimented: living in a barn on a university property, walking from barn to milking stand twice a day, hooked up to a milking machine, led back to the pen. They were conceived and came into existence primarily to produce raw material, the spider silk protein, and secondarily to reproduce more spider goats. Each generation of spider goats lives in a cyclical routine of freshening (or breeding and rebreeding), pregnancy, birthing, milking, measuring, drying out (slowing and ceasing the doe's milk production). Rinse, repeat. These practices are commonplace and systematized for most dairy animals until they become less productive (Gillespie 2018); however, with spider goats, the milk is not the end product but rather is the medium to get to the spider silk. These goats live in a system of hypersurveillance and extreme regulation overseen by the Spider Silk Lab at USU, and by mandate of the US Department of Agriculture, these transgenic goats are quarantined in a secure facility, isolated from nontransgenic species.

Over time, as was predicted, they became less productive and progressively closer to being obsolete. Theirs was not the more immediate dramatic killing like their farm animal brethren but a slower, deliberative, and fairly bureaucratic negotiation of rational considerations. These considerations punctuate the spider goats' lives. Humans made ongoing determinations of whether they are worth it, whether their value justifies the cost of their lives. These evaluations happen for each individual goat on a micro level, as described next, but also on a macro level, as I explore in the final section of this chapter.

I attended lab meetings to negotiate the *cull list* of particular goats who were not "good producers," and I witnessed the evaluation of individual goats. People analyzed spreadsheets representing the worth of the goats in grams of protein and longitudinally compared to previous herds or even that particular goat herself in her earlier cycles. The framing of which goats to cull is part of a calculus of the expense of consumption (the cost of caring for the goats) compared to the level of production (the amount of silk protein in their milk). This framing was not just for individual goats but also applied to the herd as a population.

Here I share a conversation I observed during the summer of 2019 to illustrate the evaluation of the spider goats and the consideration for the cull list:

> During a routine Monday lab meeting, Brianne, a lab technician; Amber, the herdsman; and Brittany, an undergraduate biology student, stay behind after the larger group disperses to discuss the cull list. They are going through a list of the herd and evaluating their milk productivity. Brianne offers, "718 protein is low. And 602 has a lot of fat content in her milk, so that is changing the way we have purified her, but she is pretty consistently good." She continues on, "607 is bad. We had to dump her milk."
>
> Amber asks, "What about 623? She is up in the air. She was on the cull list."
>
> Brianne responds, "We're drying her all right now with all the ones that were on the cull list, we started drying them now. But she is decent—do we want to keep her culled?"
>
> I look at them very confused. Brittany, responding to my tilted head, says, "Culling them was like getting rid of them. You don't want them anymore." Drying out a goat means giving the goat a hormone to create a "decrease in production. When we want to cull them, we want to dry them off so she doesn't get mastitis or anything, and sometimes we decided to keep her around for breeding in the next round." Drying off a goat can cause discomfort if it is done abruptly and without management as an engorged udder creates pressure.

I approached Brianne a day later and said, "I wanted to talk to you about the cull list. Why does an animal end up on the cull list?"

She sighed, "A couple of reasons. Usually because they don't produce a lot of milk or a lot of protein. If they do produce a lot of milk and they have a lot of kids and those kids need milk, we might keep them off the list, but we also usually have nontrans goats to feed them, so it depends."

Participating in these conversations about whether a specific goat is worth it, specifically whether the cost of maintaining their life is justified by their productivity, so aptly captures the slow death described. This process of becoming worn out under the demands of capitalism, where the spider goats' existence is measured on spreadsheets and quantified in grams and their biological capacity for profit as a production system is evaluated to be good or bad, results in dialogues about death that feel ordinary and almost insignificant. When Amber says, "What about 623? She is up in the air," it does not even feel like we are talking about the death of an individual animal as the larger dying off of a species—a specicide—looms.

"They Had a Pretty Good Life": Moving On

During my first May 2022 call with Justin, when I asked how the lab was doing, he was upbeat. "Everything's going along really well. Great guns. We are doing the first scale-up run of the hagfish-derived proteins." Confused, I rapidly Googled "hagfish" to make sure that they were real and I was not hearing things. A grotesque eel-like fish direct from my nightmares appeared on my screen. "Hagfish?" I asked him. "Are you still using the goats for the spider proteins, or are the goats synthesizing hagfish protein now?" Justin replied, "Ah, the goats have been retired. The goat herd became too expensive and inefficient—costing somewhere as a conservative estimate of $30K a year for a small herd of goats. They carried us a long way, and we were able to prototype, but we just couldn't scale them up."

I was obviously disorientated and also worried, but I did not want to come off as judgmental. "So the spider goats aren't doing spider silk anymore?" I tentatively asked.

"Correct," he replied. "They just couldn't put grams on the bench, and there was a deterioration of protein delivery. Part of it was genetic and breeding a small herd of goats: when something happens in the star producer and she doesn't produce milk any longer, we have lost those genetics. A vast majority of the herd was getting old, and the genetics weren't there." He explained how in a small operation such as theirs, it was hard to maintain good genetics with high variation and keep up the quality of good producers of silk protein.

"So where are the goats now?" I asked, trying to modulate the concern in my voice.

"Oh, we donated them to a program, and I believe they were given to another researcher who studies cardiac stuff, hearts and heartbeats. It didn't matter that they were transgenic."

Justin was rather clipped in his speaking, and I felt nervous. But I pushed on, asking him, "Okay, so as a form of closure, I am wondering if I could speak to the lab that has them?"

"To be honest, I don't know their fate. I don't even know the person who has them. I just donated them to a program," he stated.

"Oh, I see. So I guess I am just curious about what happened to them." I hesitate and then added, "Like, are they dead?"

He replied, "Philosophically, I didn't want to see the herd euthanized. They had a pretty good life and could contribute to more research and be moved on to another project, but I don't know where they are." This explanation of the goats being repurposed reminds me of the miraculous novel *Never Let Me Go*, by Kazuo Ishiguro (2006), in which the cloned main characters are used as organ donors with a series of donations until they "completed."

Justin then briefly explained the mechanism of the hagfish to produce this predatory slime. Scientists were able to isolate the two proteins from the hagfish, and the intermediate filament was nearly as strong as spider silk. He explained, "It's a whole lot easier to produce this protein in bacteria because it is not a ginormous molecular weight. E. Coli produces the protein, and it is so much easier to work with than spider silk, with applications largely similar to the spider silk. The balance of research is weighted pretty much to the hagfish now."

Feeling stunned, I scrambled to come up with something interesting to ask, knowing that I had already taken up Justin's time. I also felt a sense of grief and bewilderment about what had happened to the goats that I had met a few years before. As if I were writing a eulogy for the spider goats, needing good copy, I asked a leading question: "So would you say the goats were instrumental in enabling the hagfish research to happen? Like, were they a stepping stone?" I do not stand by this question as one of a particularly good ethnographer, and as I write this now, I feel embarrassed by my clear objectives to get Justin to say that the goats mattered.

"Absolutely yes, we had to go through spider silk to get here," he replied. "They just became too difficult to work with. We were able to plug a new protein into other systems, and it worked like nobody's business, and we did have to go through spider silk. But it really is just all about the production and getting the protein reliably and in a way that is economically viable."

Once I got off the phone, I felt a sense of sorrow, and I imagined the spider goats: their bodies dissected on a lab table, their hearts chopped up. Haunted by these images, I made an effort to find out more.

A week or so later, I called Randy. I had not spoken to him in almost three years. We shared our updates. Randy had retired from USU and was currently working as a part-time nonbenefited hourly employee. "It is nice," he said. "I am in for a couple hours, and Justin does all the administrative stuff. And so that means I can pick and choose what I want to do. I have a couple projects I am working on, including this fascinating project on comb jellies."

"Oh, not hagfish?" I attempted to sound in the know.

"No, this project is on comb jellies. They have an adhesive they use on their tentacles that catch prey. No one knows anything about it. So we have been able to identify some proteins that might be involved. And we are about to get a shipment from the West Coast to see where the proteins might be located. It's likely in the tentacles." His infectious enthusiasm reminded me of the delight of being with him in the lab in Utah. I listened to more details about the comb jellies and shifted the conversation.

"So I spoke with Justin about the spider goats, and I am still a bit confused about what happened to them." I stopped myself from saying more.

"Basically, you know, for the last two years, we didn't breed them. The handwriting has been on the wall for five years that they weren't producing. And we kept hoping against hope some superstars would happen along the way, and none showed up. They just became too expensive to keep for what little protein we were getting." Randy explained some intricacies of the funding for caring for the animals and how it was difficult to get any grant money specifically for goat care.

"Yes. Justin explained that the goats are being used for heart research?"

"Well, when we decided not to keep going, all the transgenic goats we had were females.[2] They are able to be used as surrogates for producing other goats for other labs." This information was slightly soothing, in that the goats got to live, and I encouraged Randy to continue to explain. "There is a whole other project in animal sciences where they are making mutations in goats that mimic human mutations around cardiac problems in humans. Our transgenic goats are not related to the embryos that they put in when they are acting as surrogates." The spider goats are now essentially acting as gestational hosts for other goats that will be specifically bred for heart research.

I asked, "So did the goats physically move? I'm just trying to imagine where they are." I am trying to get the image of them on some gruesome operating table out of my mind.

Randy reassured me, "The goats are all in the same building that you visited. The goats haven't moved anywhere. The new researchers took over the building. The goats have gone nowhere. They are actually in the same pens that they used before. They are just having different babies, not spider goats' babies."

As I stated earlier, I am still processing the lives and deaths of spider goats. As a result, finishing this chapter with a definitive conclusion is difficult, and I must rely on the speculative.

Are spider goats becoming a footnote? This animal, constructed as a system to make a product that was then too esoteric and too expensive, is now just a part of the story of invention. We have manufactured a creation and extinction event in the Anthropocene in the period of just a few decades, and it was not caused by climate change but by capitalism fueling our desires to do things cheaper.

Before I finished my conversation with Randy, I knew I had to ask a hard question. I had worked so carefully over the several years to manage my own changing feelings about the spider goats, and this ending did seem very tragic to me.

"Randy, I am just wondering if you think this is sad. I mean, you have been with this species of goat since the beginning and have seen them through many generations of the entire trajectory of the species. Is it sad for you that they will essentially die out?" I asked.

Unfailingly generous in his thoughtful responses, Randy took a moment. "I guess in my way of thinking, it is the best ending for them. Because the only other ending would have been to euthanize them, and I felt good that that is not what happened. I felt it was good that they were still useful and still able to do work raising these new sets of animals." Clearly an anthropocentric and capitalistic way to think of a good ending, Randy is seeing extending the usefulness and hence the life of the goats as being successful.[3] Because a new source of value—as surrogates—was able to be secured for these goats, their continued existence has been, at least temporarily, extended. A stay of execution?

Randy then continued, "I think the spider goats are not lost. If we had the need to have these types of goats again, we could make them, and there are better ways to make transgenic animals now than when we started with these." Here it feels like Randy is suggesting that even if, or really when, the spider goats have all died, they will not truly cease to exist because they can be reengineered anytime there is a need for them. So perhaps it is not an extinction so much as a break in their existence, a pause of sorts, in which humans maintain the possibility of re-creating this transgenic species. Maybe it is not sad because their potential is not lost? They can be reconstituted at some point whenever we might need them again.

Do we grieve and mourn these deaths? Do we celebrate science becoming ever more efficient and economically viable? What is the qualitative difference between the cull list and the giving away of the spider goats to another researcher to their presumed death? How does this slow death (versus the immediate euthanasia) change how we think about the disposability of other animals?

I believe it is important to consider these questions as a way to interrupt the business as usual (or in this case unusual) way we manage animals. Modifying animals to be living factories or commodity producers can add to their value temporarily. But as I have seen in more than one species, once we innovate a cheaper or more efficient solution, these animals are reclassified as wasteful. Furthermore, in the case of spider goats, our modification of the animals inscribes into their bodies an expiration date. These lives then become disposable, but slowly, over time, to extract every last bit of labor power from them. This slow death extends their service to capital and biomedicine, and their lives only have meaning in their usefulness to the promise of accumulation.

NOTES

1 Brianne Bell, a lab technician, explains the multiple factors that have gone into refinements and redesigns of the purification protocols:

> We have gone through several process modifications for both protein types. Changes that are incorporated into both protein purification methods are,
> - running the process for twenty hours instead of forty-eight hours
> - optimizing the ammonium sulfate needed for precipitating the spider silk proteins
> - running the milk and arginine solution near the protein isoelectric point
> - while not a process modification, both proteins are run under the "supervision" of level controls to prevent draining out the milk solution or spider silk solution; this process has changed and improved over time as we learn more about available sensors and flow control
> - the addition of PMSF to decrease the effects of protease activity on the spider silk protein
> - process at room temperature instead of in a cold room (4°C)

2 When reproducing spider goats, a nontransgenic buck is used in order not to overproduce protein in the milk. Scientists found that when they used transgenic bucks, the protein was too large and ended up causing mastitis in the nanny goats.

3 Obviously an entirely different chapter could be written about how the breeding of scientific goats creates new relations between nannies and kids, whereby nannies and kids never get to know one another (this subject is touched on in my book; see Moore 2022). Breeding kids with cardiac defects engineers suffering into the goat's body and probably changes its life expectancy and is thus another form of both immediate and slow death for those engineered offspring.

REFERENCES

Berlant, Lauren. 2007. "Slow Death: Sovereignty, Obesity, Lateral Agency." *Critical Inquiry* 33 (Summer): 754–80.

Fish, Kenneth. 2013. *Living Factories: Biotechnology and the Unique Nature of Capitalism*. Montreal: McGill-Queen's University Press.

Gillespie, Kathryn. 2018. *The Cow with Ear Tag #1389*. Chicago: University of Chicago Press.

Gruen, Lori. 2015. *Entangled Empathy: An Alternative Ethic for Our Relationships with Animals*. New York: Lantern Books.

Haraway, Donna. 1988. "Situated Knowledges: The Science Question in Feminism and the Privilege of Partial Perspective." *Feminist Studies* 14 (3): 575–99.

Harding, Sandra. 1991. *Whose Science / Whose Knowledge? Thinking from Women's Lives*. Ithaca, NY: Cornell University Press.

Ishiguro, Kazuo. 2006. *Never Let Me Go*. New York: Vintage.

Kljajevic, Nemanja V., Igor B. Tomasevic, Zorana N. Miloradovic, Aleksandar Nedeljkovic, Jelena B. Miocinovic, and Snezana T. Jovanovic. 2018. "Seasonal Variations of Saanen Goat Milk Composition and the Impact of Climatic Conditions." *Journal of Food Science and Technology* 55 (1): 299–303.

Moore, Lisa Jean. 2017. *Catch and Release: The Enduring yet Vulnerable Horseshoe Crab*. New York: New York University Press.

———. 2022. *Our Transgenic Future: Genetic Modification, Animals and the Will to Change Nature*. New York: New York University Press.

Moore, Lisa Jean, and Mary Kosut. 2013. *Buzz: Urban Beekeeping and the Power of the Bee*. New York: New York University Press.

10

Entanglements of Species and Injustice through Carceral Violence

DAVID PELLOW

This chapter considers and responds to the spectrum of multispecies violence, social death, and physical death associated with the prison-industrial complex, the linkages between government and industry in the institutional practices associated with policing, surveillance, and incarceration. While prisons, jails, and other carceral facilities are spaces where scholars have documented a range of harms committed against imprisoned humans, they are also sites of direct and indirect violence perpetrated against nonhuman animals and ecosystems. I organize these harms across four terrains: (1) the impact of prisons and jails on sensitive nonhuman animal well-being and habitat, which regularly results in the degradation of ecosystems and the physical death of animals; (2) the consumption of nonhumans by incarcerated persons via daily food service operations; (3) the killing of nonhumans through the use of prisoners as farm and slaughterhouse workers, both on- and off-site, and its effects on humans as well; and (4) the "ghostly matter" (Gordon 2008) of sedimented violence associated with prisons being located atop former industrial-scale animal-killing facilities.

Drawing on environmental justice, animal studies, and abolitionist scholarship, I consider the ways in which the drive for punishment as reflected in the US criminal legal system in particular, and in US culture and politics more broadly, shapes the experiences of both humans and nonhumans with oppression and death, as they are routinely consumed by these forces.

Environmental Justice, Animal Studies, and Abolition

Scholars have, for decades, documented the pattern in which marginalized groups (e.g., people of color, Indigenous communities, low-wealth and global South populations, LGBTQ+ people) experience environmental and climate threats that are outsized and disproportionate. These threats include living in close proximity to or working within polluting industrial facilities, greater vulnerability to extreme weather events and pesticide drift, and the health risks that accompany such exposure (Bullard 2000; Hoover 2018; Sze 2020; Taylor 2000; Whyte 2017). These inequities are referred to as examples of environmental racism, environmental injustice, and climate injustice and have sparked a powerful grassroots movement that has pushed back against corporations and governments that have perpetrated these harms and that has articulated a vision of justice that integrates ecological sustainability with equity.

More recently, scholars and activists have turned their attention to the ways in which environmental and climate injustices are occurring within and around carceral facilities, creating additional vulnerabilities and threats to the health and well-being of already-marginalized persons who are caged in inherently dangerous environments. Some of these threats include contaminated water and toxic air quality, extreme heat, proximity to hazardous waste, and low-quality nutrition (Gribble and Pellow 2022; Opsal and Malin 2019; Pellow 2017; Perdue 2018). As with the environmental justice (EJ), climate justice, and food justice movements in "free" residential communities, we are witnessing the leadership and bravery of incarcerated persons resisting institutional violence within prisons and jails, thus constituting a critical front in these grassroots political formations. And while this activism is not a recent phenomenon, it has only been recently acknowledged in the literatures on environmental, climate, and food justice. This development presents the opportunity to integrate and explore the intersections between environmental justice and abolitionist theory and politics. For example, a number of scholars have argued that the logics and aims of EJ scholarship and the EJ movement must evolve to embrace abolition as a method and goal, since much of the former has problematically relied on a framework and strategy that views the state as a site of resolution. Accordingly, for EJ scholars and activists to adopt an abolitionist framework would entail taking on a more cautious and critical orientation toward the state, developing perspectives that look to nonstatist approaches for addressing environmental injustices (Pellow 2016, 2017; Pulido 2017; Pulido, Kohl, and Cotton 2016; Ranganathan and Bratman 2019).

And while abolitionists focused on imprisonment tend to be among the most visible researchers and community advocates using this terminology today, many animal rights and animal liberation scholars and activists have adopted the language of abolition as well. These are advocates and researchers who reject any use of nonhumans—whether for consumption, food, clothing, entertainment, science, and so on—for human benefit. Claire Jean Kim embraces the broad perspective of abolition from an animal liberation orientation, writing that "animal abolition's radical instincts are entirely correct: it is right in its unforgiving critique of welfarism and right in its call for revolutionary change" (2018, 29). However, she pointedly critiques this movement for its lack of willingness to integrate a racial justice perspective into its framework and, in particular, its resistance to understanding the ways in which anti-Blackness is a major force within society and the animal rights movement. She contends that if animal liberationists linked "their cause to black liberation," they could "achieve a clearer understanding of the structures of power they are struggling against by questioning its continuing humanist assumptions" (Kim 2018, 29). Kim's work is an important step toward drawing deeper connections between social justice and animal liberation. In recent years, scholars have been using terms like "multispecies justice" and "ecological justice" to fill in some of the key gaps to build these bridges (Brisman 2008; Celemajer et al. 2021; Davis et al. 2019; Schlosberg 2014).

These concepts underscore that humans are a part of webs of multispecies kinships and relationships that require consideration and respect for all beings. Petra Tschakert (2021) embraces multispecies justice and argues that this is a major missing ingredient in much of the discourse and practice of climate and environmental justice movements. Generally speaking, these political formations have paid little attention to the health and well-being of nonhumans, and Tschakert contends that the focus on the "unfair distribution of harmful emissions" might be less effective than conceptualizing justice "as a matter of relations" (2021, 279). She sees relational perspectives as a way of recognizing and mobilizing around developing multispecies spaces that are fraught with exclusions and violence but that are also spaces of possibility for coexistence. Recalling Kim's point that animal liberationists' vision of abolition tends to lack a focus on racial justice, it must also be said that prison and slavery abolitionists tend to lack a focus on animal liberation, and the same can be said for climate and environmental justice movements, as Tschakert has noted. Thus, a much more "deeply intersectional" (Malin and Ryder 2018) approach to social change can bring these concepts and movements together in greater collaboration and conversation to find points of integration among racial, environmental, climate, and food justice and animal liberation. Elsewhere I have variously called this "multispecies abolition democracy" or "total liberation," which are terms that point to an ethic of justice that is inclusive of humans, nonhumans, and ecosystems (Pellow 2014).

The concept of "carceral logics" is a productive tool for illustrating and linking these ideas. For Lori Gruen and Justin Marceau (2022, 2), carceral logics reflect "the harmfulness of our system of mass incarceration and the harm that humans do to nonhumans." For example, Karen Morin (2016, 2017) argues that the parallels between the agricultural-industrial complex and the prison-industrial complex are stark and reveal the violence that dominant institutions perpetrate across species and spaces of the prison, the slaughterhouse, the zoo, and the research laboratory. Furthermore, the quest for punitive responses to index crimes, combined with the more generally repressive orientation of the US racial state toward BIPOC communities (independent of any alleged criminal activity), results in mass incarceration (Alexander 2020; Berger 2014; Fassin 2018; Lytle Hernandez 2017; Story 2019), a system that produces extraordinary harm, social death, and physical death among humans and across multiple species. Furthermore, as Gruen and Marceau (2022) note, when the dominant societal response to nonhuman animal abuse is occasionally elevated from the usual mode of acceptance or erasure of such harms, it tends to involve an embrace of punitive approaches that rely on the criminal legal system, which only reinforces cycles of violence. In an ethnographic study of an animal shelter in the Los Angeles area, Katja M. Guenther writes, "Even as rescuers 'save' dogs from the carceral institution of a high-kill shelter, they encourage the incarceration of those individuals and entire social categories who they believe hurt animals, namely dark-skinned, urban men" (2020, 177). Similarly, the passage of "Desmond's Law"—the first law in the US that allows animal welfare advocates to testify in court cases involving animal cruelty—was driven in part by a desire to promote carceral solutions to nonhuman animal abuse and has reportedly resulted in "a significant increase in jail time" for defendants (Gruen 2022, 402) while not producing demonstrable improvements in animal welfare. Guenther demonstrates how these practices—and the motivations behind them—reflect harmful intersections of the welfare state, the carceral state, and the anthroparchal state. Thus, carceral logics fail conspicuously to reduce harm across species.

In the rest of this chapter, I demonstrate how carceral logics impact the health and well-being of humans and nonhumans across the four terrains mentioned earlier. Taken separately and together, these terrains reflect how death-dealing at sites of industrialized violence produces harms across species and ecosystems, which should be a matter of great concern to scholars of environmental justice, animal studies, and abolition.

Prisons as Threats to Sensitive Nonhuman Well-Being, Habitat, and Ecosystems

Letcher County, Kentucky, was the site of a proposed federal prison project that was slated to be placed on land where mountaintop removal (MTR) coal mining has occurred, that is, where mountains have been destroyed to extract coal, reducing ecosystems to poisonous rubble and dust. The Letcher County site is also home to second-growth forests that serve as habitat for the Indiana bat and gray bats, both of which are endangered species (suffering from white nose syndrome), whose fate was further placed in jeopardy as a result of this proposal. Fortunately, in June 2019, a coalition of twenty-one prisoners and several allied groups succeeded in stopping the Letcher County prison project when the Federal Bureau of Prisons withdrew the project because it would have threatened the health of prisoners, nonhuman species, and local ecosystems and the environmental impact report (as required by the National Environmental Policy Act) did an insufficient job of addressing those impacts. This outcome was touted as a major victory for environmental and climate justice, but it should also be viewed as a win for animal rights and multispecies justice since the fates of humans and nonhumans were linked in this battle.

In June 2000, the activist group Critical Resistance brought a lawsuit against the California Department of Corrections in opposition to the state's proposal to construct a prison in the town of Delano, California. This grassroots action was innovative in both the stakeholders involved and the framing of the struggle, with environmental justice, animal conservation, and prison abolitionist groups collaborating to highlight the anticipated harms the prison would cause to local air quality and the region's water system and the threats it would bring to the habitat of endangered and threatened species like the Tipton kangaroo rat and the San Joaquin Valley kit fox. In addition to Critical Resistance, the coalition included the California Prison Moratorium Project, the NAACP, the Rainforest Action Network, the National Lawyers Guild, and a group called Friends of the Kangaroo Rat. Ultimately, they lost the legal battle, and the prison was constructed; but the strategy of framing prisons as a threat to human and nonhuman well-being was innovative and groundbreaking.

Both the Letcher County and Delano prison cases reveal how the very act of building a prison can threaten the habitat and the lives of a host of nonhuman species, placing in critical jeopardy the well-being of animals that are already listed as endangered. Thus, *carceral logics can harm and kill nonhumans well before any humans are even caged in a prison*, reflecting the urgent need for prison abolitionists to take seriously the issue of animal liberation and the need for animal liberationists and multispecies justice frameworks to take seriously the need for theorizing and mobilizing around the prison-industrial complex.

Consumption of Nonhumans by Incarcerated Persons

Historically, the provision of food to incarcerated persons was often linked to a system of rewards and punishments, which reflected the view that consuming nonhuman animal products was more desirable and a privilege. In nineteenth-century carceral institutions in the US, "incoming prisoners were provided typically with bread and water until they had earned the right for such luxuries as meat or cheese" (Bosworth 2002, 73). More recently, food products like "nutriloaf" have been the subject of controversy because many incarcerated persons have claimed that these amalgams of animal and plant-based products are so unappetizing that they constitute cruel and unusual punishment. Among the primary aims of producing and serving prisoners nutriloaf are meeting basic protein and caloric requirements for survival, behavior modification (e.g., nutriloaf can be consumed without the use of trays and utensils that prisoners might otherwise use as weapons), and cost reduction. One type of nutriloaf served in US prisons contains "a mixture of cubed whole wheat bread, nondairy cheese, raw carrots, spinach, seedless raisins, beans, vegetable oil, tomato paste, powdered milk and dehydrated potato flakes" (Spanos 2013, 240). Thus, prison food services generally rely on nonhuman animal products that are openly weaponized against incarcerated persons, indicating a double move that involves unacknowledged violence against more-than-just-humans to produce the food and an embrace of the use of food as discipline against humans.

With respect to using nonhumans for food in the carceral system, the California Prison Industry Authority (CALPIA) is the state agency that oversees the work assignments for thousands of incarcerated persons in the state's prison system. CALPIA produces these goods and services for federal, state, county, and city governments as well as for tribal governments, and each year, the agency makes and sells some $65 million worth of agricultural and food products, including meat, eggs, and milk. By far the largest purchaser of these goods from CALPIA is the California Department of Corrections and Rehabilitation (CDCR), demonstrating that the carceral system is at once a major producer and consumer of nonhuman animal products. Furthermore, that agency is the single largest food purchaser and provider in the state of California, delivering roughly 130 million meals each year throughout California's three dozen prisons. And while there are vegetarian options available to a small subset of incarcerated persons, the overwhelming majority of meals contain animal products, which means the California prison system is a source of considerable suffering and violence directed at nonhumans, a site where extraordinary numbers of animal bodies are consumed every day.

Of course, the state is just one of many actors involved in the production and distribution of food for carceral institutions. Corporations are heavily involved in this process as well. According to the US Department of Justice, in late 2006 or early 2007, John Soules Foods—at the time the leading fajita meat-processing company in the US, according to the firm—was alleged to have altered or mislabeled raw "beef trimmings" before selling it to wholesale purchasers. Apparently the company was having trouble getting the meat to freeze properly, so it sold it to an independent meat broker who agreed to resell it as pet food. John Soules Foods chose not to relabel the boxes containing the meat because it believed the meat broker would do so. Unfortunately, that did not happen: the first meat broker "violated the agreement and sold the boxes of pet food beef trimmings to another meat broker for human consumption," and some of that beef ended up in the Bureau of Prisons system and was served to incarcerated persons (Gilna 2014).

Complaints about the quality of food in US prisons are legion, with outbreaks of disease and sickness being reported on a regular basis. For example, in 2011, there was a salmonella outbreak at United States Penitentiary, Canaan, in Pennsylvania, which resulted in 513 lawsuits. That outbreak was caused by improperly stored chicken, which caused vomiting, nausea, chills, headaches, abdominal pain, and diarrhea (Gilna 2014). In fact, incarcerated persons are 6.4 times more likely to get sick from food-related illnesses than members of the general public (Fassler and Brown 2017). "The dehumanization of incarcerated populations has allowed the government and private contractors to serve inmates foods that are pest-infested, expired, improperly stored, in insufficient portions, and/or 'not fit for human consumption'" (Austin 2018, 58).

The preceding examples illustrate how the carceral system remains committed to the mass consumption of nonhuman animals in its daily food service operations and how the quality and safety of that food is routinely compromised. These practices signal the ways in which the othering and mistreatment of incarcerated humans, through the delivery of substandard nutrition, and the destruction of nonhuman life are entangled and inseparable in the prison-industrial complex and the animal-industrial complex—the ways in which capitalism and animal industries are linked (Noske 1989; Twine 2012). In other words, the social death of humans and the physical death of nonhumans are integrated processes in this single system.

Killing Nonhumans by Prisoners as Farm and Slaughterhouse Workers

This section of the chapter features a much lengthier examination of violence directed at nonhumans since that is the core focus of the book volume. There are numerous slaughterhouses around the nation that are run by corporations or states using incarcerated labor. This dynamic facilitates the erasure of violent labor and the mass killing of nonhuman animals since it occurs in spaces that are far removed from the public eye (Pachirat 2011).

Mt. McKinley Meats and Sausages is a state-owned facility operated by the Alaska Department of Corrections and is one of the state's three meat-processing companies (Associated Press 2015). The Lorton Correctional Complex was a prison built in the early 1900s in the Washington, DC, area, originally as a reformatory that was a Progressive-era experiment aimed at rehabilitating persons who broke the law by ensuring that they developed skills and worked hard every day. A core part of that work involved farming. In addition to harvesting crops, the prison had a dairy farm, a poultry ranch, a hog ranch, and a slaughterhouse—all of which were tended by incarcerated persons (Goran 2016). In 2001, Colorado Correctional Industries (CCI) began employing incarcerated persons to raise and harvest tilapia fish on a fish farm owned by the company Quixotic Farming. Quixotic was selling the fish to Seattle Fish corporation, which then sold it to Whole Foods. Quixotic Farming was producing approximately 1.2 million pounds of tilapia each year, and it paid workers between $0.74 and $4 per day (Knauf 2015). When some consumers found out about this arrangement, there was a major outcry, with protests in front of Whole Foods stores due to concerns about the exploitation of incarcerated persons, prompting the company to cancel its contract with the supplier (Mitchell 2015). In addition to CCI's tilapia operation, the company also produces a range of animal-based food products, including buffalo ground meat, water buffalo patties, water buffalo brats, and Italian goat sausage. CCI also produces leather horse saddles. All of these industrialized killing facilities function around the premise that hard work will serve as a rehabilitative force in the lives of incarcerated persons and facilitate profit making for the industry involved and that nonhuman animal suffering and death are of no concern and are in fact required to achieve those ends.

Rikers Island jail in New York is infamous. The jail's population is overwhelmingly made up of people of color—fully 90 percent (Broyard and Seville 2021)—and has animated protests against the harsh conditions of confinement in that facility in recent years. In the fall of 2021, protesters gathered around New York's City Hall to register protests against particularly brutal circumstances evident at Rikers Island jail, where numerous incarcerated persons have been injured or died in recent years as a result of overcrowding and poor management of the facility. According to government officials, there were at least fifteen reported inmate deaths in 2021 (Broyard and Seville 2021). Melania Brown is the sister of Layleen Polanco, a transgender incarcerated person who died in the facility, and she stated, "My sister was a human. My sister deserves to be here today. *They treated her worse than they would treat their own animals. Rikers is a human slaughterhouse*" (Cranmore 2021, emphasis added).

If Rikers Island can be called a *human* slaughterhouse, that horrifying portrayal would be incomplete without attention to the fact that it was also a *nonhuman* slaughterhouse. The island has long been the site of a large rat population, and many attempts were made to eradicate them, including the use of poisonous gas, poison bait, and hunting dogs (Steinberg 2010). But more formally, for many years, Rikers was the site of a farm where nonhuman animals were slaughtered for mass consumption. In the 1920s, there was a hog-farming operation at Rikers, as noted by then–Correction Commissioner Richard Patterson, who wrote about some two dozen prisoners who were employed to feed and raise several hundred hogs on the island. As Peter F. Amoroso—one of Patterson's successors—wrote in his 1941 report, in addition to the "variety of vegetables" that some fifty inmates raised on the one hundred-acre farm on the property, there was also "a piggery, with 700 swine, [that] produces 110,000 pounds of pork annually" (1941, 70). Amoroso's successor as correction commissioner, Albert Williams, noted that "the hennery was extended, grounds graded and a modern slaughter house installed" (1951, 32). There was a poultry farm on the island for many years as well (Kross 1954). Commissioner Amoroso also wrote about the fact that the island was the site of a growing landfill waste dump. He noted, "Original land 87 acres in extent. Increased to 400 acres by dumping ashes and other wastes. Present buildings [Penitentiary, Workhouse, Hospital] largely on original land but piling under foundations necessary in some places. Slight settlement has occurred but now apparently stopped. . . . Dumping by the Department of Sanitation stopped in vicinity of the institution and dumps are landscaped by Department of Parks in preparation for World's Fair. When broken down, dumps make tillable farm land" (Amoroso 1941, 68).

The layers of environmental and ecological injustice at Rikers Island are staggering. The island was used as a landfill, a jail, and an animal slaughter operation. In other words, on the very same stretch of earth, people were incarcerated and experienced the social death of being caged, as nonhumans were "raised" and slaughtered for consumption at the jail. This is truly a story of "when animals die."

Outside the strict confines of the formal built environment of the carceral system, we find that each year, hundreds of people who are convicted on drug-related charges are sent to work in chicken slaughter houses ("processing plants") in Arkansas, Missouri, Oklahoma, and Texas as a prison diversion project that is a collaboration between the criminal legal system and faith-based organizations like Christian Alcoholics & Addicts in Recovery (CAAIR). The guiding premise of this initiative is that hard work and religious training will "cure" these individuals of any future impulses to engage in unlawful activity. Unfortunately, the labor involved is highly dangerous, frequently resulting in serious occupational health hazards and injuries for the workers, and is necessarily focused on the mass slaughter of chickens. This case reveals the reach of the criminal legal system into corporate settings where nonhumans are being sacrificed as a method of securing cheap (unpaid) human labor while also relieving prisons and jails of overcrowding (because the workers are housed in dormitories operated by CAAIR). This case also underscores how multiple institutions and sectors, including religious organizations, are involved in the punishment of both humans and nonhumans.

CAAIR was founded in 2006–7 by Donald and Janet Wilkerson and Rodney and Louise Dunnam with the goal of assisting persons addicted to illegal drugs and alcohol with their recovery through a program that did not require admission fees or other forms of financial payment up front. CAAIR's emphasis on combining adherence to Christian beliefs with labor that involves nonhuman animal slaughter reflects a long tradition of Christian doctrine that views humans as having a divine right to subjugate more-than-humans as they see fit (Linzey 2017), an ideology known as "anthroparchy" (Guenther 2020).

The multispecies violence associated with CAAIR's programming stems from the career experiences of many of its cofounders and key staffers. Rodney Dunnam was a founding partner of CAAIR and has a "background . . . in the cattle industry and business" (CAAIR, n.d.-a). Donald Wilkerson is one of the founding partners of CAAIR and is the vice president of operations. "Donald has a farming background" (CAAIR, n.d.-b). CAAIR cofounder Janet Wilkerson was the vice president of human resources for Peterson Farms and served as a spokesperson for Simmons Food and other leading poultry companies. Jim Lovell was also a key person involved in the growth of CAAIR, with years of experience in "farming, ranching and construction" (CAAIR, n.d.-a). According to the Center for Investigative Reporting, CAAIR was "originally launched by food executives having trouble finding employees for low-pay, high-risk all-hours work at chicken processing plants" (Brown 2017). Despite CAAIR's official mission focused on supporting rehabilitation, the organization has only one licensed counselor and no certified treatment or recovery program. Judges in courts across Arkansas, Missouri, Oklahoma, and Texas have been sending around 280 young men to CAAIR annually, as an alternative to incarceration, apparently guided by a belief in that organization's mission. As one judge told a defendant named Brad McGahey, "You need to learn a work ethic. . . . I'm sending you to CAAIR" (Harris and Walter 2017b). Soon McGahey found himself working in a poultry plant, ripping and suctioning the guts, blood, and feathers from slaughtered chickens rapidly moving down a conveyor on metal hooks, the final products of which were destined for grocery stores and fast-food chain restaurants. He worked for no pay, and CAAIR received remuneration from the company. "It was a slave camp," McGahey said. "I can't believe the court sent me there." In a particularly gruesome accident, McGahey's hand was mangled in the conveyor belt at the plant (Harris and Walter 2017a).

Around two hundred men live at the CAAIR facility in a dormitory, and most of them work for Simmons Food, a company that brings in an annual revenue or more than $1 billion. Their job is to slaughter and process chickens for some of the largest and most profitable stores, restaurants, and pet-food distributors and brands, including KFC, Walmart, Popeyes Louisiana Kitchen, PetSmart, and the television celebrity cook Rachael Ray's Nutrish brand. Over a period of seven years, CAAIR's revenue was recorded as $11 million. A number of investigations and lawsuits have revealed that these so-called rehabilitation programs are not much more than state-supported forced labor camps for private companies. As one class-action lawsuit against CAAIR stated, "Despite performing demanding, dangerous, and dirty work, the residents do not receive any wages. Instead, CAAIR keeps all of the wages earned by the residents. CAAIR generates over one million dollars a year in revenue, largely based on the slave labor provided by residents. CAAIR's officers, however, do not work for free, and they pay themselves hundreds of thousands of dollars annually in compensation" (Fochtman and O'Neal 2017, 6–7).

It is well documented that jobs in slaughterhouses are among the most hazardous in the nation, and this program reflects those trends, as numerous workers have suffered a range of injuries, including bacterial infections, maiming by machines, and acid burns. In CAAIR worker Roger McMullen's workers' compensation claim, in response to the question "What is the nature of the injury or illness?" he wrote, "Can't hardly use my hands," and in response to the question "Describe the details how the injury occurred," he wrote, "Hanging froze chicken parts" (McMullen 2012). According to court records, a number of CAAIR workers were sent to prison because their injuries prevented them from working. Not surprisingly, other workers who witness those consequences do their best to work through the pain of injuries in order to avoid the same fate. "They work you to death. They work you every single day," said Nate Turner, who graduated from CAAIR in 2015. "It's a work camp. They know people are desperate to get out of jail, and they'll do whatever they can do to stay out of prison" (Harris and Walter 2017b). "You can either work or you can go to prison," McGahey remembered administrators telling him. "It's up to you." He already had made up his mind. "I'll take prison over this place," he said. "Anywhere is better than here" (Harris and Walter 2017b).

Mark Fochtman (2017) worked at a Simmons Foods chicken farm as ordered by a judge in the Washington County Drug Court in the state of Arkansas. In an affidavit as part of a suit against CAAIR, he recalled horrifying details associated with working in a slaughter operation: "My job at the chicken farm was a dirty, disgusting job. Each day I was responsible for collecting the birds from the chicken houses that had died during the previous day. On a typical day I collected over 100 dead birds. I disposed of the dead birds in an empty chicken house. That chicken house was full of thousands of decaying and rotting chickens covered in maggots." Fochtman continued, "Other employees from CAAIR also worked disgusting and dangerous jobs. For example, I remember seeing CAAIR employees who worked in Simmons' Live Hang Department returning to CAAIR with their faces covered in bird feces from when they hung live chickens on hooks above their heads as part of Simmons' poultry processing operation. The birds routinely defecated in the mouths and on the faces of those employees." Arthur Copeland was sent to work in a chicken slaughterhouse by a drug court in 2016. Like others in his position, he mistakenly believed he was going to a rehabilitation program "but instead found himself hanging more than 60 live chickens a minute along an assembly line." He sustained a serious injury while working at the chicken plant but was threatened with prison if he stopped working. He later had a drug relapse while in the program and was sent to prison (Harris and Walter 2017a).

These testimonials and reports offer a graphic representation of the intertwined nature of abuse directed at both human workers and nonhuman animals in the interest of profit making and control over disposable bodies. CAAIR has been the target of several lawsuits that allege that it violates the US Constitution and the Constitution of Arkansas, both of which prohibit forced, unpaid labor (except as punishment for a crime, but in this case, the defendants have been charged but not convicted of a crime), and they allege that CAAIR violates the state's labor law, which guarantees that employees receive minimum wage and overtime pay.

The irony is that this alternate sentencing—through what are called "diversion courts"—is largely driven by the well-intentioned efforts of many community leaders to keep nonviolent persons who violate the law—usually through drug-related activities—out of overcrowded and dangerous prison environments. The drug diversion program in Oklahoma was formalized through legislation passed by the state assembly two decades ago, which requires judges to send defendants to rehabilitation programs rather than prison. Despite how troubling the CAAIR program is, being sent to a drug diversion program is often the preferred outcome for many defendants who would otherwise face prison time.

Numerous studies indicate that there are stark racial disparities in these proceedings, with Black and Latinx defendants being far more likely to be sent directly to jail or prison while white defendants are more likely to be given the opportunity to participate in drug diversion and treatment programs (Nicosia, MacDonald, and Arkes 2013; Schlesinger 2013). The CAAIR program bears this out, with the majority of participants being white, which means that white defendants and people of color received differential but equally harsh treatment, with the former being subjected to dangerous work in slaughterhouses and the latter being subjected to the violence of human caging. And while some observers might draw a distinction between the slaughterhouse and a prison, I see them as interlinked, since both are sites of forced labor and immobility, social death, and physical death. The blurred boundaries between prisons and work camps reflect an important dimension of what scholars have long called the "prison-industrial complex" to describe the relationship between the state and corporations that collaborate and benefit from mass incarceration.

The broader impacts of animal-killing industries must also be taken into account in order to grasp the full socioecological spectrum of the violence they perpetrate. A 2018 report by the Environmental Integrity Project found that 75 percent of large meat-processing plants in the US that directly dump waste into streams and rivers routinely contaminate waterways and violate their pollution-control permits, often contributing to the death of fish and other aquatic life each year (Environmental Integrity Project 2018b). In one case, the Pilgrim's Pride poultry plant in Live Oak, Florida—part of the largest meat company on Earth, JBS—racked up thirty-seven water-pollution violations, contributing massively to the fouling of the Suwanee River. JBS also owns a hog slaughterhouse in Beardstown, Illinois, where a spill of twenty-nine million gallons of hog waste into a river killed sixty-four thousand fish in March 2015 (Environmental Integrity Project 2018b). Moreover, according to Eric Schaeffer, executive director of the Environmental Integrity Project, "This water pollution is really an environmental justice issue, because many of these slaughterhouses are owned by wealthy international companies, and they are contaminating the rivers and drinking water supplies of rural, often lower-income, minority communities" (Environmental Integrity Project 2018a). Thus, these meat-processing plant workers slaughter thousands of hogs and chickens, which creates contamination that then kills thousands of other animals off-site, in a practice that also frequently disproportionately impacts marginalized human communities because of the location of such facilities.

Meatpacking workers have significantly higher rates of severe injury and death compared to workers in other food-processing sectors, and that harm usually derives from accidents involving nonhuman animals, machines, and toxic chemicals (Carrillo and Ipsen 2021; York 2004). In a groundbreaking study (Johnson et al. 1997), researchers found poultry slaughterhouse workers have a higher than average probability of developing various forms of cancer, even after controlling for other factors such as smoking tobacco. These trends reflect the fact that both slaughterhouse workers—whether free or incarcerated—and our nonhuman relatives face exploitation and abuse, which necessitates a multispecies justice framework for understanding the socioecological impacts of capitalism and incarceration.

Ghostly Matters and Sedimented Violence: Prisons atop Former Animal-Killing Facilities

The Northwest Detention Center is a 1,575-bed migrant prison in the Seattle-Tacoma region of Washington State. The vast majority of the migrant prisoners are people of color and low-wealth persons. The facility is right next door to a federally designated Superfund site known as the "Tacoma Tar Pits," where for three decades, a company "transformed coal into gas and spewed toxic sludge into the soil" (Kamb 2012). As if its location adjacent to a toxic sludge field were not enough, the prison is also located in a flood plain and on a site packed with fill material that has been judged to have a high probability of liquefying in the event of an earthquake (Kamb 2012). Moreover, the site will also be directly in the path of any future volcanic mudslides that will occur if nearby Mount Rainier—an episodically active volcano—were to erupt. While these markers of environmental and climate injustices have been documented by journalists and activists, what has generally escaped much notice is the fact that the same site on which the prison was built used to be a meat-packing plant, previously owned by the Carstens corporation (Carstens was incorporated in Tacoma, Washington, in 1904).

In other words, this very property where humans are caged and mistreated stands on the remains of a site where the bodies of nonhuman animals were dismembered and packaged for sale and consumption. The layers of violence and social and physical death on that space are extraordinary, and they reflect at least two core imperatives of the US nation-state: control over the bodies of migrants and a commitment to the sustained and increased killing and consumption of nonhumans. As an illustration of that twin commitment, consider the policies of the Trump administration, which included an overtly racist and hostile posture toward migrants seeking entry from majority people of color nations and a public declaration of the meatpacking industry as "critical infrastructure" through Trump's April 28, 2020, invocation of the Defense Production Act, which kept that industry operating at full capacity during the COVID-19 pandemic.

The sociologist Avery Gordon argues in her book *Ghostly Matters* (2008) that past or shadowy social forces can frequently shape contemporary life in more complicated ways than most social analysts presume. She contends that "haunting" is a manifestation of those historical forces:

> Haunting is one way in which abusive systems of power make themselves known and their impacts felt in everyday life, especially when they are supposedly over and done with (slavery, for instance) . . . or when their oppressive nature is denied. . . . Haunting is not the same as being exploited, traumatized, or oppressed, although it usually involves these experiences or is produced by them. What's distinctive about haunting is that it is an animated state in which a repressed or unresolved social violence is making itself known, . . . when home becomes unfamiliar, when your bearings on the world lose direction, when the over and done with comes alive. (Gordon 2008, xvi)

The Northwest Detention Center has been rocked by numerous protests from migrant prisoners incarcerated within its walls, who are supported by allies on the outside who seek to make visible their struggles. In a manner of Gordon's haunting, the most frequent form of protest within the prison has been the hunger strike. For example, in April 2017, more than one hundred migrant prisoners in the facility went on a hunger strike to call attention to the mistreatment they routinely experience in the form of poor-quality food (Northwest Detention Center Resistance 2017). The fact that this space of brutal, racist oppression against migrants is also a space of resistance against an unjust food system, all of which is occurring on a plot of land where nonhuman animals were killed, dismembered, and packaged for consumption, suggests an unnerving and grisly example of Gordon's haunting. The afterlives of violence and killing directed at nonhumans might be said to have indirectly influenced the current struggle over and against social death.

Addressing and Resisting Intersecting Forms of Institutional Violence through Multispecies Ecological Democracy

Scholars studying environmental justice have only recently begun to take notice of the linkages between EJ struggles and the prison-industrial complex and to seriously consider the question of multispecies justice. Animal studies scholarship tends to give scant attention to broader environmental and environmental justice considerations but offers important perspectives and tools for grappling with multispecies carceral logics (Gruen and Marceau 2022; Guenther 2020; Morin 2016, 2017). And abolitionist and critical prison studies research has yet to center environmental justice or animal liberation in its orbit, so this chapter seeks to integrate key insights and lessons from each of these areas of research.

In this chapter, I have documented and analyzed a range of forms of violence—including abuse, exploitation, injury, social death and physical death—that impacts humans and nonhumans in the prison- and animal-industrial complexes. Specifically, this includes the harms that carceral systems perpetrate against sensitive nonhuman habits and ecosystems, resulting in the physical death of animals; the mass consumption of nonhuman animals by persons incarcerated in jails and prisons; the mass killing of nonhuman animals by prisoners working as laborers on farms and slaughterhouses; and the "ghostly matter" of layered, sedimented violence associated with prisons being located atop former animal-killing facilities. Each of these terrains is meant to illustrate the ways in which the killing of nonhumans is intertwined with and made possible through the abuse of humans, through a combination of incarceration and forced labor, revealing troubling intersections of speciesism with social, racial, and environmental injustice. Thus, carceral logics are evident in the ways in which institutional violence spills over the species border, reducing incarcerated persons to interchangeable cogs in a machinery that reinforces social death for human prisoners and physical death for nonhuman animals.

The recent scholarship on multispecies and ecological justice offers an opportunity to think more deeply and broadly about how scholars and advocates might address these intersecting forms of institutional violence (Brisman 2008; Celemajer et al. 2021; Davis et al 2019; Tschakert 2021). While multispecies and ecological justice is certainly a key missing element from most formulations of environmental justice and prison abolition, I would argue that its realization requires something more. Justice is, at best, a practice and a process for ensuring fairness and equity, but it requires an infrastructure for its realization. Toward that end, I propose "multispecies ecological democracy" as a term that signals a way of imagining, supporting, and practicing multispecies, ecological, and environmental justice. By "multispecies ecological democracy," I mean those practices and infrastructures that begin with the recognition that all human societies are multispecies societies and that we need processes that facilitate consideration, equity, and respect across those populations and the places, spaces, and ecosystems that we rely on for sustenance and survival.

A multispecies ecological democracy will also have to be marked by what Lori Gruen calls an "abolition ethic of care," which "encourages the development of empathy and compassion for all, no matter what species they belong to or what mistakes they have made" (2022, 413). Importantly, an abolition ethic of care also recognizes that all animals, "including human animals, have deep capacities for care" (414) and would rest on a foundational belief that we can reimagine our caring relationships within and across species in ways that do not rely on punishment or other carceral solutions to achieve justice. Feminist care theorists have produced important ideas about how best to reframe the Marxist concept of social reproduction—actions that make possible labor participation in the production process—to include "life-making activities" such as caring for family members and the fulfillment of our basic needs through families, schools, health care, and the like (Federici 2012; Gottlieb 2022; Poo 2015; Tronto 2012). And community leaders across each of these spaces have invested enormous volumes of time and energy into that work, including environmental justice advocates, who have always articulated a care politics as it relates to our daily lives (e.g., the environment includes those places where we live, work, play, learn, eat, and pray) and who have insisted on caring for the land, water, and all living things. Addressing some of those concerns is the concept and practice of the "solidarity economy," which places its primary emphases on cooperation and mutual aid, a model that is witnessing a resurgence as social inequalities, health disparities, and climate-change-driven disasters produce dislocations, evictions, hunger and thirst, and illness while governments are either absent or incapable of addressing those needs. The solidarity economy exists in the work of everyday people to mobilize medicine, clean water, food, shelter, and other critical resources to be shared with those who need it most.

The people leading this work are community advocates who are "caring with" rather than only "caring for" one another in order to reduce power differentials and increase equity. Bridging Gruen's abolition ethic of care with these Marxist feminist concepts of care offers an opportunity to imagine what a politics and practice of care and solidarity might look like if they included attention to the ways in which both humans and more-than-just-humans engage in "life-making activities." An increasing number of incarcerated and formerly incarcerated persons are drawing these connections in their writings, artwork, and speeches. Timothy James Young is an innocent African American man on death row at San Quentin State Prison. He recently collaborated with the artist jackie summell to create the Solitary Garden, a sculpture and garden project that symbolizes what a landscape without prisons could look like. As Young points out, it is also a multispecies landscape: "I think of the birds, bees, and butterflies that visit the garden, I think of the deer that are out there feasting on our spring harvest, in doing so, this reminds me of our interdependence with the non-human world" (Young 2020).

Ultimately, the realization of any form of multispecies ecological democracy will require what Kathryn Yusoff (2021) calls an "inhumanities" framework—a set of imaginings and practices that recognize that the very concept of the "human" is rooted in Western Enlightenment ideologies of racism, white supremacy, genocide, and ecocide. In other words, we must rethink and redefine what it means to be human in order to challenge speciesism, racism, heteropatriarchy, and other forms of dominance. In my view, the prison-industrial complex is an ideal place to start that conversation.

REFERENCES

Alexander, Michelle. 2020. *The New Jim Crow: Mass Incarceration in the Age of Colorblindness*. New York: New Press.

Amoroso, Peter. 1941. *Report of the Department of Correction, City of New York, Commissioner*. New York: City of New York. www.correctionhistory.org.

Associated Press. 2015. "Alaska Farmers Want Prison-Run Slaughterhouse Kept Open." November 16, 2015.

Austin, Michaela Anastasia. 2018. "Hungry, Sick and Malnourished: Prison Food as Cruel and Unusual Punishment." In *Environmental Injustice behind Bars: Toxic Imprisonment in America*, edited by David Pellow, 55–62. Santa Barbara: University of California Santa Barbara's Prison Environmental Justice Project.

Berger, Dan. 2014. *Captive Nation: Black Prison Organizing in the Civil Rights Era*. Chapel Hill: University of North Carolina Press.

Bosworth, Mary. 2002. *The U.S. Federal Prison System*. Thousand Oaks, CA: Sage.

Brisman, Avi. 2008. "Crime-Environment Relationships and Environmental Justice." *Seattle Journal of Social Justice* 6:727–907.

Brown, Elizabeth Nolan. 2017. "The Real 'Modern Slavery'? Inside America's Court-Ordered Corporate Labor Camps." *Reason*, October 5, 2017.

Broyard, Bliss, and Lisa Riordan Seville. 2021. "Rikers: The Obituaries. Fifteen People at the Jail Died in 2021." *Intelligencer*, December 27, 2021.

Bullard, Robert D. 2000. *Dumping in Dixie: Race, Class, and Environmental Quality*. 3rd ed. Boulder, CO: Westview.

CAAIR. n.d.-a. "History." Accessed September 1, 2022. http://caair.org.

———. n.d.-b. "Our Staff." Accessed September 1, 2022. http://caair.org.

Carrillo, Ian, and Anabel Ipsen. 2021. "Worksites as Sacrifice Zones: Structural Precarity and Covid-19 in U.S. Meatpacking." *Sociological Perspectives* 64 (5): 726–46.

Celermajer, Danielle, David Schlosberg, Lauren Rickards, Makere Stewart-Harawira, Mathias Thaler, Petra Tschakert, Blanche Verlie, and Christine Winter. 2021. "Multispecies Justice: Theories, Challenges, and a Research Agenda for Environmental Politics." *Environmental Politics* 30 (1–2): 119–40.

Cranmore, Crystal. 2021. "Protest Held as New York City Council Holds Hearing on Rikers Conditions." ABC7NY Eyewitness News, New York.

Davis, Janae, Alex A. Moulton, Levi Van Sant, and Brian Williams. 2019. "Anthropocene, Capitalocene . . . Plantationocene? A Manifesto for Ecological Justice in an Age of Global Crises." *Geography Compass* 13 (5).

Environmental Integrity Project. 2018a. "Three Quarters of Large U.S. Slaughterhouses Violate Water Pollution Permits." October 11, 2018. https://environmentalintegrity.org.

———. 2018b. *Water Pollution from Slaughterhouses*. Washington, DC: Environmental Integrity Project.

Fassin, Didier. 2018. *The Will to Punish*. Oxford: Oxford University Press.

Fassler, Joe, and Claire Brown. 2017. "Prison Food Is Making U.S. Inmates Disproportionately Sick." *The Atlantic*, December 27, 2017. www.theatlantic.com.

Federici, Silvia. 2012. *Revolution at Point Zero: Housework, Reproduction, and Feminist Struggle*. Oakland, CA: PM Press.

Fochtman, Mark. 2017. Affidavit filed with the Benton County Circuit Court, Arkansas. October 25, 2017. www.documentcloud.org.

Fochtman, Mark, and Shane O'Neal. 2017. Class Action Complaint against CAAIR, Inc., Simmons Foods, Inc., et al. Circuit Court of Benton County, Arkansas, October 23, 2017.

Gilna, Derek. 2014. "Bureau of Prisons Mistakenly Served Meat Intended as Pet Food." *Prison Legal News*, June 5, 2014.

Goran, David. 2016. "The Lorton Reformatory: A Historic Prison with Maximum Insecurity Built by Its Prisoners." *Vintage News*, June 16, 2016.

Gordon, Avery. 2008. *Ghostly Matters: Haunting and the Sociological Imagination*. Minneapolis: University of Minnesota Press.

Gottlieb, Robert. 2022. *Care-Centered Politics: From the Home to the Planet*. Cambridge: MIT Press.

Gribble, Emily C., and David N. Pellow. 2022. "Climate Change and Incarcerated Populations: Confronting Environmental and Climate Injustices behind Bars." *Fordham Urban Law Journal* 49 (2): 341–70.

Gruen, Lori. 2022. "Abolition: Thinking beyond Carceral Logics." In *Carceral Logics: Human Incarceration and Animal Captivity*, edited by Lori Gruen and Justin Marceau, 400–416. Cambridge: Cambridge University Press.

Gruen, Lori, and Justin Marceau. 2022. Introduction to *Carceral Logics: Human Incarceration and Animal Captivity*, edited by Lori Gruen and Justin Marceau, 1–14. Cambridge: Cambridge University Press.

Guenther, Katja M. 2020. *The Lives and Deaths of Shelter Animals*. Stanford, CA: Stanford University Press.

Harris, Amy Julia, and Shosana Walter. 2017a. "Chicken Workers Sue, Saying They Were Modern-Day Slaves." *Reveal*, October 10, 2017.

———. 2017b. "They Thought They Were Going to Rehab: They Ended up in Chicken Plants." *Reveal*, October 4, 2017.

Hoover, Elizabeth. 2018. "Environmental Reproductive Justice: Intersections in an American Indian Community Impacted by Environmental Contamination." *Environmental Sociology* 4 (1): 8–21.

Johnson, Eric S., Charles Shorter, Barbara Rider, and Ruth Giles. 1997. "Mortality from Cancer and Other Diseases in Poultry Slaughtering/Processing Plants." *International Journal of Epidemiology* 26:1142–50.

Kamb, Lewis. 2012. "A Rare Look Inside Tacoma's Northwest Detention Center." *News Tribune* (Tacoma, WA), September 9, 2012.

Kim, Claire Jean. 2018. "Abolition." In *Critical Terms for Animal Studies*, edited by Lori Gruen, 15–32. Chicago: University of Chicago Press.

Knauf, Ana Sofia. 2015. "Whole Foods Is Selling You Fish Farmed by Prisoners." *Grist*, March 3, 2015.

Kross, Anna. 1954. *Report of the Department of Correction, Commissioner, City of New York*. New York: City of New York.

Linzey, Andrew. 2017. "Is Christianity Irredeemably Speciesist?" In *The Animal Ethics Reader*, edited by Susan J. Armstrong and Richard G. Botzler, 294–300. New York: Routledge.

Lytle Hernandez, Kelly. 2017. *City of Inmates: Conquest, Rebellion, and the Rise of Human Caging in Los Angeles, 1771–1965*. Chapel Hill: University of North Carolina Press.

Malin, Stephanie, and Stacia Ryder. 2018. "Developing Deeply Intersectional Environmental Justice Scholarship." *Environmental Sociology* 4 (1): 1–7.

McMullen, Roger Paul. 2012. Form 3 Claim. Workers' Compensation Court, Oklahoma City, Oklahoma, July 25, 2012.

Mitchell, Kirk. 2015. "Whole Foods Will No Longer Sell Fish Produced by Colorado Prisoners." *Denver Post*, September 30, 2015.

Morin, Karen M. 2016. "Carceral Space: Prisoners and Animals." *Antipode* 48 (5): 1317–36.

———. 2017. "Wildspace: The Cage, the Supermax, and the Zoo." In *Critical Animal Geographies: Politics, Intersections, and Hierarchies in a Multispecies World*, edited by Kathryn Gillespie and Rosemary-Claire Collard, 73–91. New York: Routledge.

Nicosia, Nancy, John M. MacDonald, and Jeremy Arkes. 2013. "Disparities in Criminal Court Referrals to Drug Treatment and Prison for Minority Men." *American Journal of Public Health* 103 (6): e77–e84.

Northwest Detention Center Resistance. 2017. "Immigrants Held at Northwest Detention Center Launch Hunger Strike to Protest Their Conditions." Press release, April 10, 2017.

Noske, Barbara. 1989. *Humans and Other Animals*. London: Pluto.

Opsal, Tara, and Stephanie A. Malin. 2019. "Prisons as LULUs: Understanding the Parallels between Prison Proliferation and Environmental Injustices." *Sociological Inquiry* 90 (3): 579–602.

Pachirat, Timothy. 2011. *Every Twelve Seconds*. New Haven, CT: Yale University Press.

Patterson, Richard C. 1927. *Report of the Department of Correction, Commissioner, City of New York*. New York: City of New York.

Pellow, David N. 2014. *Total Liberation: The Power and Promise of Animal Rights and the Radical Earth Movement*. Minneapolis: University of Minnesota Press.

———. 2016. "Toward a Critical Environmental Justice Studies: Black Lives Matter as an Environmental Justice Challenge." *DuBois Review* 13 (2): 221–36.

———. 2017. *What Is Critical Environmental Justice?* London: Polity.

Perdue, Robert Todd. 2018. "Linking Environmental and Criminal Injustice: The Mining to Prison Pipeline in Central Appalachia." *Environmental Justice* 11 (5): 177–82.

Poo, Ai-jeen, with Ariane Conrad. 2015. *The Age of Dignity: Preparing for the Elder Boom in a Changing America*. New York: New Press.

Pulido, Laura. 2017. "Geographies of Race and Ethnicity II: Environmental Racism, Racial Capitalism and State-Sanctioned Violence." *Progress in Human Geography* 41 (4): 524–33.

Pulido, Laura, Ellen Kohl, and Nicole-Marie Cotton. 2016. "State Regulation and Environmental Justice: The Need for Strategy Reassessment." *Capitalism Nature Socialism* 27 (2): 12–31.

Ranganathan, Malini, and Eve Bratman. 2019. "From Urban Resilience to Abolitionist Climate Justice in Washington, D.C." *Antipode* 53:115–22.

Schlesinger, Traci. 2013. "Racial Disparities in Pretrial Diversion: An Analysis of Outcomes among Men Charged with Felonies and Processed in State Courts." *Race and Justice* 3 (3): 210–38.

Schlosberg, David. 2014. "Ecological Justice for the Anthropocene." In *Political Animals and Animal Politics*, edited by Marcel Wissenburg and David Schlosberg, 75–89. Basingstoke, UK: Palgrave Macmillan.

Spanos, Alexander J. 2013. "The Eighth Amendment and Nutriloaf: A Recipe for Disaster." *Journal of Contemporary Health Law and Policy* 30 (1): 222–48.

Steinberg, Ted. 2010. *Gotham Unbound: The Ecological History of Greater New York*. New York: Simon and Schuster.

Story, Brett. 2019. *Prison Land: Mapping Carceral Power across Neoliberal America*. Minneapolis: University of Minnesota Press.

Sze, Julie. 2020. *Environmental Justice in a Moment of Danger*. Berkeley: University of California Press.

Taylor, Dorceta E. 2000. "The Rise of the Environmental Justice Paradigm: Injustice Framing and the Social Construction of Environmental Discourses." *American Behavioral Scientist* 43 (4): 508–80.

Tronto, Joan. 2012. "Democratic Care Politics in an Age of Limits." In *Global Variations in the Political and Social Economy of Care*, edited by Shahra Razavi and Silke Staab, 29–40. New York: Routledge.

Tschakert, Petra. 2021. "More-than-Human Solidarity and Multispecies Justice in the Climate Crisis." *Environmental Politics* 31 (2): 277–96.

Twine, Richard. 2012. "Revealing the 'Animal-Industrial Complex': A Concept and Method for Critical Animal Studies." *Journal for Critical Animal Studies* 10 (1): 12–39.

Whyte, Kyle Powys. 2017. "The Dakota Access Pipeline, Environmental Injustice, and U.S. Colonialism." *Red Ink* 19 (1): 154–69.

Williams, Albert. 1951. *Report of the Department of Correction, Commissioner, City of New York*. New York: City of New York.
York, Richard. 2004. "Humanity and Inhumanity: Toward a Sociology of the Slaughterhouse." *Organization and Environment* 17 (2): 260–65.
Young, Timothy James. 2020. "Solitary Garden." Accessed August 1, 2022. www.timothyjamesyoung.com.
Yusoff, Kathryn. 2021. "The Inhumanities." *Annals of the American Association of Geographers* 111 (3): 663–76.

ABOUT THE CONTRIBUTORS

Bénédicte Boisseron is Professor of Afroamerican & African Studies, specializing in the fields of Black diaspora studies, francophone studies, and animal studies, at the University of Michigan, Ann Arbor. She is the author of *Afro-Dog: Blackness and the Animal Question* and *Creole Renegades: Rhetoric of Betrayal and Guilt in the Caribbean Diaspora*, as well as of numerous articles and chapters. She is working on a project tentatively titled *Black Freeganism*, about the poetics of repurposing, reclaiming, and reusing in a Black context. In 2022, she was named a Guggenheim Fellow.

Matthew Calarco is Professor of Philosophy at California State University, Fullerton. He works primarily at the intersection of Continental philosophy and animal/environmental philosophy. He is the author of *Beyond the Anthropological Difference* and *Animal Studies: The Key Concepts*, as well as the coeditor of *Exploring Animal Encounters: Philosophical, Cultural, and Historical Perspectives*. His earlier work examined philosophical concepts in animal death, summarized in *Thinking through Animals: Identity, Difference, Indistinction*.

Charlotte Coté is Professor of American Indian Studies at the University of Washington in Seattle. She is from the Nuu-chah-nulth community of Tseshaht on the west coast of Vancouver Island. She is the author of *A Drum in One Hand, a Sockeye in the Other: Stories of Indigenous Food Sovereignty from the Northwest Coast* and *Spirits of Our Whaling Ancestors: Revitalizing Makah and Nuu-chah-nulth Traditions*. She is the founder and chair of the annual University of Washington "Living Breath of wəłəbʔaltx^{w}" Indigenous Foods Symposium. She serves as series editor for the University of Washington Press's Indigenous Confluences Series.

Yair Dor-Ziderman is Postdoctoral Researcher at Safra Brain Research Center in Haifa, Israel. His work has been published in numerous journals including the *Neuroscience of Consciousness*, *Consciousness and Cognition*, *Neuroimage*, *Cortex*, and *Frontiers in Neuroscience*. His work on death and the denial of the inevitable has been featured in many popular press outlets including *Newsweek*, *Fox*, and *CNET*. He is the first author to systematically examine how the brain deals with one's own mortality, and he is also the first to determine how denial of one's death influences basic brain function.

Carrie Ducote has been working in animal shelter executive consulting for fifteen years helping shelters streamline operations and increase live release rates. She earned a master's degree in anthrozoology from Canisius College and institutional certificates in animal services executive leadership and cat lifesaving from Southern Utah University.

María Elena García is Professor of the Comparative History of Ideas at the University of Washington in Seattle. She is the author of *Gastropolitics and the Specter of Race: Stories of Capital, Culture, and Coloniality in Peru* and *Making Indigenous Citizens: Identities, Development, and Multicultural Activism in Peru*. Her next project, *Landscapes of Death: Political Violence beyond the Human in the Peruvian Andes*, considers the impact of political violence in Peru on more-than-human lives and bodies. Her work on Indigeneity and interspecies politics in the Andes has appeared in multiple edited volumes and journals.

Lisa Jean Moore is SUNY Distinguished Professor of Sociology and Gender Studies at Purchase College, State University of New York. Her scholarship is located at the intersections of sociology of health and medicine, science and technology studies, feminist studies, animal studies, and body studies. She is the author of numerous books, most recently *Our Transgenic Future: Spider Goats, Genetic Modification, and the Will to Change Nature*.

David Pellow is the Dehlsen Chair and Distinguished Professor of Environmental Studies and Director of the Global Environmental Justice Project at the University of California, Santa Barbara. His research and teaching focus on environmental and social justice, race/class/gender and environmental conflict, human-animal conflicts, sustainability, and social change movements that confront our socioenvironmental crises and social inequality. He has authored numerous books including *Total Liberation: The Power and Promise of Animal Rights and the Radical Earth Movement.* He has volunteered for and served on the boards of directors of several community-based, national, and international organizations that are dedicated to improving the living and working environments for people of color, immigrants, Indigenous peoples, and working-class communities.

Paola A. Prada-Tiedemann is Assistant Professor of Forensic Science in the Department of Environmental Toxicology, Director of Forensic Academic Programs, and Director of the Forensic Analytical Chemistry & Odor Profiling Laboratory at Texas Tech University. She is the coauthor of *Human Scent Evidence* as well as the author or coauthor of numerous journal publications and book chapters. She has presented her research at various national and international forums. She is a member of the criminalistics section of the American Academy of Forensic Sciences (AAFS), American Academy of Forensic Sciences Standards Board Dogs and Sensors Consensus Body, and Council of Forensic Educators (COFSE) and is Chair of the NIST OSAC subcommittee on Dogs and Sensors.

ABOUT THE EDITORS

KATJA M. GUENTHER is Professor of Gender & Sexuality Studies at the University of California, Riverside. She is the author of *The Lives and Deaths of Shelter Animals*, which won the 2021 American Sociological Association's Section on Animals and Society Distinguished Book Award, and *Making Their Place: Feminism after Socialism in Eastern Germany*.

JULIAN PAUL KEENAN is Professor of Biology and Psychology as well as Director of the Cognitive Neuroimaging Laboratory and the Brains, Equity, and Medicine Program at Montclair State University. He is the coauthor or coeditor of numerous books, including *The Face in the Mirror: The Search for the Origins of Consciousness*, which examines whether animals have a sense of self, and *Handbook of Research Methods in Health Psychology*. He is the founder of the journal *Social Neuroscience*. He has published in *Science*, *Nature*, and the *Proceedings of the National Academy of Sciences*.

INDEX

Page numbers in *italics* indicate Figures and Tables